RECEPTION AND TH

CW01064302

An Interdisciplinary Approach to

This collection brings together leading e..
of the humanities to offer a new perspective on the classical tradition.
Drawing on reception studies, philology, and early modern studies, the
essays explore the interaction between literary criticism and the multiple
cultural contexts in which texts were produced, discovered, appropriated,
and translated. The intersection of *Realpolitik* and textual criticism, poetic
and musical aesthetics, and authority and self-fashioning all come under
scrutiny. The canonical Latin writers and their subsequent reception form
the backbone of the volume, with a focus on the European Renaissance. It
thus marks a reconnection between classical and early modern studies and
the concomitant rapprochement of philological and cultural historical
approaches to texts and other works of art. This book will be of interest to
scholars in Classics, Renaissance studies, comparative literature, English,
Italian, and art history.

WILLIAM BROCKLISS is Visiting Assistant Professor of Classics at
Brigham Young University. He has recently completed a dissertation
on the relationship between the metaphorical associations of flowers in
Homeric poetry and the characteristics of flora in the Greek natural environment. In the future, he intends to develop his studies of metaphoricity
by exploring the contrasting treatments of everyday metaphor in Greek
poetry and philosophy.

PRAMIT CHAUDHURI is Assistant Professor of Classics at Dartmouth
College. He specializes in the Latin poetry of the early Roman empire,
set within a broader study of classical epic and tragedy. His current work
explores literary depictions of "theomachy" (conflicts between humans
and gods) and their mediation of issues such as religious conflict, philosophical iconoclasm, political struggle, and poetic rivalry. He also studies
the reception of classical antiquity in early modern epic and tragedy and
in Renaissance art.

AYELET HAIMSON LUSHKOV is Assistant Professor of Classics at the
University of Texas at Austin. She specializes in the political culture and
historiography of the Roman republic, with a particular focus on the conjunction of literary technique and historical subject matter. Her current
work includes a book-length study of the construction and experience of
political authority in the republic, focusing especially on Livy and Cicero.
She has also published on intertextuality and source criticism in Livy.

KATHERINE WASDIN is Visiting Assistant Professor of Classics at Rutgers University. She works on Latin poetry, with an emphasis on minor
and occasional genres. Her current project explores the dialogue between
Greek and Latin erotic and nuptial verse showing how and why these types
of poetry borrow from each other to express ideas of union, desire, and
community in authors such as Sappho, Catullus, the Latin love elegists,
and Claudian. She also has interests in Archaic Greek poetry, the ancient
novel, and the reception of antiquity in contemporary literature.

YALE CLASSICAL STUDIES

VOLUME XXXVI

RECEPTION AND THE CLASSICS

EDITED FOR THE DEPARTMENT OF CLASSICS BY

WILLIAM BROCKLISS

Visiting Assistant Professor of Classics, Brigham Young University

PRAMIT CHAUDHURI

Assistant Professor of Classics, Dartmouth College

AYELET HAIMSON LUSHKOV

Assistant Professor of Classics, University of Texas at Austin

KATHERINE WASDIN

Visiting Assistant Professor of Classics, Rutgers University

CAMBRIDGE
UNIVERSITY PRESS

CAMBRIDGE
UNIVERSITY PRESS

University Printing House, Cambridge CB2 8BS, United Kingdom

Cambridge University Press is part of the University of Cambridge.

It furthers the University's mission by disseminating knowledge in the pursuit of education, learning and research at the highest international levels of excellence.

www.cambridge.org
Information on this title: www.cambridge.org/9781316620779

© Cambridge University Press 2012

First published 2012
First paperback edition 2016

A catalogue record for this publication is available from the British Library

Library of Congress Cataloguing in Publication data
Reception and the classics / edited for the Department of Classics
by William Brockliss . . . [et al.].
p. cm. – (Yale classical studies ; v. 36)
Includes bibliographical references and index.
ISBN 978-0-521-76432-2 (hardback)
1. Classicism – Congresses.   2. Reader-response criticism – Congresses.
3. Literature – Congresses.   4. Music – Congresses.   5. Motion pictures –
Congresses.   I. Brockliss, William.   II. Reception and the classics
(2007 : Yale University)   III. Title.   IV. Series.
PN56.C6R43   2011
880.09 – dc23   2011033044

ISBN 978-0-521-76432-2 Hardback
ISBN 978-1-316-62077-9 Paperback

Contents

v

Notes on contributors

GORDON BRADEN is Linden Kent Memorial Professor of English at the University of Virginia. He has written widely on Renaissance literature and its classical background. His publications include *The Classics and English Renaissance Poetry: Three Case Studies* (1978), *Renaissance Tragedy and the Senecan Tradition: Anger's Privilege* (1985), *Petrarchan Love and the Continental Renaissance* (1999), and *The Oxford History of Literary Translation in English, vol. 2: 1550–1660* (forthcoming), co-edited with Robert Cummings and Stuart Gillespie.

JOSEPH FARRELL is Professor of Classical Studies and Joseph B. Glossberg Term Professor in the Humanities at the University of Pennsylvania. He specializes in Latin literature, especially poetry, and the culture of the Republican and Augustan periods. His publications include *Vergil's Georgics and the Tradition of Ancient Epic* (1991), *Latin Language and Latin Culture* (2001), and *A Companion to Vergil's Aeneid and its Tradition* (2010), co-edited with Michael C. J. Putnam.

ROBERT A. KASTER is Professor of Classics and Kennedy Foundation Professor of Latin at Princeton University. He has written mainly in the areas of Roman rhetoric, the history of ancient education, and Roman ethics. His books include *Guardians of Language: The Grammarian and Society in Late Antiquity* (1988), *Suetonius: De Grammaticis et Rhetoribus* (1995), *Emotion, Restraint, and Community in Ancient Rome* (2005), and editions, translations, and commentaries of various Latin authors, including most recently Seneca and Macrobius.

GIUSEPPE MAZZOTTA is Sterling Professor of Humanities for Italian at Yale University. He has written a number of essays about every century of Italian literary history. His books include *Dante, Poet of the Desert: History and Allegory in the Divine Comedy* (1979), *The World at Play in Boccaccio's Decameron* (1986), *Dante's Vision and the Circle of Knowledge*

(1993); *The Worlds of Petrarch* (1993); *The New Map of the World: The Poetic Philosophy of Giambattista Vico* (1998), and *Cosmopoiesis: The Renaissance Experiment* (2001).

RICHARD TARRANT is Harvard College Professor and Pope Professor of the Latin Language and Literature. His main areas of interest are Latin literature, especially poetry, Greek and Roman drama, and the transmission and editing of classical Latin texts. Among his major publications are editions with commentary of Seneca's *Agamemnon* (1977) and *Thyestes* (1985), and a critical edition of Ovid's *Metamorphoses* for the Oxford Classical Texts series (2004); he is also one of the co-authors of *Texts and Transmission: A Survey of the Latin Classics*, edited by L. D. Reynolds (1983).

RICHARD F. THOMAS is Harvard College Professor and George Martin Lane Professor of the Classics. His publications include *Lands and Peoples in Roman Poetry: The Ethnographical Tradition* (1982), a two-volume text and commentary on Virgil's *Georgics* (1988), *Reading Virgil and his Texts* (1999), *Virgil and the Augustan Reception* (2001), and two co-edited books to which he also contributed: with Charles Martindale, *Classics and the Uses of Reception* (2006), and with Catharine Mason, "The Performance Artistry of Bob Dylan", *Oral Tradition* 22.1 (2007).

EMILY WILSON is Associate Professor of Classical Studies at the University of Pennsylvania. She is the author of two monographs on classical culture and its reception, *Mocked with Death: Tragic Overliving from Sophocles to Milton* (2004) and *The Death of Socrates: Hero, Villain, Chatterbox, Saint* (2007). She has recently published *Six Tragedies of Seneca* (2010) for the Oxford World's Classics series. Her book reviews have appeared in the *Times Literary Supplement*, *London Review of Books*, and *The New Republic*.

CHRISTOPHER S. WOOD is Professor in the Department of History of Art, Yale University. His books include *Albrecht Altdorfer and the Origins of Landscape* (1993), *Forgery, Replica, Fiction: Temporalities of German Renaissance Art* (2008), and *Anachronic Renaissance* (2010), co-authored with Alexander Nagel. He is the editor of *The Vienna School Reader: Politics and Art Historical Method in the 1930s* (2000) and has translated major works by Erwin Panofsky and Hans Belting.

JAMES E. G. ZETZEL is Anthon Professor of the Latin Language and Literature at Columbia University. He has written widely on Latin literature of the first century BCE, ancient political theory, Roman intellectual life, and the history of classical scholarship. His books include *Latin Textual Criticism in Antiquity* (1981), a commentary on Cicero's *De re publica* (1995), an edition of the *Commentum Cornuti in Persium* (2004), co-authored with W. V. Clausen, and *Marginal Scholarship and Textual Deviance: The Commentum Cornuti and the Early Scholia on Persius* (2005).

Acknowledgements

This volume has been in the making for some time, and we on the editorial committee have seen many changes with it. We remain, however, steadfastly grateful to all those who made its production possible. Michael Sharp, Elizabeth Hanlon, and Christina Sarigiannidou at Cambridge University Press shepherded four editors and nine contributors to press with unfailing grace. The comments of the two anonymous referees for Cambridge University Press much improved the introduction to, and organization of, the volume; its remaining flaws are ours alone. The Department of Classics at Yale University, and especially Christina Kraus, offered support, funding, and that most precious of resources, good advice. Funding for the initial conference also came from various sources at Yale, in particular the Edward J. and Dorothy Clarke Kempf Fund, the Office of the Provost, the Office of the Secretary, the Beinecke Rare Book and Manuscript Library, and the Whitney Humanities Center. *Oral Tradition* and its editor, John Miles Foley, have graciously allowed us to reprint Richard Thomas' piece, with some modifications. Giuseppe Mazzotta's paper, originally published in *Petrarch: A Critical Guide to the Complete Works*, edited by Victoria Kirkham and Armando Maggi (2009), appears here courtesy of the University of Chicago Press. Unfortunately, conference papers by Julia Haig Gaisser, Charles Martindale, David Quint, and Claude Rawson could not be included in this collection, but we are grateful to all four for their role in our discussions and their support of the volume. Above all, we thank our contributors for their enthusiastic participation, and their kind patience.

CHAPTER I

Introduction

William Brockliss, Pramit Chaudhuri,
Ayelet Haimson Lushkov, and Katherine Wasdin

This volume collects the majority of papers from a conference held at
Yale University in 2007. That conference, also entitled *Reception and the
Classics*, sought to define and articulate the particular role of Classics and
classicists in the project of Reception Studies.[1] The field of Reception
Studies ranges over a vast stretch of time and material, from classical
antiquity to the present day, from literature to art, music, and film; it is
thus an inherently interdisciplinary field in its encompassing of a variety
of departments and disciplines, each with its own canons, practices, and
shared working assumptions. This interdisciplinary practice has formed
the intellectual foundation for the present collection: although Reception
Studies as a field has grown in scope and energy between conference and
publication, we feel that the question of where Classics stands in relation
to its peer disciplines remains alive and crucial.

Even today the practitioners of classical reception are, by and large,
classicists; and although some names outside our discipline, such as David
Quint and Kenneth Haynes, are perhaps well known to classicists, any
such familiarity generally springs from their work on explicitly classical
material or from their collaborations with classical scholars.[2] And while
many scholars rely on the classics for their own research in other fields,
the work of non-classicists in this vein has often been seen not as part
of a coherent discourse on the *nachleben* of Greek and Latin, but simply
as accounting for the sources, cultural practice and intellectual curiosity
of a Shakespeare, a Joyce, or a Petrarch, in the regular course of literary criticism. The difference between the approaches of scholars working
within various institutional categories extends to more than a temporal

---

[1] Throughout the introduction we use "Classics" to refer to the discipline and "classics" to refer to
ancient Greek and Roman works of art (usually literary).
[2] E.g., Quint, *Epic and Empire*, and "The Virgilian coordinates of *Paradise Lost*"; Carne-Ross and
Haynes, *Horace in English*; Haynes, *English Literature and Ancient Languages*, and "Text, theory, and
reception."

perspective, since each department or discipline relies also on a hoard of specialized knowledge (linguistic, cultural, archival, etc.), to which outsiders are not always privy, nor do the audiences of each field overlap.

A brief account of some of the benefits and caveats of looking across disciplinary boundaries appears in a recent book review by Ruth Scodel:

> It is a good idea for classicists, every once in a while, to read treatments of their texts by smart people who are not classicists, usually colleagues in related fields. They can profit in two very different, indeed opposite, ways: first, sometimes the comparative outsider, with a fresh perspective, can offer insights, solutions to problems, or methods of approach that the community of specialists has missed because it can be very hard to go beyond the questions that have already been defined and endlessly discussed. Second, such books can reveal how the field looks to its neighbors . . . So we sometimes find out that our scholarly neighbors are out of touch with developments in classics, and maybe are encouraged to inform them better. There is always a danger, though, that we can turn ourselves into scholarly police, patrolling our boundaries and looking for mistakes on which to pounce.[3]

Scodel is not here referring to Reception Studies *per se* but her points are nonetheless germane: as classicists and non-classicists begin to approach the same material from different perspectives, so an awareness of developments in related fields is required if we are to arrive at a better understanding of the relationship between, for instance, text and musical reception, text and translation, classical and post-classical author – to use just a few of the examples from this volume.

This collection, which is deliberately drawn from a broad disciplinary background, provides an uncommon opportunity to see experts in different fields join their perspective on classical reception to that of trained classicists. In addition to Classics, the contributors are experts in, and work within departments of, English, Italian and Art History; the original conference featured other contributions from specialists in English and Comparative Literature as well. One of the vital consequences of this diversity and interdisciplinarity is that these scholars are not operating under the same assumptions – perhaps even the shadow – of Reception Studies as seen from within Classics, nor do they face the same institutional pressures to interpret the classical text in its own right or in its own terms. A beneficial corollary of this broad expertise is a chance for readers of this volume in various disciplines to assess Charles Martindale's rigorous historicist demand that classicists' work on reception be satisfactory not just to classicists but also to post-classical scholars working in the relevant

---

[3] Scodel, Review of Johnstone, *Listening to the Logos*.

field, and (we hope to add) vice versa.[4] A viewpoint oscillating between antiquity and other periods allows us to consider not only how the classics can illuminate other periods, but also how the reception of antiquity can teach us more about the ancient world itself.

In effect, interdisciplinary collaborations help us to conceptualize the (albeit fluid) line between disciplinarity and interdisciplinarity, and to see how different institutional practices lead to different scholarly practices. In the firm belief that these questions are often best answered with recourse to practical examples as well as theoretical debate, the contributors were given maximum leeway in their choice of topics; hence the broad range of subjects and genres covered in these proceedings. However, the canonical Latin literary tradition and its subsequent reception, along an axis running from antiquity through the early modern humanistic traditions following Petrarch and up to the scholarly and artistic responses of the nineteenth and twentieth centuries, forms the backbone of the collection. In this, we hope, the volume may offer a useful complement to the considerable attention paid by reception scholars to Greek literature and culture, and especially to its reception in the performing arts.[5] For although Latin has been somewhat neglected in the most recent articulations of reception as a scholarly discourse, it has had a fundamental role in the development of the humanistic and classical traditions. The recent scholarly focus on the eighteenth century and following may reflect the privileging of Greek in those periods, while a view of reception that begins earlier in history will be more open to the importance of Latin, the lingua franca of the humanist world.[6] What we perhaps miss in the current interest in classics

---

[4] Martindale, "Introduction," pp. 1ff. Cf. Porter, "Reception studies," pp. 478–9.

[5] Here the work of the Archive of Performances of Greek and Roman Drama (APGRD) has had a significant impact, not only in the creation of a large and expanding database of information about performances of Greek and Roman drama, but also in the many volumes of essays produced under its auspices. An accidental consequence of the success of the APGRD is the proportionally greater attention given to the reception of Greek tragedy in particular (though Roman drama does feature in many of the collections). The dominance of the reception of Greek also follows from the Romantic and modern fascination with archaic poetry, which has generated its own rich study, e.g., Graziosi and Greenwood (eds.), *Homer in the Twentieth Century*; Most, Norman, and Rabau (eds.), *Révolutions Homériques*; Greene (ed.), *Re-reading Sappho*; Prins, *Victorian Sappho*. Finally, the influence of ancient Greek thought on modern literary, cultural, and political theory has formed yet another area of reception scholarship. See, e.g., Leonard, *Athens in Paris*, Miller, *Postmodern Spiritual Practices*. Among the Latin exceptions to the current Hellenocentricity is Julia Gaisser's award-winning book, *The Fortunes of Apuleius and the Golden Ass*, on the reception of Apuleius, part of which was presented as a paper at our original conference.

[6] For the privileging of Greek in the Romantic period and following see Habinek, *The Politics of Latin Literature*, pp. 15–33. But a stronger narrative of Latin's reception need not be confined to the pre-Romantic period, as the essays of Farrell and Thomas in this volume clearly demonstrate (cf. the work of Theodore Ziolkowski, in particular *Virgil and the Moderns* and *Ovid and the Moderns*). In

and empire, colonialism and national traditions is the *longue durée* of classical reception and its continuities and disjunctions over time. In this volume those continuities and disjunctions are particularly focused on the themes of philology, modes of transmission, and self-fashioning.

Another distinctive feature of this volume, therefore, is its focus on treating classical reception in the early modern period. That common choice of focus goes hand in hand with a strong Yale connection, with almost half of the contributors (and several more participants at the original conference) receiving their training or currently teaching at Yale. This particular concentration is in no small part the legacy of Thomas Greene, whose work at Yale over the latter half of the twentieth century shaped our collective understanding of the imitative and competitive relationship between classical and Renaissance literature.[7] During the very same period, Yale was also the home of the most exciting developments in literary theory, led by scholars in the departments of English and Comparative Literature, such as Harold Bloom and Paul de Man. From this twin inheritance of humanistic erudition and critical originality, Yale built a tradition of scholarship that revitalized our understanding of how early modern writers perceived their own age and literary practices as they confronted the powerful yet fragmented traces of classical culture. In a way, the birth of Reception Studies within the discipline of Classics, which can be identified with the publication of Martindale's *Redeeming the Text* in 1993, may be seen not as an outgrowth of Reception Theory or *Rezeptionsgeschichte* but rather as an importation of what had been going on in Renaissance literary scholarship for some time.[8]

If this interdisciplinary connection with Early Modern Studies has been somewhat obscured over the last twenty years, the change merits some explanation. As Constanze Güthenke has recently suggested in a review article of the field, it is high time to scrutinize the history of Reception Studies itself.[9] Martindale's own preface to *Redeeming the Text* cites the influences

fact, Latin has often provided the medium through which ancient Greek culture and language were understood, whether because of the unavailability of texts in the time of Petrarch or the exclusivity of Greek instruction in the time of Joyce (on which see the papers of Mazzotta and Farrell).

[7] Most famously *The Descent from Heaven* and *The Light in Troy*.

[8] There was, of course, a tradition of scholarship on classical reception from long before 1993 (the work of Gilbert Highet and Richard Jenkyns, to name but two, quite different, examples), but *Redeeming the Text* marked a new engagement, within Classics at least, between literary history and theory, an engagement that would be central to the rapid growth of the field of Reception Studies.

[9] Güthenke, "Shop talk," p. 113: "But just as much as acts of reception need to be contextualized and historicized, so do the theoretical approaches that have inspired Reception Studies in the field of Classics, and that privilege that sense of empathy and the lingering dream of immediacy as an approach to the past."

of New Criticism, Derridean deconstruction, Bakhtin, Gadamer, and T. S. Eliot but omits mention of his own earlier work on the classicism of Milton and Shakespeare.[10] And yet, those earlier studies, and their roots in the work of, amongst others, Thomas Greene, were never characterized by the uncritical cataloguing of sources and fixed interpretations from which the modern reception theorist might retreat in embarrassment.[11] On the contrary, as the papers by Mazzotta and Braden in this volume clearly show, the dynamism of the early modern engagement with the past – its deference and competitiveness, its sense of temporal continuity and dis-junction, its immersion in multiple sources and the mysteries generated by fragments and historical traces – shares much with our current interests in the ancient world, whether in the connection between Rome and its early history, or between Flavian culture and its Julio-Claudian antecedents, or in the retrospectives of late antique scholarship. Nevertheless, it may have served the burgeoning field of Reception Studies well to mark a break, even if only rhetorically and temporarily, from the "Classical Tradition" (as con-ventionally conceived) and the familiar complementarity of Greco-Roman antiquity and the humanist High Renaissance. The opening-up of new vistas now populated with studies of modern literature, performance, and film rightly demanded a polemicism and protreptic to theory appropriate to the 1990s. In our current, perhaps more ecumenical, climate we may be in a better position to reflect on the history of scholarship with attention to all of its strands.

Güthenke's consideration of how traditional forms of scholarship – including historiographies of the discipline – can be reconstituted in light of Reception Studies extends to that most traditional of classical disci-plines, philology: "What then can philology, especially philology of a past language, as a specific practice beyond philology at large add to the cate-gory of scholarship on scholarship?"[12] Her illustration of the convergence between philology and Reception Studies is Sean Gurd's recent book on the textual criticism of Euripides' *Iphigeneia at Aulis*.[13] We would expand that paradigmatic example of philology to include a range of technical and interpretive activities concerned with the history and forms of texts and language itself. Where Güthenke sees Reception Studies at work in Gurd's

---

[10] Martindale, *Redeeming the Text*, pp. xiii–xiv. Martindale's continued work on Renaissance texts feeds into this volume via Gordon Braden's paper.
[11] But for his final illness Greene would have contributed to Martindale's *Shakespeare and the Classics*, co-edited with A. B. Taylor, a contribution that would have increased awareness of Greene's work among classicists.
[12] Güthenke, "Shop talk," p. 110.   [13] Gurd, *Iphigeneias at Aulis*.

historiography of textual critical practices, we see the same attention to the local motivations and resources for reading classical texts in Zetzel's history of Ciceronian textual criticism, Kaster's cultural contextualization of ancient commentary, Tarrant's explication of the transference of Horace's words into music, and Farrell's demonstration of how Joyce's philological knowledge fed back into creative and imaginative expression. In each of these cases a species of philological expertise is brought into productive engagement with a historicized view of the conditions under which the ancient text or language is read or interpreted. No longer, in that light, can there be any false dichotomy between philology and history as two alternative modes of approaching a text.

At the conclusion of her seminal work on the early modern and modern history of the Latin language, Françoise Waquet argues that the future of the study of Latin as a going concern depends on a very specific intellectual project: she advocates the study of Latin for the purpose of reading untranslated, documentary texts in order to better understand European history.[14] This is undoubtedly a promising field for further research but it suggests a circumscribed view of the value of the ancient languages. That value is perhaps better represented through the lens of reception. As Wilson's essay in this volume on the Scottish reception of Vergil shows – in the same vein as Andrew Laird's work on Vergil in early modern Central America – history, both European and global, is illuminated by a knowledge not only of the language of the texts themselves but also of the local contexts in which Greco-Roman culture, such as Vergilian poetry, is read, learned, interpreted, appropriated, and disseminated.[15] Especially where literary texts are concerned, Reception Studies functions as an argument for acquiring the philological expertise to see how the relations between texts produce meanings at even the most microscopic of levels.[16] Philology and Reception Studies thus together contribute to a history that is not confined to the European and the documentary. Wherever the classical languages have been read or translated one must apply a philological scrutiny to questions of who reads, how, and why. We hope that the diverse papers presented here inaugurate a new fusion of philological with Reception Studies.

---

[14] Waquet, *Latin or the Empire of a Sign*, p. 274. For an alternative argument concerning the future of the study of Latin in relation to the history of the language see Leonhardt, *Latein*.

[15] Laird's work is well represented by *The Epic of America*, but see also a number of his recent articles. For a similarly historicist approach to the local contexts of reception (from outside Classics), cf. the work of Craig Kallendorf, notably *The Virgilian Tradition* and *The Other Virgil*.

[16] See, for instance, Wilson's acute reading of Douglas' aims in his translation of the *Aeneid* through close comparison with Vergil's Latin.

The publication of such a collection under the auspices of the Classics Department at Yale not only marks a reconnection with the tradition of Renaissance studies at the university but also sets a wider example for the revitalization of what was once called the "Classical Tradition."[17] Where once that phrase connoted the transhistorical conversations of supposedly like-minded European males, it can now be recuperated as a growing body of texts and ideas whose analysis, contestation, appropriation, understanding and misunderstanding shaped European cultural history and thereby our modern habits of thought and interpretation.[18] It is with this history in mind that we present this volume. Given the high stock of Reception Studies today and a climate that lends itself to interdisciplinary enterprises, it seems an appropriate moment to sit scholars of antiquity and post-antiquity side-by-side to see how they approach the classical tradition and to identify avenues for further exploration.

PRACTICING RECEPTION: ORGANIZATION AND THEMES

As a snapshot of various types of engagement in Reception Studies in the early years of the twenty-first century, this volume is organized into two sections, focusing on: 1. transmission, philology and the broader cultural movements that should bear on our understanding of texts and language;[19] 2. self-fashioning, or individuals' use of the classics to project an image of

---

[17] On the concept of the classical tradition and its potential pliability see Budelmann and Haubold, "Reception and tradition." Martindale, "Reception," p. 298, discusses the terminological nuances of "tradition," "reception," and other related keywords; he acknowledges that any definitional boundaries must take account of variation in usage from one author to another (citing, as an example, T. S. Eliot's use of "tradition" in the influential essay, "Tradition and the individual talent"). Carlo Caruso and Andrew Laird offer trenchant criticism of any supposed dichotomy between reception and tradition ("The Italian classical tradition, language and literary history," pp. 2–3): "The distinction between reception and tradition does not survive close scrutiny. During the Renaissance, just as much as in any later period, perennial controversies about the virtues of Ciceronianism or the superiority of Homer to Virgil show that the very nature of the classical world and its legacies was regularly contested."

[18] Recent work in Reception Studies has stretched beyond European confines, e.g., Cook and Tatum, *African American Writers and Classical Tradition*, duBois, *Out of Athens*, Goff (ed.), *Classics and Colonialism*, Greenwood, *Afro-Greeks*; but common to all receptions, irrespective of place and time, is a measure of creative response, assertion of authority, and intellectual continuity and difference – this new and more dynamic sense of the classical tradition is exemplified both by the kinds of study listed above and equally by the papers in this volume.

[19] Cf. Porter, "Reception studies," p. 473: "In fact, transmission and reception are not two faces of a single coin. Rather, they are two names for the selfsame activity. Classical studies are not merely the beneficiary of this activity. They are *subsumed* by it."

themselves.[20] These divisions are based on the differing modes of reception of classical texts, rather than any unifying and underlying theoretical framework in the modern scholarship. Some of our contributors, such as Kaster, work backwards, seeking to identify the meaning that was once attributed to a text; others, such as Zetzel and Tarrant, explore facets of the later culture and its modes of reception; while others still, for instance Thomas, bring out a dialogue between two points.[21]

All the papers in this volume explore the interplay between philological approaches to classical texts and the historicist discourse of Reception Studies.[22] While these two approaches have often appeared to be at loggerheads with one another, we hope that our volume will help to move their relationship in the direction of productive dialogue in place of mutual antagonism.[23] In general, the papers share a combined attention to the artist, to the artwork *qua* work of *art*, and to the cultural context of production and reception. This kind of criticism rejects the dichotomy constructed by partisans of a cultural studies or aesthetic approach to reception.[24] A mark of the reconciliation between philology and culture can be seen in the fact that the papers often raise issues treated at greater

[20] The choice of the term "self-fashioning" itself acknowledges a connection to Early Modern Studies, in particular the formative work of Stephen Greenblatt in *Renaissance Self-Fashioning*. This vein of work has been internalized in literary criticism for some time now, and has made itself felt in Classics with particular reference to Cicero. See Connolly, review of Dugan, *Making a New Man*, esp. nn. 2 and 3.

[21] For a sense of the variety of approaches available – in terms of theories of interpretation and their application to different kinds of objects – see Batstone, "Provocation," Hall, "Towards a theory of performance reception," Hardwick and Stray, "Introduction," Paul, "Working with film," and Porter, "Reception studies."

[22] Sheldon Pollock ("Future philology?", p. 934) offers a suggestive definition of philology: "the critical self-reflection of a discipline." The prefix *philo-*, then, would imply not only a love of language (*lógos*), but an (informed) self-love. That inward-looking aspect of the study of language is shared by the textual critic, commentator and translator, whose practices are explored below. Pollock argues that, at its best, the discipline has always been aware of both its own historicity and that of its objects of study. For an alternative definition of philology, wider than that followed by Pollock and this introduction, cf. Geoffrey Harpham, "Roots, races, and the return to philology," who argues that, in addition to close linguistic analysis, philology has always been characterized by concerns with meaning, value and cultural identity.

[23] For an attempt to reconcile traditional philology and historicizing theory, cf. Harrison (ed.), *Texts, Ideas and the Classics*. In his general introduction, Stephen Harrison calls for "mutual tolerance and understanding, in the cause of mutual interest and enrichment" between practitioners of "conventional classical scholarship and modern theoretical ideas" (pp. 1–2). (Later in the same volume, however, Michael Reeve ("Reception/history of scholarship") arrives at a rather more pessimistic evaluation of the chances that traditional philologists and scholars of reception might find enough common ground to work together.) For the latest discussion of some of these issues see the essays in Gurd (ed.), *Philology and Its Histories*, which appeared too recently to be considered here.

[24] See, for instance, the recent debate between Simon Goldhill and Charles Martindale (Goldhill, "Cultural history and aesthetics" and Martindale, "Performance, reception, aesthetics").

length in the other of the two main sections. So, for example, Farrell's essay in the first part is as much about Joyce's self-fashioning as philology and Wilson's piece in the second is as much about transmission and language as Douglas' identity. Also running through both sections is the strong fascination with the (discovered) text as a physical and powerful token of antiquity, a topic covered by Zetzel, Mazzotta, and Braden.[25]

As a rule, scholars applying reception theory to classical texts remain very much in need of the tools of traditional philology, but are able to use those tools for new, historicizing purposes. Each new modern edition of a text, for instance, adds a new voice to the continuing dialogue, expressing, with a greater or lesser degree of boldness, the particular viewpoint and interests of its editor.[26] In this volume, James Zetzel's study of the nineteenth-century rediscovery of Cicero's *De re publica* gives a clear demonstration of the potential for tendentiousness in the professedly disinterested logic of textual criticism. Cardinal Angelo Mai, keeper of the Vatican Library, attempted to appropriate the new text for a new Rome and new Italy established by Pope Pius VII after the defeat of Napoleon. He entered into a war of words with another textual critic present in Rome, the classical scholar and historian Barthold Niebuhr, who wished to assist in and thus exercise control over the editing of the new text. Niebuhr was the representative at the Vatican of Prussia, another state resurgent after the fall of Napoleon, and was eager to appropriate the text for Prussian monarchical doctrine. Zetzel shows that such scholarship is shaped by the ideologies of politics and religion, and that *Realpolitik* can determine the uses textual critics make of the texts and objects they study.[27]

Robert Kaster explores another of the traditional remits of the philologist, the commentary. He examines Servius' commentary on the *Aeneid*, focusing on his formulation of Vergil's *intentio*: to praise Augustus by praising his ancestors. Modern scholars have derided Servius' reading as naïve and reductive, but, Kaster argues, we should show due sensitivity to

---

[25] For the changing perception of tokens of antiquity – from texts to images to monuments – during the early modern period, see now Nagel and Wood, *Anachronic Renaissance* and Wood, *Forgery, Replica, Fiction*.

[26] On the interestedness of the textual critic, cf. Harrison's comments in *Texts, Ideas and the Classics*, pp. 3ff.

[27] Zetzel's contribution makes for an original and powerful instantiation of the claim Güthenke attributes to James Porter: "Porter will come around to recommend the history of scholarship as a promising field of future reception studies" ("Shop talk," p. 104). Cf. Porter, "Reception studies," p. 475. In historicizing the circumstances of the philology of the *De re publica*, Zetzel also picks up the gauntlet laid down by Sheldon Pollock for all philologists: "A double historicization is required, that of the philologist – and we philologists historicize ourselves as rarely as physicians heal themselves – no less than that of the text" (Pollock, "Future philology?", p. 958).

the world in which Servius wrote: he and his pupils lived in an honour culture, where to praise or denigrate a possession or relative of X was to praise or denigrate X her- or (especially) himself. Kaster shows that Servius, through his awareness of the potential for seemingly value-neutral statements to convey praise or blame, is able to point up interesting possible meanings for a number of passages. Although his cultural assumptions and the readings motivated by those assumptions are alien to scholars in the modern West, they may have been rather less alien to readers and audiences of Vergil's own time. Philologists have tended to mine Servius' commentary for nuggets of "truth" accidentally preserved behind the screen of his naïveté; rather than dissecting his text in this manner, we would be better advised to regard Servius as a fellow reader of the *Aeneid*, and as a reader with privileged access to meanings from which we would otherwise be excluded. Kaster's paper exemplifies how a traditional philological resource like an ancient commentary, when viewed from the perspective of Reception Studies, allows for a better understanding both of the "secondary" source itself and the "primary" text it seeks to elucidate – a relationship James Porter has described as "the remnants of an unbroken conversation that was carried on throughout antiquity."[28] On this view, both texts are in a sense primary as we pay equal attention to the conditions in which the two texts were composed and the impact of those conditions on meaning. Philologists preparing their own commentaries, rather than presenting themselves as the discoverers of objective truths "hidden" within the texts, should be aware of the historical contingency of their inferences, and might do well to declare their own hermeneutic stance as unequivocally as Servius.[29]

Joseph Farrell's essay demonstrates how James Joyce was able to reanimate even the dry, context-free philological practice of grammatical analysis. The author of *Ulysses* found a "use for Latinity" in the collision between the abstract, ahistorical logic of traditional classroom grammar drills and the most intimate thoughts of his *alter ego*, the schoolmaster Stephen Dedalus. Joyce satirized the detachment of the practice of "parsing" from

---

[28] Porter, "Reception studies," p. 473; see also pp. 475–6. Cf. Güthenke, "Shop talk," p. 109.

[29] Cf. Harrison (ed.), *Text, Ideas and the Classics*, p. 8: "It is surely better for an interpreter to declare his or her underlying viewpoint rather than to leave it to be constructed from what he or she writes or says in an apparently neutral manner." See also Charles Martindale's comments on the undeclared cultural assumptions behind Adam Parry's reading of the *Aeneid* in "The two voices of Virgil's *Aeneid*" (Martindale, *Redeeming the Text*, pp. 40–3). Modern scholars' perception of Servius' naiveté may arise not merely from the nature of his reading, but in part from the fact that he makes his opinion so clear. It is generally considered bad manners for a modern commentator's voice to obtrude too obviously (cf. Kraus, "Introduction," esp. pp. 4–7).

any external reality through a pupil's absurd association of the general Pyrrhus – he hears "*pier-us*" – and a local pier (Gabler (ed.), *Ulysses* 2.18–27). After the lesson, however, when an unlovely boy stays behind for help with his mathematics, Stephen is moved to reflect on a mother's love for even such as an "ugly and futile" specimen. The schoolmaster's pedantic analysis of the phrase "*amor matris*" as "subjective and objective genitive" suggests the awkwardness of his feelings for his own mother, and the tender reciprocity from which he feels excluded. As Farrell and others have noted, Joyce applied the philological skills he himself excelled at in the Latin classroom to the fashioning of his own distinctive diction – which is at once one of the boldest statements of modernism and an exposition of the most traditional skills of philology. In a final irony, his *Ulysses*, which at first appalled traditionalists of all stripes, is now the darling of philologists thrilled every time they can train-spot an allusion to Homer's *Odyssey*.

Richard Tarrant concludes this section with a survey of three periods in the long history of musical settings of Horace's *Odes*: the central Middle Ages, when along with other classical texts the *Odes* were often provided with neumes (musical notation); the mid sixteenth and early seventeenth centuries, when the popularity of classical texts as the basis for polyphonic choral works was at its greatest; and the first half of the twentieth century, when the choice of classical texts was often accompanied by the exploration of earlier musical styles. Tarrant considers the ways in which composers dealt with the formidable obstacles to musical interpretation of Horace's lyric odes, both because of the verbal density and metrical complexity of Horace's writing, and because of his combination of strictly repeating stanzaic form with frequent shifts of tone and register within poems. Strikingly, settings of non-Horatian texts often more closely approximate these subtle shifts, seen for example in musical adaptations of Housman's poems. The philological essence of the paper emerges from Tarrant's concern with fidelity, both to meter and to Horace's text. While the musical settings quickly abandon close adherence to the very limiting condition of meter, Tarrant identifies a few cases in which the composer captures, or even tries to capture, the poetic feel of the original.

While retaining the historicist approach to culture of the first four papers, the volume's second section shifts its emphasis to self-fashioning, that is, individuals' use of the classics to project an image of themselves. In these papers the artistic work or career comes into focus against the background of culture. Examining figures as diverse as Petrarch, Bob Dylan, and Prospero, these papers work by close attention to literary allusions and influences. Although philological concerns persist here, especially in Wilson's paper on translation, the essays in this section tend to emphasize the importance of the later authors as creators of a tradition that has been so thoroughly internalized by classicists that we are perhaps oblivious to its constructedness. That constructedness is belied by the apparent materiality of the connection between antiquity and modernity. Indeed, the past is even seen as physically present in some sense, as in Braden's suggestion that Prospero's book of magic was in fact a text of Ovid, and in Mazzotta's account of the letters discovered and conceived by Petrarch.

Giuseppe Mazzotta opens the section by showing how Petrarch's fascination with antique precedents allows him to use a Ciceronian form (the letter) along with an Odyssean mask to broadcast his erudition and sophistication. Tracing Petrarch's identification with Ulysses in the *Rerum Familiarum Libri*, Mazzotta argues that the epic hero's rhetorical guile and shifting persona function as a paradigm for Petrarch's own literary and cultural ambitions. Mazzotta's casting of classical texts as an imaginary world open to inhabitation and manipulation gains piquancy from Petrarch's almost foundational role in the history of philology as the finder of long-lost manuscripts: here discovery, in its philological and epic guises, becomes formative for Petrarch's self-conception and self-portrayal.[30] Mazzota's Petrarch, like Farrell's Joyce, draws on overarching ideas of antiquity as noble forebear, this time through the triple lenses of rhetoric, epistolarity, and epic. Yet, as with Joyce, there is no simple one-to-one correspondence between ancient and modern. The medium of literary creation in both cases allows for nuanced ideas of the value of the classical and its redefinition.

Emily Wilson's essay explores the creation of the first British translation of the *Aeneid*, Gavin Douglas' Middle Scots *Eneados*.[31] Reception theory has brought with it a renewed consciousness of the impossibility of perfect fidelity in translation, of the complete transferral of the meaning of a text expressed in one language into a text in a second language.[32] Rather,

---

[30] For a classicist's view on some of these issues see Hinds, "Petrarch, Cicero, Virgil" and "Defamiliarizing Latin literature, from Petrarch to pulp fiction."

[31] The term "British" here, and in the essay, does not refer to the unified nation which would be formed only many years after Douglas' death; rather, it simply denotes the geographical area of Scotland, England, and Wales, from which Douglas was the first person to translate the entirety of Vergil's Latin epic.

[32] On the apparent theoretical impossibility and the practical difficulties of translation, cf. Ricoeur, *Sur la traduction*. Translation is made problematic not only by the pre-existing gap between past and present, but by the shifting of those two poles as a result of the very act of translation: cf. Lianeri ("The Homeric moment?"), who sees translation as an attempt to confer on the present the authority

a translation is inevitably a re-creation, a re-reading of its model. Wilson shows how Douglas read his own concerns as a translator into Vergil's text.[33] In both his prologues to individual books and the body of his translation, Douglas casts himself as the double of Aeneas, engaged in an act of bringing across, of trans-lating an ancient culture to a new homeland. Although he professes to aim at fidelity to the *Aeneid*, he also "presents himself as Virgil's competitor, as well as his defender": he will follow him at "fut hait," as if pursuing him in a race. The translator and author are engaged in a struggle to control the meaning of the text, and to guide future readings. Such struggles provoke awareness on our part of the polysemy of both the ancient model and its translation. Translations are thus of benefit to the reader not as a crib for decoding *the* meaning of the original, but as a means to gain a multivocal, dialogic understanding of both the primary text and its successors.[34]

Continuing the theme of artistic self-definition, Gordon Braden reads the *Tempest*'s Prospero as a figure for Ovid, and the sorcerer's abjuration of magic as Shakespeare's simultaneous farewell to the classical poet and to the theatre as a whole.[35] Braden's discussion of contemporary treatises of witchcraft available to Shakespeare continues the historicist contextualization of earlier papers as a means by which to illuminate the figures of Prospero and Ovid. Shakespeare's conscious reception of Ovid the magician through Prospero becomes a form of self-reflection; adaptation becomes not merely an interpretation of the classical author but an interpretation – here a summation – of Shakespeare's own work.[36] Following up on the critique of simple source analysis laid out in his introduction, Braden's conclusion enlarges our sense of the semantic power of reception in terms of a more comprehensive rereading of a classical text and a more significant consequence of that rereading for one's own identity.

The final paper in this section, Richard Thomas' study of the late work of Bob Dylan, shows the singer-composer varying his intertexts, such as Vergil's *Aeneid*, in performance, so creating constant shifts in meaning and

---

of a classical past whose classical status and authority are, ironically, confirmed by translation itself. See also Hardwick, *Translating Words, Translating Cultures* on the effect of translation on modern cultures.

[33] Cf. Tudeau-Clayton, "Supplementing the *Aeneid* in early modern England."

[34] Cf. Martindale, *Redeeming the Text*, pp. 29ff. on "recovering" our dialogue with text, and pp. 43ff. on reading "Dante-reading-Virgil."

[35] Braden identifies Prospero's "booke" (5.1.57) with the *Metamorphoses*. Cf. Hieronimo's copy of Seneca in *The Spanish Tragedy* by Thomas Kyd (on which see Hammond, *The Strangeness of Tragedy*, pp. 17–18).

[36] Cf. Hardie, "Contrasts," pp. 163–5.

emphasis. In the process, Thomas convincingly demonstrates that Dylan's lyrics have the status of poetry. Rather than a popularizing approach to Vergil via Dylan – characteristic of some kinds of reception study – Thomas boldly adopts a canonizing approach to Dylan via Vergil. At the very same time, the pathos of Vergil's poetry comes alive through its dynamic recontextualization in modern song. Vergil may not provide as influential a paradigm for Dylan as he does for Gavin Douglas, or as Ovid or Ulysses provide for Shakespeare and Petrarch respectively, but the attentive critic can nevertheless read the reception of his text against the context of Dylan's own cultural concerns and thereby better appreciate the poetics of pathos in both artists. In Thomas' view, both the multiplicity of voices and the pathos represent fundamental features of Dylan's self-representational strategy.

Christopher Wood's envoi offers a provocation to classicists who might be tempted to rest easy with the current developments in Reception Studies. Although the project augured by Martindale's *Redeeming the Text* may have led to a more "emancipated criticism" that invites "the reader to move freely within a web of texts" (p. 165), Wood suggests that it stops short of asking a more crucial question about the very concept of "the classics" and the assumption of their transhistorical significance.

The canonical status of the classics is a working premise of current Reception Studies, as is the (potentially) canonical status of other works in various traditions from *Paradise Lost* to *Omeros*, from the *Ramayana* to *King Lear*.[37] The question of canon formation opens up two obvious scholarly paths: the first, pursued in Martindale's current work,[38] seeks to identify the basis and function of "aesthetic judgment" (p. 166) and thus to identify the theoretical criteria according to which artworks are evaluated; the second, on show in this volume, seeks to describe "histories of reading" (p. 167) and thus to describe the particular conditions of possibility of artworks and their interpretation and evaluation.[39] While acknowledging the value

---

[37] For an extremely thorough analysis of the concept of the "classical", especially as it relates to canon formation, see Porter, "What is 'classical' about classical antiquity?".

[38] Martindale, *Latin Poetry and the Judgment of Taste* and "Performance, reception, aesthetics." In a recent review published in the journal *Arion*, Martindale argues that a cultural studies model of Classics misses the special aesthetic element of classical artworks (Martindale, "Leaving Athens," p. 139): "It is doubtful, however, whether classics, or any other humanities discipline, will long survive unless its practitioners are committed to the special value of their objects of study (which in the case of works of literature and art must include their beauty). The very title 'Classics' registers a claim that those objects of study are in some sense exemplary in that regard, in a way that binds together past and present." While sympathetic to Martindale's search for the distinguishing feature of the classics in the connection between past and present, Wood eschews aesthetics in favour of a very different approach to classical artworks and their presence through time.

[39] In discussing a more radical, historicized textual criticism Güthenke, "Shop talk," p. 110 mentions "the relatively more limiting aim of just wanting to lay bare its ideological drifts." In order to

of these approaches, in the course of which he notes yet further overlaps between the theoretical outlook of Reception Studies and Early Modern Studies,[40] Wood suggests that to define "the classics" and their study by reference to the canon is to miss the fundamental feature of classical texts and art: their relationship not to other artworks but rather to the divine.

Classical art – whether texts that offer an informational or performative connection to the gods (such as an invocation to a muse or a prayer) or statuary that actually partakes of divinity – claims an intimate bond with the otherworldly and presents the hermeneutics of such art as an analogue for the interpretation and understanding of the very gods themselves, invisible, inscrutable, and just barely audible. Invoking the example of Greek statuary within the discipline of Art History together with Aby Warburg's concept of the "pathos formula," Wood argues that the classics may express just such a primordial experience – being within reach of the gods – through formulae that recur through time in various forms of representation. According to this method, rather than focusing on the unit of the artwork, the scholar traces such expressive formulae as they pulse through history and through their various manifestations. The classical is thus no longer restricted to the past and to "high" culture, not even to a whole artwork, but is rather a collapsing of moments and forms in which some powerful, originary experience is expressed.[41] On this radical view the classics become unavoidable – canonical – not because of various historical contingencies of value "but because they are *true*" in some deeper sense (p. 168).[42]

Wood's historiography of the study of the classics and his vision of Reception Studies – he even queries the adequacy of the term "reception" (p. 171) – will be controversial. But his original and direct confrontation with the value and meaning of the classics is instructive for those of us who

---

overcome this narrowness – and leaving aside her specific context of textual criticism – we might focus on the thick description of the discipline gained from the papers in this collection, the variety and confluence of motivations and resources that have driven, enabled, and characterized approaches to classical texts.

[40] See p. 167.

[41] For a very different notion of classical connectivity, drawing on Deleuze and Guattari's model of the rhizome, see duBois, *Out of Athens*. Both Wood and duBois allow for an expansive conception of the reach of classical artworks, though Wood – here closer to Martindale than duBois – sees the argument for the distinctiveness of the classics as crucial.

[42] In light of Wood's claim it may be worth approaching the question of the diminishing authority of classical texts not via the familiar narrative of pedagogy and society – a change in the constituency and habits of the elite – but rather in terms of a turn away from the sacred text. On this view, the typical polarization of sacred scripture and pagan literature occludes their shared marginalization by the secularizing process. The decline of the authority of religion concomitantly weakens classical texts' claims to contact with the divine.

have felt more comfortable evading the difficult questions concerning the identity of our discipline and our place within humanistic study, questions which this volume addresses from the different perspectives of transmission and philology, authorial self-fashioning and cultural history, and even, at its close, a new hermeneutics.

PART I

Reception between Transmission and Philology

CHAPTER 2

"Arouse the dead": Mai, Leopardi, and Cicero's commonwealth in Restoration Italy

James E. G. Zetzel

A CHRISTMAS PRESENT FOR THE POPE

On December 23, 1819, Monsignor Angelo Mai (not to become a cardinal until 1838 as head of the secretariat *De propaganda fide*), the recently appointed keeper of the Vatican Library, sent a letter to his employer, Pope Pius VII, to announce important discoveries that he had made in two manuscripts in the library.[1] One of them (Vaticanus Latinus 5750) contained portions of the letters of Fronto, of the so-called Bobbio scholia on Cicero's orations, of Symmachus, and of Ulfila's Gothic Bible: these were all palimpsests, the lower (erased) script of parchments that had then been recopied with the Acts of the Council of Chalcedon. Although the texts found were new, the manuscript in fact was one with which Mai was familiar: he had found the rest of the same book a few years earlier in the Ambrosian Library in Milan.[2] The second manuscript, however, was new to him, and he gave it pride of place in his letter: under a copy of Augustine's *Enarrationes in Psalmos* (on Psalms 119–140) he found 151 leaves of a single work, Cicero's long-lost dialogue *De re publica*.[3]

---

[1] The text of Mai's letter, preserved in Vat. Lat. 9540 foll. 3–6, is printed in Mercati, *M. Tulli Ciceronis de re publica libri e codice rescripto vaticano 5757 phototypice expressi*, vol. I, pp. 225–8 and reprinted in Cortesi, "Epistolario di A. Mai," pp. 295–7 as letter no. 263. It will be apparent to those who know more about Italian history, intellectual history, and Leopardi in particular that they indeed do know more about those subjects than I do. My goal is to trace the reactions to one text in a number of contexts; while I am sure that I have oversimplified some (perhaps all) of them, I hope that I have not seriously misunderstood them. Audiences at Columbia, New York University, and Yale have kindly listened to and made useful suggestions about earlier versions of this essay; I am grateful to all. I am particularly grateful to Rolando Ferri, who read the final draft and saved me from many errors. Jonathan Galassi's fine translation of Leopardi (*Giacomo Leopardi: Canti*, transl. J. Galassi, New York 2010) appeared too late to be used here.

[2] On Vat. Lat. 5750 and Milan, Ambros. E.147 sup., see Reynolds (ed.), *Texts and Transmission*, p. 173 with bibliography.

[3] For a full description of the manuscript (both upper and lower texts), see Mercati, *M. Tulli Ciceronis de re publica libri e codice rescripto vaticano 5757 phototypice expressi*, vol. I, pp. 175–222; the information about it given here derives from his account unless otherwise noted.

Although new discoveries of ancient works still occasionally receive attention, it is hard now even to imagine the degree of interest aroused by Mai's first report of the existence of the manuscript in 1819 and by his subsequent publication of a full edition of the remains of *De re publica* in 1822.[4] The discovery of the palimpsest of *De re publica* came near the end of the last great age in which previously unknown ancient texts were unearthed from the libraries of Europe and in which an active and deliberate search for such manuscripts was conducted. In part, the impetus came from the discovery in the previous century of the carbonized papyrus rolls from Herculaneum, which not only revealed important new texts, but showed that much was to be gained from the patient study of fragmentary and difficult manuscripts.[5] A more immediate occasion for the discovery of palimpsests was the disruption of European libraries by the Napoleonic Wars: large numbers of manuscripts had been requisitioned by the conquering French and their return to the libraries from which they had been liberated – or comparably, in France, the vast expansion of the Bibliothèque Nationale resulting from the expropriation of monastic libraries – required the reshelving, and thus almost inevitably the inspection, of entire collections.[6] The existence of palimpsests had been known for more than a century, and some had been published. But it was Mai's own energy and ambition that raised the search to a new level of intensity: the extraordinary number of texts, their importance, and the speed with which he published them beginning in 1814 turned an antiquarian curiosity into a serious and widely followed search.[7]

The discovery of *De re publica* was in a different category from the others. The correspondence of Fronto, of which Mai announced the discovery of a second portion in the same letter in which he described finding *De re publica*, did indeed provide a considerable sample of an author whose reputation in antiquity had been high, but of whom nothing had survived in the normal channels of transmission.[8] Portions of three sets of Ciceronian

---

[4] Printing began on January 15, 1822; see Mercati, *M. Tulli Ciceronis de re publica libri e codice rescripto vaticano 5757 phototypice expressi*, vol. I, p. 212 and below, n. 14. On the wider resonance of the discovery, see particularly Treves, "Ciceronianismo e anticiceronianismo nella cultura italiani del secolo XIX," pp. 404–21.

[5] It is worth noting that Humphry Davy, who was involved in the study of the Herculaneum papyri, visited Rome early in 1820 and was shown the palimpsest of *De re publica* by Mai; cf. Mercati, *M. Tulli Ciceronis de re publica libri e codice rescripto vaticano 5757 phototypice expressi*, vol. I, p. 193, n. 1.

[6] B. G. Niebuhr in 1819 reported that he had been unable to use the Vatican library for the past two years in part because the books were being arranged on their new mahogany bookcases; see Harnack, *Geschichte der königlich Preussischen Akademie der Wissenschaften zu Berlin*, vol. II, p. 405.

[7] On Mai's discoveries and methods, and on previous discoveries of palimpsests, see Timpanaro, *Aspetti e figure della cultura ottocentesca*, pp. 225–71.

[8] Fronto was renowned as an orator; the correspondence that survives did little to enhance his reputation. In this context, however, Fronto is remarkable for having been preserved (to the extent

orations were discovered in three different libraries, and in 1816 B. G. Niebuhr, stopping in Verona en route to Rome, discovered the palimpsest of the jurist Gaius in the Biblioteca Capitolare.[9] *De re publica* stood apart. Much was known about it, not only from the separate preservation of the *Somnium Scipionis* (the conclusion of *De re publica*) attached to Macrobius' commentary on it, a text highly valued for its eschatological content, but also from the huge number of quotations from it in ancient texts, most significantly in Augustine's *City of God*.[10] It was known to have been one of the masterpieces of one of the greatest stylists of antiquity, and Cicero's own repeated reference to his own work made it a text greatly to be sought after – and indeed it had been sought for since the Renaissance in libraries of Italy, Germany, and beyond. By the eighteenth century, it was believed that it was, other than the fragments, gone for good, to the extent that Joseph Bernardi had attempted to reconstruct it through gathering the various statements on political theory that Cicero had made in his surviving works.[11] One further circumstance made it even more significant. The period of Mai's discoveries was not only the last great age of manuscript searches, it was the last time that the content of classical texts was of direct interest, not only to classicists, but to the educated public in general. In particular, it mattered to statesmen as well as to Latinists to know what a great statesman of the Roman republic thought about the conduct of public affairs.

Even before anyone had read the new text – in fact, as will become clear, particularly before anyone had read it – the simple fact of its discovery was a matter of great importance, and one that the Vatican clearly thought worth publicizing. Cardinal Mercati was surely right to describe it as a Christmas present for the Pope.[12] The discovery received wide publicity, and the text itself was – after the relatively long delay before Mai's publication of it in 1822 – rapidly disseminated. The Pope, or rather his Secretary of State Cardinal Ercole Consalvi, had Mai's letter of 23 December published

---

he is preserved) in not one but three palimpsests: see Reynolds (ed.), *Texts and Transmission*, pp. 173–4.

9 Fragments of Cicero's orations were discovered by Mai in Milan (Ambros. R. 57 sup.), published in 1814; by Niebuhr in Vat. Pal. Lat. 24, published in 1820; and by Peyron in Turin D. IV.22 (destroyed by fire in 1904), published in 1824. See Reynolds (ed.), *Texts and Transmission*, p. 56. Scipione Maffei had indicated the presence of the text of Gaius before Niebuhr discovered it; see Timpanaro, *Aspetti e figure della cultura ottocentesca*, pp. 254–5.

10 On the quotations of *De re publica*, see Heck, *Die Bezeugung von Ciceros Schrift De re publica*.

11 Bernardi, *De la république ou du meilleur gouvernement*. See Mai (ed.), *M. Tulli Ciceronis de re publica quae supersunt*, pp. xix–xxiii, Mercati, *M. Tulli Ciceronis de re publica libri e codice rescripto vaticano 5757 phototypice expressi*, vol. I, pp. 206–9 on earlier searches for *De re publica*. I cite Mai's edition from Wendell Clausen's copy, given to me by his son Raymond.

12 "*Strenna natalizia*," Mercati, *M. Tulli Ciceronis de re publica libri e codice rescripto vaticano 5757 phototypice expressi*, vol. I, p. 209. Cortesi ("Epistolario di A. Mai," p. 297, n.) also quotes *L'Osservatore romano* for December 28, 1934: "*un grande dono natalizio*."

in *Diario di Roma* only six days later (December 29). Even before that, on December 28, B. G. Niebuhr, then in Rome as Prussian Minister to the Vatican (1816–23) and himself an active but frustrated participant in the search for palimpsests, wrote to the Berlin Academy to report the discovery; he had clearly read Mai's letter before its official publication.[13] Mai himself, in preparing the text for publication, took the unusual step of arranging (with Niebuhr's help) for simultaneous publication of his edition in Germany; by the end of 1823 it had been reprinted in Paris, London, and Boston. In France, the first translator of *De re publica* in 1823, A.-F. Villemain, described in the preface of his book the excitement with which he had awaited the arrival of the text: "The pages were sent to me from Rome . . . I waited for them impatiently; I was like a somewhat literate Gaul, someone living in Lyon or Paris who had a link of remembered clientship or hospitality with some Roman citizen, who received serially in separate installments the latest book by the great Proconsul."[14] Within a few weeks of his discovery, Mai had shown Niebuhr a few pages of *De re publica*, and at least one other visitor, Humphry Davy, was allowed to admire a portion of the manuscript.[15] Less illustrious people also wanted to see it, but were rebuffed. In particular, Mai's young correspondent the scholar and poet Giacomo Leopardi wrote to Mai on January 10, 1820, asking to see the manuscript or the edition which he expected to appear rapidly.[16] Ten days later, Mai politely declined, but in the interval, Leopardi had produced his magnificent *canzone* "Ad Angelo Mai, quand'ebbe trovato i libri di Cicerone della repubblica" – surely the greatest accolade ever written for the discovery of an ancient text.[17]

---

[13] Harnack, *Geschichte der königlich Preussischen Akademie der Wissenschaften zu Berlin*, vol. II, p. 405; the chronology is noted by Mercati, who also quotes the letter (*M. Tulli Ciceronis de re publica libri e codice rescripto vaticano 5757 phototypice expressi*, vol. II, p. 209, n. 1).

[14] "*On m'envoyait les feuilles de Rome . . . Je les attendais avec impatience: j'étais comme un Gaulois quelque peu lettré, un habitant de Lugdunum ou de Lutetia qui, lié avec un citoyen de Rome par quelque souvenir de clientèle, ou d'hospitalité, aurait reçu de lui successivement, et par chapitres détachés, le livre nouveau du célèbre proconsul.*" Villemain, *La République de Cicéron*, p. lxxv [wrongly paginated lxv]; quoted from the first (1823) edition by Treves, "Ciceronianismo e anticiceronianismo nella cultura italiani del secolo XIX," p. 408. All translations are my own unless otherwise noted. It was published in Stuttgart as well as Rome in 1822; in Bonn, Leipzig, Harlem, Paris, London, and Boston in 1823. On Mai's role in the multiple publications, see Mercati, *M. Tulli Ciceronis de re publica libri e codice rescripto vaticano 5757 phototypice expressi*, vol. I, pp. 228–9.

[15] Niebuhr to Savigny, January 8, 1820 (Vischer (ed.), *Briefe aus Rom*, pp. 514–5); on Davy, see above, n. 5.

[16] Brioschi and Landi (eds.), *Leopardi*, pp. 361–2. Mai's answer at *ibid.*, pp. 363–4.

[17] I cite "Ad Angelo Mai" (*Canti*, no. 3) from Gavazzeni and Lombardi (eds.), *Canti*, pp. 126–47. A note in Leopardi's hand on a copy of the first edition (cited by Carducci, "Le tre canzoni patriottiche di Giacomo Leopardi," p. 155) calls it "*Opera di dieci o dodici giorni.*"

"SCOPRITOR FAMOSO"

Leopardi was 21 when he wrote "Ad Angelo Mai"; he had been in correspondence with Mai before, in connection with Mai's earlier discoveries at Milan. Self-taught in his father's library in Recanati, Leopardi was already the best philologist in Italy, as well as having been recognized by some as one of Italy's greatest poets despite his youth.[18] The *canzone*, the last of Leopardi's political poems, is long (180 verses) and complex; he wrote it just after he had heard of the discovery of *De re publica* but long before he saw the text. The first stanza gives an idea of the tone of the poem:[19]

> *Italo ardito, a che giammai non posi*
> *Di svegliar dalle tombe*
> *I nostri padri? ed a parlar gli meni*
> *A questo secol morto, al quale incombe*
> *Tanta nebbia di tedio? E come or vieni*   5
> *Sì forte a' nostri orecchi e sì frequente,*
> *Voce antica de' nostri,*
> *Muta sì lunga etade? e perchè tanti*
> *Risorgimenti? In un balen feconde*
> *Venner le carte; alla stagion presente*   10
> *I polverosi chiostri*
> *Serbaro occulti i generosi e santi*
> *Detti degli avi. E che valor t'infonde,*
> *Italo egregio, il fato? O con l'umano*
> *Valor forse contrasta il fato invano?*   15

Daring Italian, why do you never cease awakening from their tombs our ancestors? And leading them to speak to this dead age, on which weighs such a fog of weariness? And how do you come so loudly to our ears, and so often, ancient

---

[18] The literature on Leopardi is vast, and I am decidedly not expert. For a convenient biography in English, see Origo, *Leopardi*; for introductions to Leopardi as classicist and philologist, see Timpanaro, *La filologia di Giacomo Leopardi* and Treves, *Lo studio dell'antichità classica nell'ottocento*, pp. 471–89 (with bibliography). The most famous discussion of "Ad Angelo Mai" is that of Francesco De Sanctis, conveniently excerpted in Gallo (ed.), *De Sanctis: Opere*, pp. 1164–76; see also Carducci, "Le tre canzoni patriottiche di Giacomo Leopardi" (originally published in 1898; on its context see Treves, "Ciceronianismo e anticiceronianismo nella cultura italiani del secolo xix," pp. 412–13). For a recent discussion of the poem, see Alcorn and Del Puppo, "Giacomo Leopardi's historical poetics in the canzone 'Ad Angelo Mai.'" Earlier correspondence between Mai and Leopardi: Gervasoni (ed.), *Angelo Mai*, pp. 138–9 (dedication of Leopardi's translation of Fronto; not in Brioschi and Landi, *Leopardi*); Brioschi and Landi, *ibid.*, pp. 26–31 (= Gervasoni, *ibid.*, pp. 149–55, a detailed letter on Mai's edition of Fronto), p. 54 (= Gervasoni, *ibid.*, p. 171), pp. 115–16 (= Gervasoni, *ibid.*, pp. 187–8), pp. 135–6 (= Gervasoni, *ibid.*, pp. 214–15), pp. 154–5 (= Gervasoni, *ibid.*, pp. 224–5), pp. 188–9 (= Gervasoni, *ibid.*, pp. 250–1), pp. 253–4 (= Gervasoni, *ibid.*, p. 292, from Leopardi); pp. 23–5 (= Gervasoni, *ibid.*, pp. 143–6), pp. 62–3 (= Gervasoni, *ibid.*, pp. 172–3), pp. 120–1 (= Gervasoni, *ibid.*, pp. 190–1, from Mai). On their relationship, see also Gervasoni, *ibid.*, pp. 21–8.

[19] In line 3, the early editions (prior to 1835) have "*favellar*" rather than "*parlar.*"

voice of our people, mute for so long an age? Why such awakenings? In a flash, the pages have become fruitful; it is for the present season that the dusty cloisters have preserved hidden the noble and sainted words of our ancestors. And with what valor, great Italian, has fate infused you? Or perhaps fate is futile set against human valor?

Leopardi contrasts the glory of antiquity with the tedium of the present day and the great and holy ancestors of Italy with the dusty world of monastic culture that had concealed (if it had also thereby preserved) their voices for centuries. He describes the recovered texts as "santi" – saints – and the process of discovery as a resurrection.[20] Pagan is set against Christian, past glory against present smallness and decay. The only question is whether this resurrection has a purpose – or if Mai is a hero struggling against the inexorable fate of Italy. Much of the poem is an evocation of the great poets of the Italian past, now gone and not replaced. He sees only one poet since Tasso worthy of the Italian name: Alfieri, who had died in 1803. "Death," says Leopardi in the last stanza of the poem (168), "saved him from seeing worse":

> Vittorio mio, questa per te non era
> Età nè suolo. Altri anni ed altro seggio   170
> Conviene agli alti ingegni. Or di riposo
> Paghi viviamo, e scorti
> Da mediocrità: sceso il sapiente
> E salita è la turba a un sol confine,
> Che il mondo agguaglia. O scopritor famoso,   175
> Segui; risveglia i morti,
> Poi che dormono i vivi; arma le spente
> Lingue de' prischi eroi; tanto che in fine
> Questo secol di fango o vita agogni
> E sorga ad atti illustri, o si vergogni.   180

My Vittorio, this was neither the time nor the land for you. Another time and another place fit lofty talents. Now we live content to rest, and ruled by mediocrity: the sage has declined, and the mob risen, to a single plane that the world levels. O famed discoverer, continue onward: arouse the dead, since the living are asleep; give force to the mute tongues of the heroes of old; so that this age of mud either long for life and rise to noble deeds, or feel some shame.

Leopardi views Mai's recovery of the living memorials of the Italian past as a step in the reawakening of Italy from the somnolent and sterile culture of the Restoration. The revival of Cicero is a model and occasion for a revival

---

[20] De Sanctis (Gallo (ed.), De Sanctis: Opere, p. 1170) aptly compares the reference to martyrs in Luigi Mercantini's "Inno di Garibaldi" of 1859.

of Italian letters and the Italian nation. Not surprisingly, the poem to Mai, with its implicit republicanism and overt nationalism, was banned by the Austrian government of Lombardy.[21]

TWO MEN IN SEARCH OF A PALIMPSEST

What Leopardi hoped for, in the recovery of a text representing the greatness of the Italian past, was some revival of the idea (and indeed the nation) of Italy, a return of Cicero's *res publica*, not just Cicero's *De re publica*. And Leopardi was not alone in his hope for a new and better Italy; we will return to the context of "Ad Angelo Mai" shortly. But the discovery of the palimpsest was not pure chance; and Mai, although he was the one who found it, was not the only person looking for it. The discovery of *De re publica*, in fact, brought together two men of profoundly different backgrounds and profoundly different scholarly goals. Mai, the newly appointed prefect of the Vatican Library, was one; the other was the Prussian Minister to the Vatican, the great historian Barthold Georg Niebuhr.

From the very outset, the two men had different goals and expectations. In his letter to the Pope, Mai described the importance of what he had found: "Politics, jurisprudence, history, antiquarian studies, ethics, and good Latinity have much to look forward to from the publication of this important Work of Cicero that has been lamented for so long."[22] Niebuhr, in his letter to the Berlin Academy, alluded to this, and expressed his apprehension that there might be found in *De re publica* rather more of ethics and philosophy than of solid factual gains for Roman history.[23] The difference in the desires of the two men reflects their different orientations, and casts some light on the ambivalence felt about *De re publica* when it eventually appeared in print. Niebuhr's guarded reaction was in part based on personal frustration. Even before arriving in Rome, in the course of

---

[21] On Leopardi's difficulties with his publisher Brighenti, a spy for the Austrians whose reports led to the suppression of "Ad Angelo Mai," see Carducci "Le tre canzoni patriottiche di Giacomo Leopardi," pp. 167–72, Origo, *Leopardi*, pp. 133–7. On the political circumstances and organization of Restoration Italy, see below, pp. 32–3.

[22] "*La politica, la giurisprudenza, la storia, l'antiquaria, la morale, e la buona latinità molto devono aspettarsi dalla publicatione di questa importante e tanto compianta Opera di Cicerone.*" Mercati, *M. Tulli Ciceronis de re publica libri e codice rescripto vaticano 5757 phototypice expressi*, vol. i, p. 226 = Cortesi, "Epistolario di A. Mai," p. 296; see above, n. 1.

[23] Harnack, *Geschichte der königlich Preussischen Akademie der Wissenschaften zu Berlin*, vol. ii, p. 405. At least according to Niebuhr (letter to Bekker of 18 March 1820, Vischer (ed.), *Briefe aus Rom*, pp. 535–6), Mai feared precisely the reverse: "*Vom Inhalt aber konnte er schlechterdings noch nichts präcises angeben ausser einem sehr erfreulichen Umstand, der ihm sehr misfiel, nämlich dass keine Speculation darin sey, sondern alles historisch, Darstellung der römischen Verfassung.*"

his journey from Berlin in 1816,' he had found in the Cathedral Library of
Verona the palimpsest of Gaius' *Institutes*, and he, like others (particularly
Amedeo Peyron in Turin), hoped that more new ancient texts would emerge
from thorough research in the great manuscript collections of Europe. But
his desire to scour the Vatican Library for more such manuscripts met with
resistance. On arriving in Rome, he wrote to Consalvi asking for permission
to use the catalogue of Vatican manuscripts and to be permitted more time
in the library than the three hours daily that it was open; when Consalvi
demurred, he made a specific request to look at the one manuscript that
he knew contained palimpsested material, Palatinus Latinus 24, offering to
give financial security for his good behavior. As he explained to the Berlin
Academy, "The Library has never been so inaccessible and so carefully
guarded as it is now . . . The librarian understands the rules of Clement
XIII to mean . . . that his principal duty is to secure the books from coming
into the hands of any foreigner."[24] He went on to report that he had, as a
result of his letter to Consalvi, received permission to look at Pal. Lat. 24,
and had found some palimpsest pages of Cicero's speeches and of Seneca.
But that was all he could do: the catalogue was not available to outsiders,
particularly to foreign Protestants, and after his one discovery he had no
success in breaching the defenses of the Vatican. His correspondence reveals
no further attempt for the next three years, until Mai's arrival as prefect in
November 1819. Within a few weeks, the two men resolved the differences
occasioned by Niebuhr's critical comments on Mai's Milan publications,
and Niebuhr wrote a flattering letter to Mai in Latin on November 30 –
although his letters to others show that his opinion of the new Primo
Custode remained distinctly unflattering.[25]

Niebuhr's overtures to Mai were too late. Mai had probably not found
De re publica by November 30, but within a week or two he almost certainly
had and Niebuhr, like the rest of the world, learned of the discovery from
Mai's letter to the Pope. In reporting the news to the Berlin Academy,
Niebuhr did not bother to conceal his chagrin that it was Mai rather than

[24] Letter of November 20, 1816 (Harnack, *Geschichte der königlich Preussischen Akademie der Wis-senschaften zu Berlin*, vol. II, pp. 390–1 = Vischer (ed.), *Briefe aus Rom*, pp. 103–5): "*Nie ist diese Bibliothek so unzugänglich gewesen und so streng bewacht worden als jetzt. Mann kann behaupten, dass der Bibliothekar das Reglement Clemens'* XIII . . . *so versteht, als mache es ihm zur Hauptpflicht, die Bücher dadurch zu sichern, dass er jeden Fremden hindert, sie in die Hände zu bekommen.*"
[25] Letter of November 30 to Mai in Mercati, *M. Tulli Ciceronis de re publica libri e codice rescripto vaticano 5757 phototypice expressi*, vol. I, pp. 224–5; Vischer (ed.), *Briefe aus Rom*, pp. 488–91; Cortesi, "Epistolario di A. Mai," pp. 291–3. The original text in Vat. Lat. 12895, fol. 57. Mercati, *M. Tulli Ciceronis de re publica libri e codice rescripto vaticano 5757 phototypice expressi*, vol. I, pp. 209–15 gives the Vatican view of Niebuhr's relationship with Mai. A brief summary of Niebuhr's views in Walther, *Niebuhrs Forschung*, pp. 519–20.

he who had found it, and he expressed his belief that he would have been able to do a better job in editing *De re publica*: "As much as I would have given to have been the one to make this discovery, I am at least still full of the most vivid joy – even though the edition will probably be poor – that this work of Cicero was discovered in my lifetime."[26] In the event, Niebuhr did in fact play a large part in the editing of the text, offering Mai emendations and interpretations, and composing the index to Mai's edition. It merely confirmed his already low opinion of Mai when he found that (other than in connection with the index) his assistance was almost entirely unacknowledged, and he made sure that his friends knew both of his contributions and of Mai's lack of gratitude.[27]

Niebuhr's apprehensions about the discovery and edition were not based purely on frustration and jealousy. By 1819, Niebuhr was already at work on the revision of his *History of Rome*; he had begun to develop a program of research designed to identify and to catalogue the ancient materials, both in manuscript and epigraphic, that still existed. A disciple of the new German scholarship exemplified by F. A. Wolf, Niebuhr was not only an expert on early Roman history, but was becoming more and more concerned with the transmission of knowledge of the ancient world; he was in this period not only organizing a search for manuscripts in the libraries of Europe, but studying late antique and early Byzantine texts. His endeavors ultimately

---

[26] Harnack, *Geschichte der königlich Preussischen Akademie der Wissenschaften zu Berlin*, vol. II, p. 405 (summarized in Vischer (ed.), *Briefe aus Rom*, p. 503): "*Wie viel ich nun auch darum geben würde, wenn ich er wäre, der diesen Fund gethan hätte, so bin ich doch wenigstens voll der lebhaftesten Freude, obgleich die Ausgabe wahrscheinlich schlecht werden wird, dass das Werk Ciceros in meinen Tagen gefunden ist.*" Niebuhr's frustration is even clearer in his letters to Dore Hensler on January 1, 1820 (Vischer (ed.), *Briefe aus Rom*, pp. 507–8) and to Savigny on January 8 (*ibid.*, p. 514). The latter makes it clear that Niebuhr exaggerated his difficulties: he had, in fact, inspected hundreds of manuscripts in the Vatican, but he had not looked in this section because it consisted of unimportant manuscripts that had been acquired only in the seventeenth century.

[27] Niebuhr's most trenchant opinion of Mai – which also reveals his anti-Italian bias – appears in a letter to Lord Colchester of September 10, 1822 (Vischer (ed.), *Briefe aus Rom*, p. 783; written in English): "As a true Italian, his [Mai's] mind is governed alternately by vanity and avarice: but however provoking it be to us, who have the good fortune to belong to nations differently animated, to be obliged to satisfy in him these vile passions, still it must be done, or he will withhold whatever he has discovered." He goes on to give one of his several confidential accounts of how much he had helped Mai with the edition of *De re publica*. Niebuhr's name appears on only four pages of Mai's edition: in connection with his work on Gaius (Mai, *M. Tulli Ciceronis de re publica quae supersunt*, p. xxxviiii); at 2.10.20, for restoration of the damaged text (*ibid.*, p. 148); at 2.22.30 on the Servian constitution (*ibid.*, p. 173); and in very small type, at the end of the errata, a notice thanking Niebuhr for the index: "*Qui sequuntur Indices historiae ac latinitati perutiles auctorem habent ill. Niebuhrium, qui tanto et librum meum honore et me beneficio dignatus est, ut laborem huiusmodi in summis suis occupationibus ulto perferre non dubitauerit*" (*ibid.*, p. 337). A more generous appraisal of his contribution appeared in the nearly simultaneous Stuttgart edition, which Niebuhr organized (Walther, *Niebuhrs Forschung*, p. 519, n. 66).

led to the great collections of both inscriptions and texts that characterize
German scholarship later in the nineteenth century. His interest in *De re
publica* obviously emphasized the possible gain for the study of early Rome,
but involved also ancient law and political theory, as well as the significance
of the manuscript itself.[28]

If Niebuhr can be taken as a representative of the new scholarship
of Germany, Angelo Mai is emblematic of a different strain of classical
learning. Italian classical scholarship in the early nineteenth century was not
distinguished. The great antiquarians of the previous generation (notably
Ennio Quirino Visconti) had died; there were very few Latinists of any
philological ability and almost no competent Hellenists.[29] The classical
learning of the day tended either to concentrate on the reproduction of
an elegant Latin style without the detailed knowledge of the history of
the language that was being developed in Germany, or on a cultivated
antiquarianism and the search for coins, monuments, and inscriptions
without any historical or literary context in which to understand them. A
product of Counter-Reformation classicism, Mai was far more comfortable
composing elegant verses and Ciceronian prose than he was in dealing with
the genuine technical problems of editing a palimpsest and restoring a
damaged and difficult text. Mai had not deliberately become the "*scopritor
famoso*" which Leopardi christened him in his *canzone*. He had entered
the Ambrosian Library as a student of oriental languages, and his interests
were ecclesiastical rather than classical. His education, even by the norms
of the day, was poor preparation for his career, having been disrupted by
the Napoleonic wars; although his Latin was good – at least in verse and
prose composition – his Greek was poor and his philological training (like
that of almost all his Italian contemporaries) non-existent.[30] In Milan, he
discovered a number of important texts among the Bobbio palimpsests,
including Ciceronian orations and scholia, Symmachus, and various Greek
texts, which he published with a speed equalled only by his carelessness.
The Greek texts in particular were filled with grammatical errors; the Milan
editions were severely criticized by those, including Niebuhr, who knew
the ancient languages better than he did. But the fame he acquired from

---

[28] For Niebuhr's interests in this period, Walther, *Niebuhrs Forschung*, pp. 489–523; on the effect of
De re publica on his research, see esp. pp. 519–23.

[29] On the situation of classics in Italy in the early nineteenth century, see Treves, "Ciceronianismo e anticiceronianismo nella cultura italiani del secolo XIX," and *Lo studio dell'antichità classica nell'ottocento* (esp. pp. vii–xxix); Timpanaro, *Classicismo e illuminismo nell'ottocento italiano*,
pp. 1–41.

[30] On Mai's background, see Gervasoni, *Angelo Mai*, pp. 1–9; Treves, *Lo studio dell'antichità classica
nell'ottocento*, pp. 347–63; Timpanaro, *Aspetti e figure della cultura ottocentesca*, pp. 233–9.

these publications led to his being offered in 1818 the position of Primo Custode at the Vatican; he delayed his move for a year, until he could complete his work at Milan, and arrived in Rome to take up his new position on November 7, 1819 – barely six weeks before he sent the Pope his announcement of the discovery of the palimpsests of Vat. Lat. 5750 and 5757.

Both the substance and the speed of the discoveries were as gratifying to Mai himself as to the Vatican hierarchy, since they amply justified the appointment of an outsider – at the time, Milan was part of the Austrian Empire, while Rome was of course the center of the Papal States.[31] Mai himself seems to have claimed at the time that his discoveries were a fortunate accident, but in fact they were less the result of divine assistance than the product of careful preparation and the organization of the Vatican library itself. In Milan, Mai had found palimpsested texts in manuscripts that had come from the library of the Monastery of St. Columbanus at Bobbio, a seventh-century Irish foundation, and it was generally known not only from the collection in the Ambrosiana but from another set of Bobbio manuscripts in the National Library of Turin that the combination of thrifty habits and poor technique in preparing parchment had made the Bobbio collection a fruitful source for palimpsests. The Vatican Library had only a few manuscripts from the same source, a group of some twenty-nine books that had been sent to the Vatican in 1618 at the request of Pope Paul V. The texts they apparently contained (in the upper script) were not distinguished, and in fact not important enough for them to be requisitioned by the French in 1797. On the other hand, within the Vatican collection they formed a distinct group, numbered in order from Vat. Lat. 5748 to 5776, and all but a few had identical seventeenth-century bindings of red morocco.[32] What is more, there was a catalogue of these manuscripts in the Vatican, which Mai almost certainly used, but which was not accessible to anyone else (including the frustrated Niebuhr) without the permission of the Primo Custode – who was Mai himself.[33] In his desire to establish himself in his new and important position, the small

---

[31] On the risk Consalvi took in appointing him, see Cortesi, "Epistolario di A. Mai," p. 297 n. For a full account of his move from the Ambrosiana to the Vatican, see Ruysschaert, "Il passaggio di Mai dalla Biblioteca Ambrosiana alla Biblioteca Vaticana."

[32] On the Vatican Bobbio collection and its organization, see Mercati, *M. Tulli Ciceronis de re publica libri e codice rescripto vaticano 5757 phototypice expressi*, vol. i, pp. 139–42.

[33] Niebuhr's letter to Amedeo Peyron in Turin, February 18, 1821 (Vischer (ed.), *Briefe aus Rom*, pp. 615–16): "*Tous les papiers qui regardent l'histoire de la bibliothèque sont exclusivement entre les mains du premier conservateur, et M. Amati ne pourrait y parvenir pas plus que Vous, Monsieur, si Vous veniez à Rome: car je ne parlerai pas de moi. C'est sans doute la liste des 28 manuscrits qui a conduit M. Mai à la découverte des deux manuscrits dont l'un contient les fragmens de Republica, et l'autre*

and distinct Bobbio collection was the obvious place for Mai to seek further palimpsests, and he did so both rapidly and successfully.

As a scholar, Mai's goals were not those of Niebuhr and the new school of philology. Despite his nod in the letter to Pius VII to the gains that might accrue from his discoveries to the knowledge of the ancient world, his own aims were simply to find new texts and to publish them as rapidly as possible. He treated his fragile materials with disastrously effective chemicals – a procedure which he shared with Niebuhr and all other students of palimpsests in the period – that ultimately rendered the palimpsests unreadable by anyone else, and largely impenetrable to later and less invasive techniques.[34] What was in the long run more harmful than the chemicals, however, was that Mai's own transcripts of these difficult texts were inaccurate, his emendations were poor, and his reports of the manuscripts such as to render his editions highly misleading. And, whether out of recognition of his own lack of ability or for some less disreputable reason, he was not willing to allow anyone else to see the palimpsests to check his work. Even after he had left the Ambrosiana, he kept others away from the palimpsests he had found there, and it was a very long time before more careful transcriptions could be attempted. The edition of *De re publica*, in fact, stands out among Mai's many publications for its care and accuracy as well as for a commentary that is still of considerable value. That may be the result in part of his greater experience, in part of the fact that the palimpsest of *De re publica* is far more legible than most of the manuscripts with which he dealt, and in part of the greater familiarity which he (like other Italian classicists of his generation) had with Cicero than with most of the other new texts. But it was also a far better edition, and took much longer than Mai's normal practice, because of the almost entirely unacknowledged assistance rendered him by Niebuhr himself.

"CICERO IS A LADY"

For Mai as for his employers, however, the discovery of *De re publica* (and the other texts found in Vat. Lat. 5750) was important not only as a vindication of Mai's appointment and a significant addition to the

---

ceux de Fronton, du Scholiaste, etc.: *je me rappelle que dans le temps il me dit que la découverte avait été accidentelle, et qu'il se montra instruit des circonstances de la transaction qui a valu cet envoi à la Vaticane...*" Peyron in fact did get the list, which he included in the preface of his edition of the Turin fragments of Cicero's speeches in 1824; Mercati, *M. Tulli Ciceronis de re publica libri e codice rescripto vaticano 5757 phototypice expressi*, vol. I, p. 140, n. 2.

[34] On the technique of reading palimpsests, see Timpanaro, *Aspetti e figure della cultura ottocentesca*, pp. 224–33, 248–62.

knowledge of antiquity, but as a link between the Rome of the Papal States and the Rome of antiquity. In his letter to Pius VII, after listing the areas of scholarship that might be affected, Mai announced his plans for publication: "I will immediately arrange for its publication, and it will be happy to appear under the eyes of Your Holiness, the Ruler and Defender of the Roman States."[35] The papacy as patron of classical learning in the post-Napoleonic age would continue the renaissance that had been felt to exist under the papacy of Paul V and perhaps, more ambitiously, the role of the papacy in the Renaissance. The oppressively fulsome letter of dedication of the *editio princeps* of *De re publica* to Pius VII makes the intra-Vatican significance of the discovery all too clear: after thanking the Pope for his job and promising to be worthy of it, Mai invites him to receive the dedication of Cicero's work "that comes to you as if inherited by right" ("iure veluti hereditatis Tibi obvenientem"), listing the previous popes who had tried to have it found – Silvester II and Clement VI – or Paul V who had had the palimpsest brought to Rome. He goes on to list the ancient political works translated under the sponsorship of other popes: Plato under Leo X, Aristotle under Eugenius IV: "what remains is for our Cicero (and even though he is in poor condition, the glory of his name is bright far and wide) to enter eagerly the protection of Pius VII" ("iam superest ut noster Tullius (qui male licet affectus, splendore tamen sui nominis longe rutilat) in PII VII clientelam lubens veniat"). If Cicero as *cliens* to the papacy were not revolting enough, Mai proceeds to draw connections between the subject matter of *De re publica* and the government of Pius VII:

In fact, in our day there is nobody who does not address You as the father and restorer of Roman rule: the dawn of your benevolent reign instantly summoned it back to life although it had been mourned as dead . . . And therefore, because you have governed so well and with such courage, not only has the glory of your name filled the world, but all men feel a special love for You. Lo: religion, after suffering so many disasters, has been revived; the provinces have been organized in peace and joy; the city has been enriched by countless adornments; laws have been composed with the highest fairness and wisdom; the study of literature and the arts has been renewed. Cicero himself, MOST HOLY FATHER, seems to offer thanks to You for being enhanced by new resources in your library.[36]

---

[35] *"che io immediatamente dispongo per la stampa, e che sarà lieta di comparire sotto gli occhi della Santità Vostra Sovrano e Vindice degli Stati Romani."* Mercati, *M. Tulli Ciceronis de re publica libri e codice rescripto vaticano 5757 phototypice expressi*, vol. I, p. 226 = Cortesi, "Epistolario di A. Mai," p. 296.

[36] *"Iamvero nostris temporibus parentem Te ac restitutorem romanae dominationis nemo est qui non appellet: quam flebiliter extinctam lux prima benefici regni tui in vitam subito revocavit . . . Igitur ob rempublicam tam bene tamque fortiter gestam cum implesti orbem terrarum nominis tui gloria, tum est*

The link between Cicero and Pius VII, between classical Rome and the
Restoration of the Papal States after the Napoleonic Wars, between Caesar
and Christ, aroused appropriate nausea in the enlightened sensibilities of
some Italian contemporaries. In response to an inquiry from his friend
Giuseppe Montani in 1823, Pietro Giordani, one of the leading men of
letters in Italy, offered his opinions of the new text and its discoverer, had
some strong comments about the dedication. Montani had said that it
made him laugh; Giordani replied, "it's more worthy of Brother Barnaba
than of Marcus Tullius. But, good God, how can one want to link Cicero
and Brother Chiaramonti?"[37]

The link between Cicero and Chiaramonti was ludicrous not merely
because of the oleaginous flattery of Mai's dedication and the feverish desire
of the Vatican to reinforce its image as the preserver and inheritor of the
mantle of ancient Roman glory (and political power in Italy), but because –
as Giordani saw and disliked – it was also intended to confer legitimacy on
the empty Ciceronianism of Counter-Reformation education: the classics
as a source of elegance rather than of ideas. The discovery of *De re publica*
had been given quite a different interpretation in Leopardi's poem, as an
event of patriotic importance to the (not yet extant) Italian nation.

Within the poem, Leopardi's repeated address to Mai as "Italian" is
deliberate. In 1819, Italy existed only as a geographical division; indeed, it
did not have a unified government between sometime in late antiquity and –
in fact, if not in name – the establishment of the modern kingdom of Italy
in 1861. In the Napoleonic era, Italy achieved a greater unity than it had in
centuries, in the Kingdom of Italy ruled by Eugene Beauharnais as a vassal of
Napoleon. The Restoration settlement achieved at the Congress of Vienna
was organized on the principle of legitimacy – which essentially meant the
restoration of previous monarchies and the reorganization of Italy under
Austrian domination. The Savoy and Piedmont (Turin) remained part
of the Kingdom of Sardinia; Venice and Lombardy (Milan) – indeed the

*amor erga Te singularis omnium hominum. Ecce autem religione quam tot clades adflixerant recreata,
provinciis in laeta pace compositis, urbe innumeris ornamentis ditata, scriptis summa aequitate pru-
dentiaque legibus, renovatis litterarum et artium studiis; ipse Tibi iam Cicero, PATER BEATISSIME,
novis in tua bibliotheca copiis auctus gratulari uidetur"*. Mai (ed.), *M. Tulli Ciceronis de re publica
quae supersunt*, pp. iii–vi.

[37] "*Ch'ella sia piuttosto degna di fra Barnaba che di Marco Tullio. Ma, santo dio, come voler unire Cicerone
e frate Chiaramonti?*" "*Fra Barnaba*" and "*frate Chiaramonti*" both refer to Pius VII, born Gregorio
Luigi Barnaba Chiaramonti. The text of Giordani's letter (on which more below) is given by Treves,
Lo Studio dell'antichità classica nell'ottocento, pp. 435–43; the quotation from p. 437. On the letter, in
addition to Treves' comments in his edition, cf. Treves, "Ciceronianismo e anticiceronianismo nella
cultura italiani del secolo XIX," pp. 414–18; on Giordani, see particularly Timpanaro, *Classicismo e
illuminismo nell'ottocento italiano*, pp. 41–117 and Treves, *Lo studio dell'antichità classica nell'ottocento*,
pp. 399–416, with bibliography.

whole north of Italy except the Piedmont – became part of Austria; Tuscany was returned to the Habsburg family. Further south, Cardinal Consalvi managed to negotiate the restoration of the Papal States – a large swath of central-northern Italy – and the Kingdom of Naples was restored.[38]

Metternich's system of Europe was reactionary, absolutist, and Christian; the integrity of each member state was guaranteed, by force if necessary, and all the ensuing popular (or even constitutionalist) revolts were internationally suppressed. When, in 1848, Pope Pius IX was expelled from Rome and a republic was established, armies of France, Austria, and Naples all came to restore the reassuringly reactionary papacy. From 1815 until the Risorgimento, the rationalism and anti-clericalism of the Enlightenment were rejected; the papacy ruled with as little secular aid as possible; the Jesuit order was restored. In Lombardy (Milan), whatever initial tolerance for Italian local interests the Habsburgs showed quickly diminished under threat of disorder, and strict censorship was the order of the day. In the Papal States, things were much worse; and the relatively liberal Consalvi failed completely to prevent the restoration of all the bad administrative practices of the pre-Napoleonic period: indeed, it went further, and such dangerous practices of the Enlightenment as street-lights and vaccination were abolished.

In various parts of Italy, revolutions soon followed, some led by the secret societies (the Carbonari), some by liberal factions of various stripes: in Naples and in Sicily in 1820, in Piedmont in 1821. Even in relatively non-repressive Lombardy, the Austrian government rapidly became more authoritarian, and its censorship generally viewed intellectual activity of any kind – which indeed tended toward romanticism and the desire for progress in Italian culture – as subversive. The influential liberal journal *Il Conciliatore* lasted for little more than a year; it was suppressed a few months before the discovery of *De re publica*.

The enthusiastic immediate reactions to Mai's discovery of *De re publica*, such as that represented by Leopardi's *canzone*, have very little to do with the content of the text itself; and as will become clear, the later reactions to the text as revealed in Mai's publication of it were very different. Three years before the discovery, in 1816, Pietro Giordani had contributed several articles to the new journal *Biblioteca Italiana* (including the preface to the first volume), produced by and for the intellectual leaders of Milan under the editorship of Giuseppe Acerbi and with the direct financial support of the Austrian government. In a highly rhetorical "Letter of an Italian to Nicolò Bettoni," Giordani had given a list of illustrious

---

[38] On the history of Italy in this period, see Woolf, *A History of Italy 1700–1860*, pp. 229–74.

Italians that Bettoni might have included in his collection of portraits of eminent contemporaries; Giordani's supplement included not only Botta (author of a history of the United States) and the sculptor Canova, but Mai himself, then director of the Ambrosiana.[39] In a lengthy review in the same year, he praised Mai's publications of the Ambrosian Plautus and various Greek texts (Isaeus and Themistius) of which he had discovered manuscripts.[40] Giordani's praise was in some respects hyperbolic; and the essay on Bettoni in particular received a critical response, also in the same year, in Pietro Borsieri's *Avventure letterarie di un giorno*.[41] Leopardi's poem is closely related to Giordani's effusions, in part because of Leopardi's intense admiration for and friendship with Giordani himself; like Leopardi's two previous patriotic poems – also composed under the influence of Giordani – it reflects the intense Italian nationalism of the day; and when Leopardi writes of arousing the dead, he may be recalling Giordani's words in 1816 about Mai's (first) discovery of Fronto: "Since our Mai has disinterred, or revived, or created Fronto – and he has made us hear a school of Latin eloquence so greatly praised by the ancients but unknown to us, and has brought us in to the private apartments of Marcus Aurelius, that great, wise, and good Emperor – he has gained much honor for Italy, and has earned the gratitude of all Europe, at least to the extent that it is civilized."[42]

But even aside from motives arising from personal antipathy to Mai or from disgust at the ecclesiastical attempt to appropriate *De re publica* for propagandistic purposes, the text itself was, when it finally appeared,

---

[39] *"I ritratti d'illustri Italiani viventi: lettera di un Italiano a Nicolò Bettoni a Padova"* in Gussali (ed.), *Giordani*, vol. IX, pp. 362–5.

[40] "I Frammenti Plautini e Terenziani, le Orazioni d'Iseo e di Temistio pubblicate dal Mai," in Gussali (ed.), *Giordani,*, vol. IX, pp. 376–95.

[41] Borsieri, *Avventure letterarie di un giorno*, pp. 25–7 = Calcaterra, *Manifesti romantici e altri scritti della polemica classico-romantica*, pp. 284–9; both editions have helpful notes. Note particularly Borsieri, p. 26: *"Dunque perché il sig. Mai sa di latino e di greco, ed ha la fortuna di frugare in una Biblioteca [sc.* the Ambrosiana] *in cui tutti non frugano; perché ha la pazienza di rilevare dai vecchi codici i caratteri mezzo cancellati o dalla barbarie dei monaci o dallo mano del tempo, sarà egli per questo un grand'uomo da far trasecolare l'Europa e insuperbire l'Italia?"* The attack ends with a poem punning on Mai's name (p. 27) *"Puro scrittor d'articoli / Fai giganti i mezzani, e grandi i piccoli, / E s'io chieggo: Tal fallo emenderai? / Tu mi torni a ripetere,* Mai, Mai." On Borsieri's attack see also Treves, "Ciceronianismo e anticiceronianismo nella cultura italiani del secolo XIX," p. 411 and *Lo studio dell'antichità classica nell'ottocento*, pp. 354–5; Timpanaro, *Aspetti e figure della cultura ottocentesca*, p. 40, n. 51.

[42] *"Quando il nostro Mai ha diseppellito, o risuscitato, o creato il Frontone: e ci ha fatto udire una scuola d'eloquenza latina, tanto celebrata dagli antichi e a noi incognita, e ci ha introdotti ne'proprj appartamenti di Marco Aurelio, quell'Imperatore sì grande e savio e buono; egli acquistò molto onore all'Italia, e da tutta l'Europa, quanto ella è civile, meritò gratitudine"* in *"Sul discorso precedente: lettera di un Italiano ai compilatori della* Biblioteca Italiana," Gussali (ed.), Giordani, vol. IX, pp. 339–47 at p. 342. The "previous discourse" is Giordani's own translation of Mme. de Stael's essay on translation.

something of a disappointment. Cicero was the paradigmatic text of classicism; and in the new cultural world of nationalism and romanticism, Cicero was a hollow shell. As Silvio Pellico wrote to his brother in the final, censored days of *Il Conciliatore* in 1819:

The provocations we suffered, the delays imposed by the double censorship on the publication of *Conciliatore*, the continual reports that we were about to be suppressed, opened the eyes of even the blindest, and "romantic" was recognized as a synonym for "liberal," while nobody dared call himself "classicist," except for the ultras and spies.[43]

The classicism of the Counter-Reformation and the Restoration was empty: mere elegance without attention to the thought of the ancient texts. Giordani and his friends were concerned with the vacuity of Italian culture and education in their day and they viewed the creation of a national Italian culture as central to the eventual formation of an Italian state. Hence, for *De re publica*, the name of Cicero and the link with the church so deeply desired by Mai and the Vatican were handicaps. Giordani's letter to Montani is in this respect an important document. After ridiculing the dedication and praising Mai's work in shaping his edition and commentary, he turned to the text and found it wanting. That was true not merely because of its fragmentary state, but because of what Giordani thought about Cicero himself:

So let's imagine the work complete. You will ask me, how does it seem to you? A work of Cicero, I will say . . . a treasure of eloquence, a small fund of political wisdom. Cicero as a writer is a god: Cicero the author is a fine figure of a man – but no more than that. In fact, as I look back at him, he turns into a woman. I adore two ladies in the whole world. Which? Madame Roland and Cicero. Yes indeed, believe me. Cicero is less of a man than Marie Roland. When he writes, it is the grace of a lady that so allures and seduces . . . He is always in the midst of a world of beauties and graces that he has created. But three lines of Aristotle, six of Thucydides, and I will say more, a paragraph of Hobbes, a page of Rousseau contain more nourishing substance than a flowery volume of this most lovable Cicero.[44]

---

[43] *"Le provocazioni da noi sofferte, i ritardi posti all'uscita del Conciliatore dalla doppia censura, la voce continua che fossimo per essere soppressi, apersero gli occhi anche ai più ciechi, e* romantico *fu riconosciuto per sinonimo di liberale, nè più osarono dirsi* classicisti *fuorchè gli ultra e le spie"*: Branca, *Il Conciliatore: foglio scientifico-letterario*, vol. I, p. xli. The translation is partly taken from Woolf, *A History of Italy 1700–1860*, p. 249.

[44] *"Imaginiamola dunque intera quell'opera. Mi domanderai, che ti par ella? Un'opera di Cicerone, voglio dire . . . un tesoro di facondia, un piccolo capitale di sapienza politica. Cicerone scrittore è un dio: Cicerone autore è un bell'uomo; non più. Anzi egli a guardarlo dentro mi s'infemminisce. Io adoro due donne in tutto il mondo – quali? – La Roland, e Cicerone – oh! – sì, credimi. Cicerone è meno maschio di Maria Roland. Quando egli scrive, no ci è grazia di donna che alletti e seduca tanto . . . Egli è sempre in mezzo a un mondo di bellezze, di grazie, create da lui. Ma tre righe d'Aristotile, sei righe di*

For good reason, Giordani blurs Cicero himself with the empty Ciceronianism of his day, against which he fought hard. Cicero, he said, was
eloquence itself; but that was itself a damning criticism at a time when
Cicero meant nothing more than that. He found Ciceronian elegance of
style effeminate, comparing him to Madame Roland: beauty and grace
were detrimental to content. The authors whom he prefers to Cicero are
indicative: Thucydides, Aristotle, Hobbes, Rousseau are all (except perhaps
the last) difficult to read and comprehend, dense and suggestive. Cicero
was not, from his point of view, their equal, except in the sheer seductive
beauty of his style.

Disappointment in *De re publica* was not limited to Giordani, who had
his own polemical and anti-Ciceronian goals with respect to the restoration of Italian letters; rather, it was widespread among the first readers of
the text. Leopardi, whose 1820 poem had hailed the discovery with such
enthusiasm, devoted some of his finest philological work to the emenda-
tion and elucidation of the text, when it appeared; but he also wrote to his
father in December 1822, soon after its publication, disparaging the book:
"I haven't bought Mai's *Republic*... The price, on terrible paper, is 33 paoli:
the contents have nothing new, and Cicero himself says the same things in
a hundred other places. The result is that the genuine utility of the book is
not worth the price."[45] In effect, the letter is a palinode, an expression of
Leopardi's disappointment with the text that actually appeared. Price and
the quality of paper may have played a lesser role in his verdict than his
own falling out with Mai over a question of plagiarism; but even so, it was
the content of *De re publica* that he found wanting. There was nothing
new, nothing of "genuine utility."

WHAT PRICE CONSTITUTIONALISM?

The sense that *De re publica* was useless was not limited to Leopardi and
it is not without some justification. Mai's initial announcement and the
resulting publicity about the discovery had led readers to believe that rather

---

*Tucidide, dirò più, un paragrafo d'Hobbes, una pagina di Rousseau contengono più sostanza nutritiva,
che un volume fioritissimo di questo amabilissimo Cicerone"* Treves, *Lo studio dell'antichità classica
nell'ottocento*, p. 441. For the context, see also Treves, "Ciceronianismo e anticiceronianismo nella
cultura italiani del secolo XIX," pp. 414–18.

[45] *"Non ho comprato la* Repubblica *del Mai... Il prezzo, in carta infima, è di paoli trentatrè: la materia
non ha niente di nuovo, e le stesse cose dice il medesimo Cicerone in cento altri luoghi. Di modo che l'utilità
reale di questo libro non vale il suo prezzo."* Leopardi to Monaldo Leopardi, December 20, 1822;
Brioschi and Landi (eds.), *Leopardi*, p. 598. Quoted (among others) by Treves, "Ciceronianismo e
anticiceronianismo nella cultura italiani del secolo XIX," p. 414.

more of *De re publica* had been found than was in fact the case; the *North American Review* – which printed the longest and most detailed notice of the new text, far fuller than Lachmann's comments in *Göttingische gelehrte Anzeigen*[46] – explained:

The high expectations entertained of the work upon all these grounds have been, as is usual in similar cases, partly disappointed, and partly gratified. The treatise is in fact much less complete than we had been led to suppose, from the manner in which it was announced. In the notices, that appeared from time to time in the newspapers, it was spoken of as in substance the entire treatise, although disfigured by some breaks and blemishes. It appears, however, at present, that the discovered fragment is only about a fourth part of the whole essay . . . [47]

Niebuhr himself, although he knew more about the manuscript than most readers, was disappointed when he saw the small size of the published text, barely equal to seventy-five pages of printed editions of Cicero. He was even more disappointed when he read the full text, for it contained relatively little that interested him. His reaction is in part owing to the fact that he had misread one of the pages that Mai had allowed him to see in 1820, interpreting *Rep.* 2.39 (fol. 107/8) as saying that Cicero was going to give a full account of the Servian constitution, when in fact it says precisely the opposite; he had hoped for an authoritative account of early Roman government – his own particular interest – from the hand of a leading Republican statesman, but the surviving text is confusing, oblique, and textually corrupt. In the event, he reported to Savigny, there was virtually nothing new about Roman history in the new text, and very little about *ius publicum*. Only in its style ("*ausgesucht schön*") and in its implications for Cicero's views of the situation in his own day was anything to be gained from it.[48] Six months later he sent a copy of the printed edition to his friend the Comte de Serre with the comment that it was "a work that contains things of great beauty and solid truths; but if someone wrote it

---

[46] *Göttingische gelehrte Anzeigen* 1824, no. 44 (March 15) pp. 433–40. A handwritten note in the copy in the Columbia University Library identifies the author as Lachmann, which seems probable.

[47] Everett, "Review of Mai (ed.), Ciceronis de Re Publica," pp. 34–5. The author (not given in the original text; from Cameron, *Research Keys to the American Renaissance*) was Alexander Everett. The reason for *NAR*'s interest in *De re publica* is unclear: on the one hand, it may reflect American interest in a constitutional theory so close to that underlying the United States Constitution, or in fact the admiration for Cicero and *De re publica* of the most eminent Bostonian statesman, John Adams; on the other hand, more cynically, it is worth noting that the first American edition of *De re publica* was published in the same year by Oliver Everett, not coincidentally also the publisher of *NAR* itself and the father of the reviewer.

[48] Niebuhr to Savigny, May 23, 1822 (Vischer (ed.), *Briefe aus Rom*, pp. 748–50).

nowadays, it would not make its author's reputation."[49] Stylistic elegance
and moral commonplaces – the hallmarks of Ciceronianism – were in fact
used as a stick to beat the disappointing and fragmentary new text. The
North American Review thought that the fragmentary condition of *De re
publica* was unfortunate, but that

> as the works of Cicero are more valuable for the generous feelings and high poetical
> enthusiasm which constantly inspire them, than for the originality or scientific
> enthusiasm of the matter, they are less injured than many others would be by being
> read in a mutilated form... Every separate fragment is a chapter in the great book
> of universal experience commented on by this illustrious observer. The value of
> the commentary lies in the power and charm of the style. It is like a fine poem of
> which we know the fable; and we read any detached passage with nearly the same
> interest and pleasure whether we possess the whole or not.[50]

The reality of new discoveries often fails to meet anticipation, but the
case of *De re publica* is more complex than most. Cicero stood for many
things: as a politician and orator, he was emblematic of the Roman republic and of eloquence itself; as a stylistic model, he was also associated with
the most conservative trends of European education and culture at the
time that *De re publica* was discovered. And this text in particular aroused
extraordinary expectations: as possible new evidence for early Roman history and society and as an exposition of political theory that might, in fact,
prove enlightening or useful for present circumstances. In that respect,
the woefully fragmentary condition of the text that Mai published, even
including all the previously known quotations, was a serious disappointment. What the palimpsest contained of *De re publica* consisted of most of
the first two books, a small portion of the third, and tiny scraps of Books
4 and 5; but as Niebuhr and Giordani among others observed, the most
interesting and useful portion of *De re publica* would have been the second
half of the work, and that was (and is) almost entirely lost. The portions of
the dialogue that were contained in the new palimpsest, as far as content
was concerned, seemed stale and unprofitable: an account of the theory
of constitutions that seemed to contain very little not previously known
from Polybius Book 6, and a narrative of the earliest stages of Roman
history – well preserved for the regal period, but fragmentary thereafter –
that closely matched, except for some details of the organization of the
Servian constitution, what was already known from Livy and Dionysius

---

49 "*Ouvrage qui renferme de grandes beautés & de vérités solides, mais qui, si on l'écrivait de nos jours,
    ne ferait point la reputation de son auteur.*" Niebuhr to de Serre, November 30, 1822 (Vischer (ed.),
    Briefe aus Rom, p. 810).
50 Everett, "Review of Mai (ed.), Ciceronis de Re Publica," pp. 35–6.

of Halicarnassus. And the general observations that Cicero made about public service, justice, and the role of the statesman – in the surviving portions, at least – corresponded very closely to what he had written in other, better preserved texts such as *De oratore*, *De legibus*, and *De officiis*, texts that were extremely influential for the humanists and their successors, but the relevance of which to present-day political life had long since been eclipsed.

Cicero was not altogether a successful politician in his own career (perhaps an understatement), but unlike other ancient writers on government, with the exception of Polybius, he was at least experienced in public affairs, and what he wrote *de re publica* might be expected to have practical value, even in the nineteenth century. A few years before the palimpsest was discovered, Thomas Jefferson wrote to John Adams about Plato's *Republic*, which he was then rereading, and fulminated against "the whimsies, the puerilities, and unintelligible jargon of this work." Having only contempt for institutional Christianity, he was not surprised that Plato had been taken up by the early church, "but how could the Roman good sense do it? And particularly how could Cicero bestow such eulogies on Plato? Altho' Cicero did not wield the dense logic of Demosthenes, yet he was able, learned, laborious, practised in the business of the world, and honest."[51] Adams' explanation was that Cicero's academic affiliations required him to praise Plato, but he had doubts about Cicero's attitude in *De re publica*:

In his two Volumes of Discourses on Government We may presume, that he fully examined Plato's Laws and Republick as well as Aristotles Writings on Government. But these have been carefully destroyed; not improbably, with the general consent of Philosophers, Politicians and Priests. The Loss is as much to be regretted as that of any Production of Antiquity.[52]

The two men were quite old when the palimpsest was discovered, and outlived its first publication by less than four years. Jefferson owned a copy of the edition published in Boston in 1823, but there is nothing in their correspondence to show that they in fact read it.[53] The implications of their letters, however, are clear. They expected that Cicero would

---

[51] Jefferson to Adams, July 5, 1814; Cappon, *The Adams–Jefferson Letters*, pp. 432–3.

[52] Adams to Jefferson, July 16, 1814; Cappon, *The Adams–Jefferson Letters*, p. 438. The two "Volumes of Discourses" are *De re publica* and the incomplete *De legibus*.

[53] Jefferson's copy of the 1823 Boston edition is in the Library of Congress; the flyleaves inscribed to Thomas Jefferson Smith can be found at http://memory.loc.gov/ammem/collections/ jefferson_papers/mtjser7.html#vol8 (consulted July 21, 2009). I am grateful to Mortimer Sellers for this reference.

have offered, in addition to criticisms of Plato's metaphysical and mystical speculations, the ideas of a practical man about real government: Roman good sense, and realistic views of how government worked and should be constituted.

From the point of view of Adams, who in the 1780s had cited in his massive *Defense of the Constitutions of Government of the United States of America* some of the fragments of *De re publica* as part of his own argument for a mixed constitution,[54] the text that was printed in 1822 would – aside from its fragmentary condition – have been eminently satisfactory; but Adams was perhaps the last great political figure to subscribe wholeheartedly to the classical theory of civic republicanism as represented by Machiavelli, Montesquieu and Harrington. In the 1820s, however, such a theory seemed very much out of date, and profoundly impractical. Even Alexander Everett, while accepting the traditional three-fold classification of constitutions, thought that Cicero's account of the ideal government was not very useful: "The value of this [the mixed constitution], as of the other forms of government, must be settled by an accurate examination of its theory, and practical effects; which is not attempted in the work before us."[55] He went on, in a lengthy footnote, to point out that debates over the comparative merits of constitutional forms tend to be verbal rather than substantive, and to illustrate this with the report of a debate in France in 1791 between Thomas Paine and Abbé Sièyes over the meaning of "monarchy" and "republic." This remarkable review continues with a discussion, equally damning, of Cicero's version of early Roman history in Book 2 of *De re publica*, again finding the traditional accounts (shared by Livy and Dionysius) dubious, and again citing the modern research of Niebuhr on Roman history and Schlegel on Indo-European linguistics as cause for doubting the ancient stories.[56]

Both in terms of recent (German) scholarship on antiquity that cast doubt on Cicero as a historian, and in terms of recent (French) history that cast doubt on the validity of the traditional ideas of constitutional forms, *De re publica* seemed in 1822 far less admirable than it would have had the palimpsest been discovered fifty years earlier: as in his lifetime, so in his rediscovery, Cicero's political timing could be terrible. The progress of Niebuhr's views as he gradually worked through the proofs of Mai's edition

---

[54] Adams, *Works of John Adams, Second President of the United States*, vol. IV, pp. 295–6, cites from the fragments then known.

[55] Everett, "Review of Mai (ed.), Ciceronis de Re Publica," p. 56.

[56] Everett, "Review of Mai (ed.), Ciceronis de Re Publica," pp. 61–2.

in 1822 is instructive. After having read only the first book, Niebuhr was moderately optimistic about the discovery:[57]

What I have read hitherto does not extend beyond the first book: and this, with all the disadvantages of a mutilated work, I do not hesitate to call equall to any thing which Cicero ever wrote. So far, the Roman history gains nothing by it: I expect much from the second book, although Cicero's knowledge of the ancient history of his people was evidently limited, and depended upon the information which he drew from Atticus. The book, were it entire, would produce, at this very moment, considerable attention, from its political principles: Cicero shows himself so declared a friend to limited monarchy, praising, in plain words, that very royalty whose name sounded so ill in Roman ears, that, unless he already then absolutely despaired of his country, one must suppose that he meant to advise the establishment of royalty, & the abolition of annual magistrates. He inveighs not less against factious aristocracy, than against democracy.

It is perhaps not irrelevant that the recipient of this letter, Lord Colchester, had been Speaker of the House of Commons, and Niebuhr seems to be tailoring his reading of the palimpsest to suit the beliefs of his audience. The idea that Cicero advocated a constitutional monarchy (very much of the British sort, it would appear) is bizarre in itself and is contradicted in Book 2; but in any case at this point Niebuhr thought Cicero's work both interesting and relevant. Two months later, when he had read the palimpsest through, he was less enthusiastic (and less clear) about Cicero's goals; he read *De re publica* as an attempt to restore the long-lost constitution of the middle republic that was produced at the wrong time: "I firmly believe that the work had a highly practical significance which is unclear only because the lost books were the most significant part. Sadly the thought could not be realized since Pompey and Caesar were both alive, and Fate had to be brought to pass."[58] Niebuhr, as someone who felt himself to be in political exile from Berlin, was not unsympathetic to Cicero's point of view; the sentence just quoted continues, "as it always must be brought to pass if apathy is as widespread as it is, for example, in our times" ("*wie es immer erfüllt werden muss wenn die Abgestorbenheit so weit gedichen ist wie z.B. in unsern Zeiten*"). At the end of the year, however, his opinion of Cicero as a political thinker had fallen even further; as he

---

[57] Public Records Office, London, Colchester Papers; PRO 30/9/12/12, p. 2. The letter is unpublished; only a summary in Vischer (ed.), *Briefe aus Rom*, pp. 720–1. The letter is written in English; the emphasis is Niebuhr's.

[58] "*Ich glaube ganz gewiss dass das Werk eine hohe praktische Bedeutung hatte, die nur dunkel ist weil die verlornen Bücher der bedeutendste Theil waren. Leider war der Gedanke, da Pompeius und Cäsar zugleich lebten, unausführbar, und das Fatum musste erfüllt werden*": to Savigny, Vischer (ed.), *Briefe aus Rom*, p. 750.

wrote to de Serre in November, if it were written now it would not enhance the author's reputation.[59]

Niebuhr's somewhat melancholy, if limited, sympathy with Ciceronian republicanism was not the universal reaction, and indeed he seems to have been in the minority. Ten years later, in surveying republican literature in a review of John Dunlop's *History of Roman Literature*, the anonymous reviewer for the conservative *Quarterly Review* made no bones about the feebleness of Cicero's ideas of Roman government:

> We are induced to enter more fully on this subject, because we think (especially since the delightful and interesting additions made by the palimpsest discoveries of Mai to the treatise De Re Publicâ) too much credit has been given to the Romans for proficiency in political science, and for the possession (at any period) of rational liberty. It is true that Cicero has accurately, and with his wonted elegance and clearness, stated some of the most pregnant maxims of polity, but with singular deficiency in perceiving the inadequacy of any given institution for carrying such principles into effect, and in devising any permanent means for supporting a principle, or for neutralizing hostile forces. The whole history of the republic exhibits a succession of expedients temporarily to counteract – not of principles permanently to alter – the originally vicious nature of the constitution, which gave to the assembled people, or subsequently to their agitators, the tribunes, the whole power of the state.[60]

Cicero's work was judged, in short, both in terms of the contemporary value of his political theory and in terms of the failure of the government which he described as the best: if someone writing in the last years of the Roman republic, with all its chaos and disorder, could describe the Roman constitution as the best possible even while witnessing its degeneration, then how could one respect him – or it? The constitutional theory itself – the traditional categories of monarchy, aristocracy, democracy, and the mixed constitution – might still have some theoretical truth, but it was scarcely applicable to Metternich's Europe, and its terminology was so vague as to have little real meaning. Above all, the political debate in Cicero was carried on in the lofty language of virtue and merit, of natural aristocracies and proportional justice. Those terms had relevance in the eighteenth century, but the French Revolution and its aftermath had turned political thought in different directions: European politics after the Congress of Vienna concerned nationalism, the balance of power, and the maintenance of a conservative status quo in which the issues of participatory government and the relationship between ethics and politics seemed obsolete.

---

[59] Vischer (ed.), *Briefe aus Rom*, p. 810, quoted above, n. 49.
[60] Anonymous, Review of John Dunlop, *History of Roman Literature*, pp. 83–4.

Niebuhr's reference to "Fate" (above, n. 59) suggests one final point. The Hegelian account of world history which labelled Caesar as a world-historical figure inevitably consigned Cicero and the last throes of Roman republicanism to the dustbin of history. Cicero had failed to see the course of fate and destiny, to recognize the progress that Caesar's victory represented both for Rome and for civilization; the Hegelian verdict of Theodor Mommsen in the third volume of his *Roman History* (published in 1856) described Cicero, in a memorable and damning phrase, as "a statesman without insight, idea, or purpose" (*"Staatsmann ohne Einsicht, Ansicht und Absicht"*) and his theoretical views were consequently damned as irrelevant and misguided.[61] It is perhaps significant that, at just the same time, Villemain, the French scholar who had earlier described his intense anticipation of *De re publica* as it appeared in 1822, returned to the subject in 1857, and used *De re publica* in order to attack the popular dictatorship of Napoleon III, "the pretense of 'the will of all,' in the name of which is suppressed the will of each person."[62] The coup that brought Napoleon III to power not only led to serious questioning of the traditional division of constitutional forms into monarchy, aristocracy, and democracy, but it gave a long dominance in Europe to Caesarism over Ciceronianism – and it should not be forgotten that Napoleon III himself wrote a history of Julius Caesar.[63] The theory of *De re publica* was obsolete, just as was its author. By the time of Mommsen, and even by the time *De re publica* was published, its time had passed. By the 1820s ancient constitutional theory,

---

[61] I cite Dickson's English translation of Mommsen, *History of Rome*, vol. v, p. 504. Mommsen's discussion of Cicero (pp. 504–10) is so one-sided as to be self-parody, combining the worst excesses of the romantic and the professor ordinarius; it is thus a good index to the extremes of anti-Ciceronianism. For Mommsen, not only is Cicero politically inconsistent, but "a dabbler . . . by nature a journalist" (pp. 504–5); "Cicero had no conviction and no passion; he was nothing but an advocate, and not a good one" (p. 505); "the dreadful barrenness of thought in the Ciceronian orations must revolt every reader of feeling and judgment" (p. 506). But even Mommsen shows a grudging respect for *De re publica*: while calling it "a singular mongrel compound of history and philosophy," he had to admit that it showed "comparative originality, inasmuch as the elaboration shows throughout Roman local colouring, and the proud consciousness of political life, which the Roman was certainly entitled to feel as compared with the Greeks, makes the author even confront his Greek instructors with a certain independence" (p. 508). Mommsen's absurdity comes through most clearly in the statement that "The Romans possessed no great Latin prose-writer" (p. 506) – no doubt in comparison to Mommsen's own Latin. For a brief and lucid summary of Cicero's defeat at the hands of Hegelianism, see Girardet, *Die Ordnung der Welt*, pp. 228–30, citing Mommsen's verdict. See also the useful comments of Schmid, "Cicerone e la filologia tedesca," pp. 130–2.

[62] "*Cette prétendue volonté de tous, au nom de laquelle, on supprime la volonté de chacun*": reprinted in Villemain, *La République de Cicéron*, pp. viii–ix from *Revue des Deux Mondes* for 1857. Cf. Momigliano, *Secondo contributo alla storia degli studi classici*, p. 276, n. 11.

[63] On Napoleon III, Caesarism, Mommsen, and Villemain, see Momigliano, *Secondo contributo alla storia degli studi classici*, pp. 273–8.

not just Cicero, seemed quaintly antique. I end by quoting Hegel, in about 1830: "Nothing is more misguided than to look for models among the Greeks, the Romans, or Orientals for the constitutional structures of our own time."[64] In Metternich's Europe, not even the resurrection of Cicero could resurrect republican liberty.

[64] Hegel, *Introduction to the Philosophy of History*, p. 50.

CHAPTER 3

Honor culture, praise, and Servius' Aeneid

Robert A. Kaster

One night in the early 1920s a musician in Paris was startled awake by the sound of pounding at his hotel room door. Going to open it, he found a heavily built man holding a smallish dog. The man was the musician Sidney Bechet, who had heard that the room's occupant was bragging around town that his dog was the "most dog" – that is, the meanest dog there was. Since Bechet believed *his* dog to be the most dog, he took the other man's boast to be a slur upon his animal and so, by an obvious extension, a slur upon himself. He intended to settle the matter there and then.

Bechet is remembered today as a genius of the soprano saxophone. A slightly older contemporary of Louis Armstrong, born and raised in the Creole culture of New Orleans, he is just about the only jazz musician of the period who is generally held to have been Armstrong's peer in the richness of his tone and the brilliance of his improvisations. He is also remembered for being a person as difficult as his recalcitrant instrument. This reputation was earned in a series of incidents like the Parisian dog affair that caused him to be jailed or deported repeatedly in his mostly expatriate career: the series reached a climax of sorts in 1929 when he was jailed in Paris for 15 months, and then deported, for wounding three people in a duel he fought with a banjo-player after they disagreed over a song's harmonic structure.[1]

Sidney Bechet came to mind willy-nilly as I was thinking about the subject of this essay. Biographical sketches of him usually take the line that he had a "fiery temper," that he was "undisciplined" or "unfortunately belligerent," and I suppose by contemporary (North-American, middle-class) standards all that is true. But I came to think about Bechet because I suspect that his behavior was not just a quirk of personal temperament.

---

[1] For Bechet's own side of the contretemps with the banjo-player, Mike McKendrick, see his engaging oral autobiography, *Treat it Gentle*, pp. 150–2.

I suspect, in fact, that he was a man who found himself in the wrong time and the wrong culture. A man truly at home in an honor culture, Bechet had the misfortune to live in a world where the concept of honor had been radically thinned by the transient relationships, impersonal exchanges, and rationalized routines of modernity – the same routines and exchanges that help us indulge the luxury of a private self and insulate that self from the knocks and jars of everyday transactions.

If I go to buy an automobile, I do not expect the exchange to turn on considerations of honor: that is, the kind and quality of the car I drive away does not depend on the value the dealer places on me as a person, and the exchange is not made in consideration of some obligation to the dealer I now feel bound to discharge, in a way that will in turn depend on how I value the dealer and my relationship with him. It's the worth of the car that's at stake in the transaction, not my worth or the dealer's, and that worth is determined in some rationalized, quantifiable way, expressed in the impersonal metric of dollars. By the same token, if I happen to disagree with you about a song's harmonic structure, I assume that we will resolve the disagreement by the objectively task-specific process of consulting the sheet music, not by fighting a duel. Sidney Bechet fought a duel, not just because looking at the sheet music was not an option (he could not read music), but most of all because the harmonic structure was not, at base, the matter at issue. The issue was his word and his honor. That honor radiated out like so many nerve endings from every detail of his being, projecting his ego into the world for others to judge and admire, and at the same time leaving it exposed, in countless ways, to caressing and to bruising alike. It is not for nothing that more duels were fought in New Orleans than in any other American city.

The very touchy honor of Sidney Bechet and the reception of classical texts join up, in my mind, in the perhaps unlikely person of the grammarian Servius, as he is represented by his commentary on the *Aeneid*. Produced in the early fifth century, the commentary gives us the only full pre-Christian reading of the poem that also draws extensively on the preceding four centuries of Vergilian exegesis. (I should note, parenthetically, that I will be concerned only with the so-called vulgate Servius[2] and will leave out of account the supplementary notes found in the interpolated commentary known as the Servius Auctus or Servius Danielis. Doing so will allow us to concentrate on a text that is fairly straightforwardly the product of a single man working at a roughly determinate point in time.)

---

[2] Thilo and Hagen (eds.), *Servii Grammatici*.

Servius' reading of the poem starts from a famous – or notorious – statement about the poet's "intention" (*Aen.* 1 praef.):

intentio Vergilii haec est, Homerum imitari et Augustum laudare a parentibus. namque est filius Atiae, quae nata est de Iulia, sorore Caesaris, Iulius autem Caesar ab Iulo Aeneae originem ducit, ut confirmat ipse Vergilius [1.288] *"a magno demissum nomen Iulo."*

Vergil's intention is this: to imitate Homer and to praise Augustus by reference to his ancestors. For [Augustus] is the son of Atia, Julius Caesar's niece, while Caesar descends from Aeneas' son, Iulus, as Vergil himself confirms by referring to "the name derived from great Iulus."

Now, whatever your view of Vergil's stance vis-à-vis Augustus, you are bound to think that that is a rather reductive view of the poet's "intention." But having started from that premise, Servius as reader returns to it again and again, from one end of the poem to the other. For example:

Aen. 1.286, in the prophecy of Jupiter:

N A S C E T V R *ad illud respondet "certe hinc Romanos olim" et omnis poetae intentio, ut in qualitate carminis diximus, ad laudem tendit Augusti, sicut et in sexti catalogo et in clipei descriptione.*

W I L L   B E   B O R N [the verb] looks back to that [phrase used by Venus: 1.234] "surely hence one day Romans," and as I said in my remarks on the poem's character, the poet is entirely intent on praising Augustus, as in the sixth book's catalogue [*sc.* of heroes] and in the description of the shield.

Aen. 4.234, in Jupiter's message to Aeneas at Carthage, conveyed by Mercury:

A S C A N I O N E *propter illud quod frequenter diximus, ipsi imperium deberi. ideo autem hoc asserit poeta, ut laudando Iulum Caesarem laudet, quia ab eo originem ducit, ut* [1.288] *"Iulius a magno demissum nomen Iulo."*

[Mentioned here] because supreme rule is his due, as I have said a number of times. Moreover, the poet makes this claim so that by praising Iulus he might praise Caesar, the latter being descended from the former, thus "the name derived from great Iulus."

Aen. 7.170, in the description of Latinus' palace at Laurentum:

T E C T V M   A V G V S T V M   I N G E N S *domum, quam in Palatio diximus ab Augusto factam, per transitum laudat.*

V A S T,   I N S P I R I N G   D W E L L I N G He praises in passing the house that Augustus built on the Palatine.

Aen. 12.166, with reference to Aeneas:

ROMANAE STIRPIS ORIGO *hoc ad laudem Augusti respicit.*

SOURCE OF THE ROMAN STOCK This is said with respect to the praise of
Augustus.

With that premise securely in place, too, Servius regularly finds exquisite –
or if you prefer, far-fetched – touches that Vergil supposedly incorporated to
bring honor to Augustus. For example, in the catalogue of Italian warriors
at the end of Book 7, when the narrator refers to Aricia, the nymph-mother
of the mysterious figure Virbius, Servius offers (*Aen.* 7.761–2):

QVEM MATER ARICIA MISIT *civitas iuxta Alba. "mater" autem propter Augustum
dicit, qui fuerat ex Aricina matre progenitus: ac si diceret, quae tanti auctor est generis.*

WHOM MOTHER ARICIA SENT However, he uses the word "mother" because
of Augustus, whose mother was from Aricia, as if to say "[Aricia], from which so
great a lineage issued."

And when – during Aeneas' tour of the future site of Rome – the narrator
winks at the reader by pointing out the cows "lowing in the fashionable
Carinae" northeast of the forum, Servius finds Augustus lurking (*Aen.*
8.360–1):

LAVTIS MVGIRE CARINIS . . . *"lautas" . . . dixit aut propter elegantiam aedificio-
rum, aut propter Augustum, qui natus est in †curiis† veteribus et nutritus in [lautis]
Carinis.*

He used the epithet "*lautas*" either because of the smartness of the buildings [in
the quarter] or because of Augustus, who was born in †*curiis*† and raised in the
Carinae.[3]

On the strength of Vergil's "intention" Servius also regularly interprets
historical references so as to assure us that they could not have been offensive
to Augustus; alternatively, he finds an Augustan allusion where it is at least
unclear that any was intended, and then exerts himself to make the allusion
anodyne. We can consider just two examples from Book 6.

When near the end of the so-called Catalogue of Heroes Anchises
addresses "great Cato," we can be sure that Cato the Elder is meant
because of the mainly middle-republican focus of this segment and Cato's

---

[3] Thilo and Hagen (eds.), *Servii Grammatici*, vol. II, p. 253, printed *in curiis veteribus et nutritus in
lautis carinis* but expressed in the apparatus a preference, I think correct, for bracketing *lautis* (i.e., as
an interpolation that crept in from the lemma). I do not know, however, what sense Thilo attributed
to *curiis* (or Curiis), while the reading *cunis* found in some MSS seems scarcely more plausible (one
could suppose that Servius wrote "*natus est Curibus veteribus*," but the historical error is too gross).
The textual question is irrelevant to the more general point concerning Servius' readiness to find
unexpected "honorific" notices of Augustus.

hostility to Carthage, which looms large among the figures about to be mentioned; but those are not considerations that engage Servius' attention (*Aen.* 6.841–3):

> *quis te, magne Cato, tacitum aut te, Cosse, relinquat?*
> *quis Gracchi genus aut geminos, duo fulmina belli,*
> *Scipiadas . . .*

> Who would leave you unsung, great Cato, or you, Cossus,
> Who the line of Gracchus or the paired descendants of Scipio,
> Two thunderbolts of war . . . ?

MAGNE CATO *Censorium dicit, qui scripsit historias, multa etiam bella confecit: nam Vticensem praesente Augusto, contra quem pater eius Caesar et dimicavit et Anticatones scripsit, laudare non poterat.*

GREAT CATO He means the Censor, who wrote histories and concluded many wars: for in Augustus' presence he could not praise Cato of Utica, against whom his father, Caesar, both fought and wrote the *Attacks on Cato*.

Or take the moment, earlier in his time in the underworld, when Aeneas learns of the punishments the wicked suffer in Tartarus. After a number of examples drawn from myth, the list concludes with a catalogue of generic offenders against proper human relations in civil society. Meeting the last category – "those who pursued impious arms and did not scruple to deceive their masters' right hands [i.e., their loyalty]" – one might think that if any specific historical events are meant, they are the several slave rebellions that terrified generations of Romans from the second century BCE on down to the last and greatest, the revolt of Spartacus, finally put down the year before Vergil was born. But with Augustus never far from his mind Servius sees things differently (*Aen.* 6.608–14):

> *hic, quibus invisi fratres, dum vita manebat,*
> *pulsatusve parens et fraus innexa clienti,*
> *aut qui divitiis soli incubuere repertis*
> *nec partem posuere suis (quae maxima turba est),*
> *quique ob adulterium caesi, quique arma secuti*
> *impia nec veriti dominorum fallere dextras,*
> *inclusi poenam exspectant.*

> Here were those who hated their brothers, while life remained,
> Or struck a parent and wove a deceitful snare for a client,
> Or engrossed all for themselves the wealth they'd found
> And set aside no portion for their kin (a very great throng),
> Those, too, cut down as adulterers and those who followed impious
> Arms and did not scruple to deceive their masters' right hands:
> Here imprisoned, they await their punishment.

QVIQVE ARMA SECVTI IMPIA NEC VERITI DOMINORVM FALLERE DEX-
TRAS hoc loco <u>videtur</u> blandiri Augusto, quia contra Caesarem, patrem eius, multi
quibus ignovit, <u>arma</u> susceperant; ... ut "arma impia" civilia dixerit bella, quae
moverunt Pompeiani contra acceptae veniae fidem. <u>sed non procedit</u>. nam si "arma
impia" dixit bellum civile, tangit et Augustum et Caesarem, qui et ipsi civilia bella
tractarunt. <u>item</u> si culpat eos qui contra fidem datae veniae dimicaverunt, tangit
Augustum: <u>nam</u> transierunt ad eum ab Antonio duo milia equitum, per quos est
victoriam consecutus ... fecit <u>praeterea</u> iniuriam Augusto vel Caesari si eos "domi-
nos" dixit, quod apud maiores <u>invidiosum fuit</u> ... <u>melius ergo</u> est ut bellum a Sexto
Pompeio ... in Siculo freto gestum accipiamus. nam occiso patre Siciliam tenuit et
collectis inde servitiis vastavit sex annis ultro citroque Siciliam, postea victus est ab
Augusto et Agrippa ... et hoc sensu tam "arma impia," quam "dominorum" congruit
commemoratio. (emphasis added)

Here <u>he seems</u> to ingratiate himself with Augustus, since many of those his father, <u>Caesar</u>, had pardoned took up arms against him; ... so that by "*arma impia*" he meant the civil wars that the Pompeians stirred up, contrary to the promises made when they accepted pardon. <u>But that doesn't work</u>. For if by "*arma impia*" he meant civil war, he touches upon both Augustus and Caesar, who also had a hand in civil wars themselves. <u>Likewise</u> if he faults those who went to war contrary to the promises made when they accepted pardon, he touches upon Augustus: for two thousand knights went over to him from Antony, and they were instrumental in his victory ... <u>Furthermore</u>, he insulted Augustus or Caesar if he called them "masters," which was an invidious term among our ancestors ... <u>It's better, then</u>, to take him to mean the war waged by Sextus Pompey ... in the Straits of Messina. For after his father was killed, Sextus occupied Sicily, gathered slaves from there, and laid waste ... to Sicily for six years, though he was later defeated by Augustus and Agrippa ... And this interpretation squares as much with the phrase "treacherous arms" as with mention of "masters." (emphasis added)

Let's set aside the fact that alluding to Sextus Pompey's use of slaves is a move Vergil is unlikely to have made – unless we assume he also wanted to remind his audience that Augustus himself had used 20,000 slaves to man his own fleet in the same war (Suet. *Aug.* 16.1). No, the real point of interest here is the behavior of Servius, who starts from an unwarranted premise – that the lines *must* be about Augustus – which he then extends by assuming that they *must* be favorable to him. The resulting hermeneutic gymnastics seem to me remarkable, though perhaps not as remarkable as the fact that several of Vergil's most distinguished modern commentators have followed him.[4]

---

[4] See Norden (ed.), *Aeneis, Buch* VI, p. 289 ("*Hierzu bringt Servius eine jedenfalls aus guter Zeil stammende Bemerkung ...*"), Williams, *The Aeneid of Virgil*, vol. I, p. 497, Austin, *P. Vergili Maronis Aeneidos, liber sextus*, p. 195; cf. also, e.g., Berry, "The criminals in Virgil's Tartarus," p. 416.

Now, when we see Servius' initial formulation of Vergil's "intention" and then trace the sorts of analysis that it seems to prompt, we might well think that, as one of our scholarly forebears, he's pretty much doing one of the things we do in reading the poem; he's just not doing it very well. That is, given the obvious fact that Vergil expressly incorporates Augustus in his poem at several points, we make it our premise that he must have had a particular view of the *princeps*: we wonder what that view was, and we try to define it. The difference is that Servius seems to have made the freshman mistake of assuming what it was properly his burden to prove, taking the view as given and spinning out his analyses from there. We perhaps shake our heads and make clucking sounds: ah, poor Servius.

If that is our impulse, however, I suggest that we restrain ourselves: not because Servius gets it right, exactly, but because our starting points and aims and Servius' starting points and aims are perhaps not at all as congruent as they seem. Let us suppose instead that Servius imagined Augustus to be like the grandees of his own day – his students' fathers – only more so; and let us suppose that those grandees were, in matters of honor, much closer to Sidney Bechet than to any reader of this essay (or its author) – that in matters of honor, in fact, they made even [insert preferred name here], that most thin-skinned of modern academics, look like a whacking great rhinoceros. Those two very reasonable suppositions, as I think they are, put us in a world where the scope for merely neutral comment or observation is radically reduced; where just about everything can be seen to be drenched in value; and where anything that has value attached to it potentially reflects on one's own value, expressed in the medium of praise and blame. It is a world where my saying to you "nice tie" or "good dog" does not simply rank the tie or dog in question relative to other ties or dogs but is understood to be intended to rank *you*, of whom the tie or dog are merely extensions. It is a world, in fact, where even if I do not compliment your tie or dog in so many words, I can be assumed to be thinking about them – just because they are yours, and therefore supremely important – and I therefore can be taken to allude to them even if I do not speak of them expressly. In such a world, the very obvious fact that Vergil mentions Augustus *must* mean that he intends either to praise or to blame him; and the equally obvious fact that he does not blame him must mean that he intends to praise him. QED.

Servius of course does not speak explicitly in such terms, nor should we expect him to. There are, however, two absolutely pervasive elements of his commentary that tend strongly to corroborate the suggestion that I have just made about his cultural presuppositions, and by extension those of the tradition to which he was heir. First, there is the fact that the poem, seen through Servius' eyes, is indeed drenched in value and value judgments, so that Servius sees praise where we – or certainly, I – see merely a simple description or a statement of fact. Second, there is Servius' extraordinary sensitivity to the tactical uses of praise. Let me use the rest of my space to give just a few examples of these two salient features.

For the perception that praise is everywhere, waiting to be found even in language that seems merely descriptive, consider the following examples.

In Book 4, the narrator says of the personified Fama that (*Aen.* 4.174–5):

> *Fama, malum qua non aliud velocius ullum:*
> *mobilitate viget virisque adquirit eundo.*

> Gossip, swifter than any evil: it quickens with movement
> And gains strength in its travels.

Servius somewhat unexpectedly finds this to be an instance of praise *a contrario*:

MOBILITATE VIGET . . . *laudat a contrario: cum enim omnia labore minuantur, haec crescit.*

GAINS STRENGTH IN ITS TRAVELS . . . for though toil makes all things less, [*Fama*] grows.

In Book 5, describing the huge corselet that Aeneas awards as one of the prizes in the boat race, the narrator says:

> *vix illam famuli Phegeus Sagarisque ferebant*
> *multiplicem conixi umeris; indutus at olim*
> *Demoleos cursu palantis Troas agebat.*

> The servants Phegeus and Sagaris scarce carried it,
> Many-layered, as their shoulders strained
> Under the load; but Demoleos once wore it
> As he drove the scattering Trojans at a run.

to which Servius responds first by noting,

PHEGEVS SAGARISQVE *nominatim dicendo addidit laudem,*

PHEGEVS SAGARISQVE By mentioning them by name he added praise,

and then by remarking

CVRSV PALANTES TROAS AGEBAT *ad Aeneae qui eum [sc. Demoleos, cf. 260–62] vicit pertinet laudem.*

DROVE THE SCATTERING TROJANS AT A RUN This looks to the praise of Aeneas, who defeated him.

In Book 8, as Aeneas reaches the site of Rome, he finds gathered Evander and (*Aen.* 8.104–6),

> *Pallas huic filius una,*
> *una omnes iuvenum primi pauperque senatus*
> *tura dabant, tepidusque cruor fumabat ad aras.*

> Together with him his son, Pallas,
> Together all the foremost youth and the poor senate
> Offered incense; the warm gore steamed at the altars.

Servius offers alternative explanations of the epithet *pauper*:

IVVENVM PRIMI PAVPERQVE SENATVS ... "*pauper*" ... *aut ad numerum retulit, centum enim sub Romulo fuerunt: aut re vera "pauper," per quod Romani imperii ostenditur parsimonia, pro laude tunc habita*

THE FOREMOST YOUTH AND THE POOR SENATE Either he applied the epithet "pauper" to the number – for there were one hundred [senators] under Romulus – or "pauper" is to be taken literally, to make plain the austerity of Roman might, which was then regarded as praiseworthy,

where the discovery of praise is joined with a nice historicizing touch, implying the distance between Vergil's day and Servius' own. And when soon thereafter, in his first address to Evander, Aeneas assures him (*Aen.* 8.129–30),

> *non equidem extimui Danaum quod ductor et Arcas*
> *quodque a stirpe fores geminis coniunctus Atridi.*

> For my part I felt no fear because you were a leader of Greeks
> And an Arcadian, joined in your lineage to the twin sons of Atreus.

Servius finds another unexpected occasion of praise that seems to have little or nothing to do with the context:

DANAVM QVOD DVCTOR ET ARCAS *nec quod multitudinem haberes extimui, nec quod esses Arcas ... et hoc ad laudem Euandri pertinet, qui qualitate morum meruit non timeri.*

LEADER OF GREEKS AND AN ARCADIAN I felt fear neither because you have many men nor because you are an Arcadian ... And this looks to the praise of Evander, who deservedly was not feared because of the nature of his character.

For examples of Servius' readiness to find tactical uses of praise consider what follows. The first line of approach is familiar from any instance of ancient panegyric: what can be called normative praise, or praising a given quality with the aim of urging the person praised to display it. In Book 11, for example, the reply of Diomedes to the Latin embassy is reported to have begun with these words (*Aen.* 11.252):

> *O fortunatae gentes, Saturnia regna...*
>
> O happy nations, realms of Saturn...

Servius understands Diomedes' oblique approach:

O FORTVNATAE GENTES... *id est "o viri semper pace gaudentes!" nam legimus* [8.324–5] *"aurea quae perhibent, illo sub rege fuere saecula, sic placida populos in pace regebat." et bene hoc laudat, quod eis persuadere desiderat.*

O HAPPY NATIONS... That is, "O men ever rejoicing in peace!" For we read, "Under that king were the ages men call 'golden,' thus he ruled the peoples in placid peace." And [Diomedes] does well to praise that which he wants to commend to [his listeners].

But the uses of praise that Servius brings to the reader's attention are much more varied, and include the following:

Praising person X to make a point about person Y
At the end of Book 10, when the dying Mezentius bids a tearful farewell to his horse, he imagines the animal sharing his fate (*Aen.* 10.865–6):

> *neque enim, fortissime, credo,*
> *iussa aliena pati et dominos dignabere Teucros.*
>
> Nor indeed, my bravest, you will deign,
> I'm sure, to bear another's orders and Trojans as masters,

Servius makes the tactical point explicit:

NEQVE ENIM FORTISSIME CREDO *quod dignaberis habere dominos Teucros, scilicet ignavos: nam hoc intellegimus ex eo quod dixit equo "fortissime." plerumque enim ex alterius personae vituperatione vel laude, quid de alia dicatur, agnoscimus, ut hoc loco Troianos vituperatos ex equi laude cognoscimus.*

NOR INDEED, MY BRAVEST, I'M SURE That you will deign to have Trojans as master, that is to say, cowards: for this is what we infer from his addressing the horse as "bravest." For often from the blame or praise of one character we recognize what is being said about another, as in this case we recognize from the praise of the horse that the Trojans have been blamed.

Praising person X for quality A to excuse mention of quality B
At the start of Book 4, the love-struck Dido exclaims at the physical impression that the hero makes (*Aen.* 4.11),

quem sese ore ferens, quam forti pectore et armis!

What fine looks and bearing, what gallant chest and shoulders!

FORTI PECTORE ET ARMIS . . . *bene virtutis commemoratione excusat supra dictam pulchritudinis laudem.*

GALLANT CHEST AND ARMS . . . She does well to excuse the preceding praise of his beauty by mentioning his martial courage.

Servius obviously reads *forti pectore* metonymically, and takes *armis* to be a form of *arma*, not *armus*, for he explains that the mention of Aeneas' martial prowess excuses the less creditable praise of his beauty just preceding.

Praising person X for A while implicitly blaming him for B

In Book 6, Lucius Junius Brutus is described as (*Aen.* 6.820–1):

> *. . . natosque pater noua bella mouentis*
> *ad poenam pulchra pro libertate uocabit.*

> . . . the father [who] will, for fair liberty's sake, summon
> His sons to punishment when they stir up warfare anew.

According to Servius:

PVLCHRA PRO LIBERTATE *ingenti arte loquitur consideratione personarum: factum enim laudat dicens "pulchra pro libertate," personam vituperat.*

FOR FAIR LIBERTY'S SAKE He speaks with enormous skill, from contemplation of the characters involved: for in saying "for fair liberty's sake," he praises the deed but blames the character.

Praising person X for A to imply that he lacks B

Finally, in the prelude to the duel at the start of Book 12, Servius finds a fair amount of craftiness in the opening Latinus chooses when he addresses Turnus as a "young man of extraordinary spirit" (*Aen.* 12.19–21):

> *o praestans animi iuuenis, quantum ipse feroci*
> *uirtute exsuperas, tanto me impensius aequum est*
> *consulere atque omnis metuentem expendere casus.*

> O young man of extraordinary spirit, the more you
> Yourself excel in fierce *virtus*, the more unstintingly
> Do I ponder, rightly, and fearfully weigh all outcomes.

O PRAESTANS ANIMI . . . sane magnae moderationis est haec oratio: nam et laudat
Turnum quasi virum fortem, et tamen eum a singulari certamine dehortatur: dicens
enim "praestans animi" latenter ostendit eum inferiorem esse virtute.

O . . . OF EXTRAORDINARY SPIRIT . . . This is, of course, a superbly balanced
speech, for he both praises Turnus as a hero and yet seeks to dissuade him from
the duel: in using the phrase "extraordinary spirit" he implicitly shows that he's
inferior in *virtus*.

– despite the fact that the very next words out of Latinus' mouth stress
Turnus' surpassing *virtus*, while he at no point in his speech suggests that
Turnus is the lesser warrior.

A certain amount of this, of course, will be unsurprising to anyone who
has read the ancient rhetoricians on praise and blame. But that does not
mean that this is "merely" rhetorical criticism. Servius is not as sensitive as
he is to praise and its uses because he knew his rhetorical theory; rather,
rhetorical theory was as interested as it was in praise and blame because
of the culture from which it emerged, an honor culture in which few
statements about a person or his attributes were value-neutral. In that
culture, speaking of a person's ancestors almost inevitably meant that one
would be taken to be praising them or blaming them, and thereby praising
or blaming the person himself.

It is perhaps also worth reflecting that the honor culture within which
Servius read the poem was – despite all the other ways the world had
changed – not very different from the honor culture within which Vergil
wrote it.

CHAPTER 4

Joyce and modernist Latinity

Joseph Farrell

For at least the past couple of hundred years, ancient Greece – by which
I mean Greek literature, Greek studies, Greek philosophy, and especially
the Greek language – has generally held a position of greater prestige in
Western culture than has any of the Latin or Roman counterparts. This may
be truer in some national cultures than in others. Whether it is generally
the case in those nations where romance languages are spoken I would not
say. In Germany it seems certainly to have been true for a long time, but
that is not the subject of this paper.[1] My concern is with the Anglophone
world, which is itself not monolithic; but in respect of attitudes towards
Greece and Rome, the prevailing trends have long been similar in British
and American culture and in colonial cultures as well. This situation is
sometimes explained as a product of the Romantic movement at the turn
of the eighteenth and nineteenth centuries, and cultural historians have
amply documented the Romantic fascination with things Greek.[2] During
much of the time since, even if the Romans have had their advocates, many
have expressed the opinion or have simply assumed that Greek literature,
Greek art, and even the Greek language, are simply more beautiful, in an
intrinsic sense, than their Latin and Roman counterparts.[3]

---

[1] The literature on this phenomenon is too vast even to summarize here. See, for example, Hildebrand
"Hellas und Wilamowitz"; Janicaud, *Hegel et le destin de la Grèce*; Seidensticker and Vöhler (eds.),
Urgeschichten der Moderne.

[2] Another enormous area; see for instance Jenkyns, *The Victorians and Ancient Greece*; Hermand and
Holub, *Heinrich Heine, The Romantic School and Other Essays*; Wallace, *Shelley and Greece*; Güthenke,
Placing Modern Greece.

[3] For the most part, Roman art and literature have been regarded as derivative Greek models and therefore as inferior. The articles on "Greek art," "Roman art," "Greek literature," and "Latin literature" in
the 11th edition of the *Encyclopedia Britannica* provide a convenient overview of mainstream opinion
just before the dawn of the Modernist period. As of this writing, the issue of originality vs. deriva-
tiveness is being actively rethought by specialists, but it is not clear that traditional attitudes have
changed all that much among the broader community of interested parties. The Wikipedia entry
on "Roman art," for instance, begins thus: "While the traditional view of Roman artists is that they
often borrowed from, and copied Greek precedents (much of the Greek sculpture known today is

57

The focus of this paper is the work of James Joyce, and its purpose is to raise the possibility that Joyce is at least a partial and paradoxical exception to this rule. The paradox arises from the fact that Joyce is a consummately Modernist writer who is in many respects representative of Modernist aesthetics and values; but in respect to his creativity in using Latin, I believe, he is something of an exception.

The general issue has to do with the position of antiquity within a culture of self-conscious modernity. This relationship has received some useful attention from literary historians, but certain basic issues demand further thought. On the one hand, the very word "modern" seems to be the definitive antonym of "ancient," and certainly an important element of the Modernist movement involved a reaction against some aspects of "the past." But we cannot speak of early Modernism as rejecting antiquity, even if the Modernist reception of antiquity was highly and characteristically selective. Much of what the early Modernists did reject about the past involved the immediate past; but once again, in their general attitude towards the Greeks and the Romans, the early Modernists were very much the descendants of their Victorian predecessors. What was the immediate context of the early Modernist reception of "classics"?

The decisive formulation was pronounced by that consummate "eminent Victorian" Matthew Arnold. In *Culture and Anarchy*, Arnold expressed the view that two forces in particular shaped the contours of British culture in his day, forces to which he gave the names "Hebraism" and "Hellenism."[4] Both terms require definition. By Hebraism, Arnold meant not Judaism, but the idea of obedience to a code of duty symbolized by the Ten Commandments, the Book of Leviticus, and the kashrut, but also by the moral code of Christianity and by the nominally secular but formidably Christianized social codes of the European nation-states. With this force Arnold contrasted Hellenism as an impulse towards intellectual inquiry not out of duty, desire for gain, or any reason other than the sheer joy of it. "The governing idea of Hellenism," he wrote, "is spirit of consciousness, that

---

in the form of Roman marble copies), more recent analysis has indicated that Roman art is a highly creative pastiche relying heavily on Greek models but also encompassing Etruscan, native Italic, and even Egyptian visual culture. Stylistic eclecticism and practical application are the hallmarks of much Roman art" (http://en.wikipedia.org/w/index.php?title=Roman_art&oldid=300615191, retrieved July 6, 2009 15:54 UTC). Even the apparent champions of the Romans tend not to base their opinions on aesthetics: see, for example, Ziolkowski, *Virgil and the Moderns*, pp. 119–45 on T. S. Eliot's famous designation of Virgil as "the classic of all Europe," and, especially, on the reaction that it produced.

[4] On the contemporary background of Arnold's formulation see DeLaura, *Hebrew and Hellene in Victorian England*.

of Hebraism, strictness of conscience."[5] Arnold believed that a healthy culture balanced these forces, but that the England of his day suffered from an excess of Hebraism. This view won followers among the aesthetically minded, who (we are told) began to speak of old-fashioned Victorian moralists as "Jews" and of the socially liberated avant-garde as "Greeks," according to a kind of slang shorthand derived from Arnold's terms.[6]

What, then, was the attitude towards classics that these Arnoldian "Greeks" espoused? A few years ago I made a first pass at this question by commenting on certain passages from Virginia Woolf and W. B. Yeats.[7] I argued that both Woolf and Yeats represented a strong tendency among the early Modernists to esteem ancient Greek much more than Latin culture on the grounds of its greater inherent beauty, authenticity, and immediacy. The contrast is drawn most clearly by Yeats in a famous passage, a fictitious letter to his son's schoolmaster directing him to teach the boy no Latin, but Greek instead and, if he should do well in Greek, Irish – "it will clear his eyes of the Latin miasma."[8] In this same passage Yeats complains that "our schoolmasters read Greek even to-day with Latin eyes," and opines that "Greece, could we but approach it with eyes as young as its own, might renew our youth." Woolf develops this idea, making it clear that such opinions have to do with the fact that, for the majority of educated people in their day, Greek remained somewhat remote and inaccessible, certainly in comparison with the Latin that most of them had been compelled to learn at school (to whatever degree of accomplishment in each case).[9] The reception of Greek therefore was conditioned by the fact that it was more recherché and was fully accessible only to a select few, while conversely Latin suffered from its status as a too-familiar and compulsory subject. This paper resumes my former argument and applies it to the works of Joyce in order to extend, but also to complicate, the impression that Yeats and Woolf create.

---

[5] I cite from Super (ed.), *Complete Prose Works*, vol. v, p. 165.

[6] See Gifford and Seidman, *Ulysses Annotated*, p. 16, where it is stated that "By 1900 'Greek' had become Bohemian slang for those who preached sensual-aesthetic liberation, and 'Jew' had become slang for those who were antagonistic to aesthetic values, those who preached the practical values of straightlaced [sic] Victorian morality." This note is frequently cited as evidence for the colloquial usage, which I have not traced back to primary sources.

[7] Farrell, *Latin Language and Latin Culture from Ancient to Modern Times*, pp. 32–6.

[8] Yeats, *Explorations*, pp. 320–1.

[9] See, for instance, the essays "The perfect language" in McNeillie (ed.), *The Essays of Virginia Woolf*, vol. II, pp. 114–19, and the more famous "On not knowing Greek" in McNeillie (ed.), *The Common Reader*, pp. 23–38; cf. Poole, *The Unknown Virginia Woolf*, pp. 173–84.

The indispensable starting point for this investigation is Joseph Schork's work on Latin and Greek elements in Joyce's writing.[10] In an important chapter entitled "Buck Mulligan as 'Grammaticus Gloriosus'" Schork places Joyce in a very particular position with regard to Greek and Latin and also with respect to Anglo-Irish political and social relations.[11] At school Joyce excelled in Latin, which was both a compulsory subject and a generally recognized mark of intellectual achievement. But he had no Greek, which was not commonly taught in Irish schools. An acquaintance of Joyce, Oliver St. John Gogarty, who was in many ways also his intellectual and social rival, received part of his education in England, where he did learn Greek; and in the opening chapter of *Ulysses*, the character who is based on Gogarty, Buck Mulligan, lords his superior education over Joyce's avatar, Stephen Dedalus: "Ah, Dedalus, the Greeks! I must teach you. You must read them in the original. *Thalatta! Thalatta!*"[12] Stephen, of course, as we later learn actually makes his living as a teacher, in fact teaching Latin and ancient history at a boys' school. Mulligan's remark thus alerts the reader to Stephen's ignorance of Greek as a kind of defect which his expertise in Latin cannot (in Mulligan's eyes) make whole. In the process it also orients the reader towards the Hellenic plot of adventure and discovery in which Stephen is involved. Does this gesture, then, also betoken Joyce's Modernist nostalgia for classical Greek culture, and his envy of those, like Gogarty, who were able to flaunt it?

Joyce more or less confessed such envy on more than one occasion. In a letter to his friend Harriet Shaw Weaver, editor of *The Egoist*, he wrote, "I forgot to tell you one thing. I don't even know Greek though I am spoken of as erudite."[13] Elsewhere Joyce's friend Frank Budgen recounts an anecdote to illustrate that Joyce's ignorance of Greek "was a sore point with him." Budgen once told Joyce that one thing he regretted about his schooling was that he was never able to learn Greek. Joyce thereupon regretted his own lack of Greek, but then, according to Budgen: "as if to underline the differences in our two cases . . . he said with sudden vehemence: 'But just think: isn't it a world I am peculiarly fitted to enter?'"[14] On such evidence

---

[10] Schork, *Latin and Roman Culture in Joyce* and *Greek and Hellenic Culture in Joyce*, with a summary of the main conclusions in Schork, *Joyce and the Classical Tradition*; Arkins, *Greek and Roman Themes in Joyce*, O Hehir and Dillon, *A Classical Lexicon for Finnegans Wake*; on the latter cf. Schork, *Latin and Roman Culture in Joyce*, pp. 10–11 and *Greek and Hellenic Culture in Joyce*, p. xiv. See also Ruggieri, *Classic Joyce*.

[11] Schork, *Latin and Roman Culture in Joyce*, pp. 28–39.

[12] *Ulysses* 1.79–80; I cite from Gabler (ed.), *Ulysses: The Corrected Text*.

[13] *Per litteras* June 24, 1921; see Gilbert (ed.), *Letters of James Joyce*, vol. 1, p. 167.

[14] Budgen, *James Joyce and the Making of Ulysses*, pp. 358–9.

it would be tempting to conclude that Joyce's attitude towards the Greek language is just like that of Virginia Woolf, W. B. Yeats, and of many other artistic contemporaries. Did Joyce's ignorance and desire also cause him to overestimate the richness of Greek and breed contempt for the too familiar Latin of his school and church?

This system of values is unquestionably among *Ulysses'* governing ideas. Indeed, the novel's design is explicitly informed by Arnoldian (and for that matter Nietzschean) attitudes towards "Hellenism" and "Hebraism."[15] The titular allusion, after all, casts one Leopold Bloom, a character whose Jewishness is thematized throughout, in the role of Odysseus, the great Greek wanderer.[16] Bloom's Telemachus, an aspiring writer, bears the impossibly "Hellenic" name of Stephen Dedalus, a name that traces his spiritual progress from the "Hebraic" world of the Christian Church (represented through reference to the ur-martyr Stephanos) back to that of pagan mythology (in the form of Daidalos, the original artist). This theme of movement from "Hebraic" to "Hellenic" culture is again loudly advocated in chapter 1 by Mulligan when he comments on Stephen's "absurd name, an ancient Greek!" (1.34). But Mulligan acknowledges this absurdity with evident jealousy when he comments on his own (to this point) suppressed "Christian" name, which is that of an ancient Hebrew prophet: "My name is absurd too: Malachi Mulligan, two dactyls. But it has a Hellenic ring, hasn't it?" (1.41–2).[17] The parallelism thus established between the two characters invites further comparison; and in this context it seems clear enough that Stephen's name is more self-evidently "absurd" (i.e., impossibly Greek), while Mulligan must argue rather tendentiously for the curious status that Stephen's Hellenic nomenclature more obviously confers. The point may be that Stephen is, as it were, an *anima naturaliter Graeca* while Mulligan is a mere pretender.[18] Lest there be any doubt what all of this means, the reader is soon informed that Stephen, gazing out a window of the Martello tower, sees "a deaf gardener, aproned, masked with Matthew Arnold's face" (1.172–3). And just after that Mulligan declares, now in a

---

[15] On this theme in *Ulysses* see Theoharis, *Joyce's Ulysses*, pp. 142–99; Davison, *James Joyce, Ulysses, and the Construction of Jewish Identity*, pp. 106–26.

[16] Hildesheimer, *The Jewishness of Mr. Bloom*; Nadel, *Joyce and the Jews*; Reizbaum, *James Joyce's Judaic Other*; Ó Gráda, *Jewish Ireland in the Age of Joyce*.

[17] Gifford and Seidman, (*Ulysses Annotated*, p. 14) note that the name has Irish as well as Biblical resonances.

[18] As a further thrust at Mulligan's (and so of Gogarty's) pretensions, this time as a Latinist, it is argued that Joyce deliberately allowed an egregious solecism to stand in a passage of apparently expert Ciceronian parody that he put in the mouth of that character (Schork, *Latin and Roman Culture in Joyce*, pp. 28–39).

Nietzschean vein, "I'm the *Übermensch*" (1.708).[19] A clearer statement of the novel's "Hebraic/Hellenic" program could hardly be desired.

The other side of the novel's apparent preference for Greek over Latin culture soon shows itself as well. Chapter 2 opens with Stephen teaching a lesson to a group of students whose command of history and of Latin seems shaky at best. He asks one of them, a boy named Armstrong, "What was the end of Pyrrhus?" What Stephen wants to know is how the great Greek general died. But Armstrong completely misunderstands, thinking that the question is about Latin grammar, not Greek history; and, misconstruing what Stephen means by "end," he subtracts the case-ending *-us* from Pyrrhus' name, and finds that the result is a perfectly good English word: "Pyrrhus, sir? Pyrrhus, a pier . . . A thing out in the waves. A kind of bridge. Kingstown pier, sir" (*Ulysses* 2.18–27).

One glimpses in this passage just the sort of classroom that Yeats hoped his son might be able to avoid. Schork has coined a phrase that aptly captures this aspect of Joyce's attitude: "the Parser's Revenge," or "the ability of a clever Latin student to use the tricks of his linguistic dedication to poke fun at the entire enterprise, especially to mock the ridiculously pedantic methods of instruction and the language-masters who expounded them."[20] In the context of *Ulysses*, there is an undeniable element of self-loathing involved in this mockery. Stephen, Joyce's stand-in, is portrayed as a Latin adept who is ignorant of Greek, and as a cog in an educational machine that uses Latin as a means of processing students into relatively standardized members of a spiritually atrophied society. His question about "the end of Pyrrhus" results in nothing but the "mirthless high malicious laughter" of his charges, which effectively dissolves the lesson. But the question that poor Armstrong flubbed is not permanently forgotten, even if the answer to it does not come until much later. In chapter 7, the "Aeolus" episode, a certain Professor MacHugh represents the eponymous hero of Pyrrhic victories not as the disappointed imperialist that he really was, but as a kind of rebel martyr against the Roman tyranny over Greece (which would not in fact come into being until generations after his campaigns). In so representing "the end of Pyrrhus" the embittered professor speaks for all who feel oppressed by Latinity and who long for the beauty and freedom that, as they believe, "Hellenism" represents:[21]

---

[19] On Joyce and Nietzsche see Davison, *James Joyce, Ulysses, and the Construction of Jewish Identity*, pp. 106–26.

[20] Schork, *Joyce and the Classical Tradition*, p. 12. The concept first appeared in Schork, *Latin and Roman Culture in Joyce*, pp. 1–12.

[21] *Ulysses* 7.551–71.

We were always loyal to lost causes, the professor said. Success for us is the death of the intellect and of the imagination. We were never loyal to the successful. We serve them. I teach the blatant Latin language. I speak the tongue of a race the acme of whose mentality is the maxim: time is money. Material domination. *Domine!* Lord! Where is the spirituality? Lord Jesus? Lord Salisbury? A sofa in a westend club. But the Greek!

KYRIE ELEISON!

A smile of light brightened his darkrimmed eyes, lengthened his long lips.

The Greek! he said once again. *Kyrios!* Shining word! The vowels the Semite and the Saxon know not. *Kyrie!* The radiance of the intellect. I ought to profess Greek, the language of the mind. *Kyrie eleison!* The closetmaker and the cloacamaker will never be lords of our spirit. We are liege subjects of the catholic chivalry of Europe that foundered at Trafalgar and of the empire of the spirit, not an *imperium*, that went under with the Athenian fleets at Aegospotami. Yes, yes. They went under. Pyrrhus, misled by an oracle, made a last attempt to retrieve the fortunes of Greece. Loyal to a lost cause.

He strode away from them towards a window.

At this point, the case that the author of *Ulysses* retained any fondness or admiration for Latinity may look pretty bad. Joyce frequently and undeniably gives voice to "Hellenic" characters who disparage Latinity openly, as does MacHugh, identifying it as he does with forces and institutions that exist in order to inculcate a "Hebraic" sense of duty. And there is no question that Stephen Dedalus must wrestle with his own complicity in these institutions as well as with his personal ambitions and integrity. But there are indications throughout Joyce's work that Latin is empowering as well, both for Stephen and for Joyce himself; and the rest of this paper will be devoted to exploring some of these.

To begin with some simple, formal observations, it is clear that Latin in various forms plays a huge and varied stylistic and textural role in all of Joyce's mature work.[22] Often it appears in satirical contexts that verge on the grotesque. Such elements evidently grew out of Joyce's own early experience with the language and its place in his educational and social milieu. One amusing aspect is the habit among his friends of conversing in a kind of student argot called "dog Latin." Thus in the *Portrait* Stephen overhears the following declaration of an unnamed medical student: "Ego credo ut vita pauperum est simpliciter atrox, simpliciter sanguinarius atrox, in

[22] As is abundantly illustrated by Schork, *Latin and Roman Culture in Joyce.*

Liverpoolio" (*Portrait*, p. 216).[23] Here too perhaps the point is to undermine pretension and to make glaringly clear the contrast between the archaic values of the education to which Joyce and his peers were subjected and the world in which they actually lived. But it has also been observed that Joyce's own inimitable style is closely implicated in the kind of linguistic play that such passages represent. In a reminiscence of Joyce, his friend Eugene Sheehy speculates that the author's own youthful conversations in dog Latin could have been "the first intimation of the vocabulary of *Finnegans Wake*."[24] It is unquestionably true and has been amply documented that the deracinated linguistic amalgam that is the language of the *Wake* draws heavily on the resources of Latin, both directly and by analogy.[25] Coming at the issue from another angle, one critic has convincingly analyzed the famously Latinate English style employed in chapter 14 of *Ulysses* (the "Oxen" episode) as using the linguistic history of Latin, from the "Song of the Arval Brethren" to medieval chronicle, to chart self-reflexively the development of Joyce's own style – this time in even more explicit anticipation of the *Wake*.[26] An impulse towards parody of the schoolroom is still an important point of reference – the passages in question read like a capable student's effort to convince a skeptical teacher that he really understands the syntax of a piece of Latin that he is translating in class[27] – but this is parody of a more generous sort than we find in the lampooning of characters like Buck Mulligan.[28] And crucially, such passages offer evidence that Joyce's own sense of familiarity and comfort with Latin is one factor, and evidently not the least powerful one, that made possible the development of his unprecedented literary style.[29]

---

[23] I cite from Anderson (ed.), *A Portrait of the Artist as a Young Man*.

[24] Sheehy, *The Joyce We Knew*, p. 22; cited by Schork, *Latin and Roman Culture in Joyce*, p. 217.

[25] O Hehir and Dillon, *A Classical Lexicon for Finnegans Wake*, pp. xi–xiii.

[26] Downing, "Joyce's use of Latin at the outset of 'Oxen,'" pp. 255–66. Downing develops the insights of Joyce's first great explicator, Stuart Gilbert; see the following note.

[27] Or, as Gilbert puts it (commenting on the passage that begins "Universally that person's acumen," *Ulysses* 14.7–17), "this appalling sentence reads like the literal translation of a tract on child welfare written in medieval Latin – reminiscence of the *Epistolae Obscurorum Virorum*, for instance – by a demented German docent" (*James Joyce's Ulysses*, p. 298). Gilbert gives evidence that Joyce gave considerable thought to calibrating the literary–historical effect of this passage in terms of Latin style when he cites a letter from Joyce to Frank Budgen describing the style of this passage, evidently at an early stage of composition, as "Sallustian–Tacitean." But, as Gilbert notes, "no style could be further than this" from either of those models, and he concludes that this was one of the changes that Joyce made while working on the episode (p. 298 n.).

[28] Gilbert, again, hits the mark: "the greater part seems to be devoid of satiric intention; that willful exaggeration of mannerism which points a parody is absent and the effect is rather of pastiche than of travesty" (*James Joyce's Ulysses*, p. 296).

[29] On the further stylistic relationship between "Oxen" and *Finnegans Wake*, see the letter of Stanislaus Joyce dated August 1924 in Ellman (ed.), *Letters of James Joyce*, vol. III, pp. 102–3, cited by Downing, "Joyce's use of Latin at the outset of 'Oxen,'" p. 261.

To this extent at least I would suggest that Joyce's Latinity and his attitude towards it share the characteristic *jouissance* that marks his approach to language in general. This *jouissance* is compatible with the "Parser's Revenge," but goes beyond the low entertainment of retribution through parody and contributes to something much more positive and creative. A similar impulse does its work on other planes. Joyce does represent characters who worship Greek and hate Latin, but this is only one side of the story. In the first place, as we have seen, the pretensions of such characters are often satirized. To go further, it may be indicative that Stephen, arguably the most consummately Latinate character in Joyce's work, is in a sense more "Greek" than the "Greeks." The name of Dedalus, glossed in the epigraph to *A Portrait of the Artist as a Young Man* by a quotation from Ovid (*ignotas animum dimittit in artes*, "he directs his mind towards unfamiliar arts," *Met.* 8.188), and orthographically a none-too-classical corruption of the Greek name, follows suit.[30] The title of *Ulysses* – not, that is, *Odysseus* – points in the same direction. Many times where one might expect Joyce's work to gaze upon Greek more openly, it squints instead through a Roman lens.[31] Joyce is in this respect a specimen of the type that Yeats lamented when he wrote that "our schoolmasters read Greek even to-day with Latin eyes." Yeats of course implicates himself in this critique of those who must "clear our eyes of the Latin miasma," and it would be easy to assume that Joyce shared such sentiments and focused them above all on the character of Stephen Dedalus as an embodiment of Latinate self-loathing and longing to transcend itself, to throw off the shackles of duty, conventional thinking, and social constraint, and to realize one's better nature – to become, at last, Greek. It is Stephen above all who yearns for the imagined simplicity, clarity, and wholeness that defines the Modernist canon of artistic excellence; and it would be easy to read this longing as congruent with Virginia Woolf's Hellenophile rhapsodies. But when, in *Portrait*, the young Stephen states his artistic principles, he draws upon the philosophical legacy of Aristotle as presented by Aquinas, whom he quotes in Latin and expounds at some length.[32] Nor is there any indication that he is frustrated by an understanding of Aristotle, whom he does not even mention by name, that is filtered through a Latinate, scholastic exegesis.

---

[30] On the epigraph itself and its larger significance see Senn, *Joyce's Dislocutions*, pp. 73–8.

[31] The sheer volume of Greek and Latin in the *Wake* is documented by O Hehir and Dillon, *A Classical Lexicon for Finnegans Wake*, pp. xi–xii.

[32] Anderson (ed.), *A Portrait of the Artist as a Young Man*, pp. 211–14, citing Aquinas, *Summa theologica* I, q. 39, a. 8, corp.; cf. Noon, *Joyce and Aquinas*, p. 105.

For Stephen, steeped as he is in Latin culture, this situation is both a fact of life and even a source of sustenance. It would be wrong to suppose that he devalues Greek culture, just as it would be wrong to deny that Joyce himself regretted his lack of it. But there is little if any indication that Stephen feels quite the same way as the disappointed Professor MacHugh about "the blatant Latin language." Stephen is only the most prominent among the many characters who habitually think in Latin and whose use of the language is rich and varied, surpassing in importance all other foreign tongues and tapping veins of significance inaccessible to English – even to Joycean English – alone. Moreover, in presenting "stately, plump Buck Mulligan" as the embodiment of philhellenic aspiration, Joyce can hardly be felt to be endorsing the Romantic notion of what it means to go Greek. Rather, it is reasonable to suppose that the narrator's satirical presentation of self-styled Arnoldian "Greeks" like Mulligan represents Stephen's, and Joyce's, skeptical stance towards the breed. Mulligan's Greek is represented by the most conventional and banal elements of the schoolboy's lexicon – Homer's *epi oinopa ponton*, Xenophon's *Thalatta! Thalatta!*, the scansion of his proper name as a pair of dactyls – and by a scheme to take the Grand Tour on borrowed funds.[33] He prattles cheerfully and insincerely in classical Greek slogans and mottoes, while Stephen broods tortuously over some of the greatest monuments of Latin culture. Mulligan's mockery, of course, is bilingual: his first utterance is in Latin as he intones a phrase from the entrance antiphon to the Roman Catholic Mass (*Introibo ad altare Dei*), a passage comparable to his Homeric and Xenophontic tags in its triteness: as part of the introductory prayers to the Tridentine Mass, the phrase is among the most familiar in Christendom.[34] This bit of vulgar blasphemy is answered by Stephen's exquisite and haunted recollection of verses from the funeral service, the Ordo Commendationis Animae, in connection with his mother's death: *liliata rutilantium te confessorum turma circumdet: iubilantium te virginum chorus excipiat* ("may the company of martyrs, shining and bearing lilies, surround you; may the chorus of virgins, rejoicing, greet you").[35] Mulligan's Greek *and* Latin sources are generic, unimaginative, and obvious; Stephen's specific, pointed, and recherché.

It is true, of course, that Joyce sometimes presents Latin merely as a learned language that few people actually manage to learn (as in "Pyrrhus, a pier"). But Stephen, crucially, has learned it and learned it well – better (the novel implies) than the more expensively schooled Mulligan, whose Latin (as Schork argues) is on at least one occasion signally exposed as

---

[33] Gabler (ed.), *Ulysses*, pp. 80 and 42–3, respectively.   [34] Gabler (ed.), *Ulysses*, p. 5.
[35] Gabler (ed.), *Ulysses*, pp. 276–7, 736–8; Thornton, *Allusions in Ulysses*, pp. 17–18.

defective.[36] Stephen's expertise, we may infer, gives him access not only to the resources of Latinity itself, but to those of Greek culture as well. It may be paradoxical to say, particularly in the light of the opinions expressed by Joyce's contemporaries, but it seems possible that for Stephen and for Joyce the Latin adept possesses a means of more complete access even to Greek culture than does the slipshod scholar who gets caught up in reductive Arnoldian binaries.

In any case, Joyce's Latinity is by no means always or even regularly parodic or parodied, and at times it appears as an avenue of privileged access not only to conventionally defined cultural attainments, but to the much more inaccessible recesses of the psyche and the spirit. Near the end of the *Portrait*, Stephen and a friend named Cranly are found having a somewhat troubled discussion when they are interrupted by the sound of a girl singing in the distance:[37]

Behind a hedge of laurel a light glimmered in the window of a kitchen and the voice of a servant was heard singing as she sharpened knives. She sang, in short broken bars, *Rosie O'Grady*.

Cranly stopped to listen, saying:

– *Mulier cantat.*

The soft beauty of the Latin word touched with an enchanting touch the dark of the evening, with a touch fainter and more persuading than the touch of music or of a woman's hand. The strife of their minds was quelled. The figure of woman as she appears in the liturgy of the church passed silently through the darkness: a white robed figure, small and slender as a boy, and with a falling girdle. Her voice, frail and high as a boy's, was heard intoning from a distant choir the first words of a woman which pierce the gloom and clamour of the first chanting of the passion:

– *Et tu cum Jesu Galilæo eras.*

And all hearts were touched and turned to her voice, shining like a young star, shining clearer as the voice intoned the proparoxyton and more faintly as the cadence died.

The singing ceased. They went on together, Cranly repeating in strongly stressed rhythm the end of the refrain:

> *And when we are married,*
> *O, how happy we'll be*
> *For I love sweet Rosie O'Grady*
> *And Rosie O'Grady loves me.*

– There's real poetry for you, he said. There's real love.

---

[36] See n. 18 above.   [37] Anderson (ed.), *A Portrait of the Artist as a Young Man*, pp. 244–5.

In Stephen's reverie, a simple scullery maid is transformed by the power and beauty of Cranly's ironic and offhand Latinate comment (*mulier cantat*, "a woman is singing") into a figure of mythical significance, both pagan and Christian.[38] Appearing in a window "behind a hedge of laurel" she is a type of Daphne, the living symbol of poetic inspiration, and in the power of her song to soothe nature and the human heart she stands comparison even to Orpheus.[39] But she is also and more explicitly "liturgical": a servant herself, in Stephen's reverie she becomes another servant girl, the one who in the Gospels accuses Peter of being Jesus' follower (*et tu cum Jesu Galilæo eras*, "you were also with Jesus the Galilean"), before whom Peter famously denies Jesus three times.[40] Stephen remembers this passage not from the New Testament but from "the liturgy of the church."[41] And, of course, he, Stephen, *is* Peter in this reverie. His conversation with Cranly has been about love and faith, two of the three cardinal virtues, and specifically about Stephen's inability to feel or to express either emotion. The exchange just discussed follows an earlier one in which Stephen observes that he has just quarreled with his mother over refusing to make his Easter duty:[42]

– It is a curious thing, do you know, said Cranly dispassionately, how your mind is
   supersaturated with the religion in which you say you disbelieve. Did you believe
   it when you were at school? I bet you did.
– I did, Stephen answered.
– And were you happier then? Cranly asked softly, happier than you are now, for
   instance?
– Often happy, Stephen said, and often unhappy. I was someone else then.
– How someone else? What do you mean by that statement?
– I mean, said Stephen, that I was not myself as I am now, as I had to become.
– Not as you are now, not as you had to become, Cranly repeated. Let me ask you
   a question. Do you love your mother?

[38] Attridge (*Joyce Effects*, p. 76) comments perceptively on Joyce's deployment of a Latin phrase at this point. For a different approach to the scene cf. Gottfried, *Joyce's Comic Portrait*, pp. 74–5, who finds the scene "almost comically overdone" and downplays the significance of Cranly's *mulier cantat* in terms of Latinity as such. But these approaches need not be regarded as dichotomous: see Schlossman, *Joyce's Catholic Comedy of Language*.

[39] The Latinity of the passage is closely linked to the theme of musicality: see Bowen, *Musical Allusions in the Works of James Joyce*, pp. 44–5; Nestrovski, "Joyce's critique of music," p. 267.

[40] The passage is quoted from the Vulgate text of Matthew 26:69.

[41] On the liturgical use of this passage see Gifford, *Joyce Annotated*, p. 267.

[42] In the Roman Catholic Church the phrase "Easter duty" refers to an obligation to receive Holy Communion at least once a year during the Easter season; the exact span of time involved is defined by local authorities. In this way as well, Stephen's refusal of his mother's wish parallels Peter's denial of Jesus during the Passion.

Stephen shook his head slowly.

– I don't know what your words mean, he said simply.[43]

Stephen's inability to deal with this question recurs hauntingly in *Ulysses* when, shortly after (yet again) the failed history lesson about Pyrrhus, the boys are let out to play – but one named Sargent stays behind for help with his arithmetic.[44] He is an evidently unimpressive young man. "Ugly and futile: lean neck and thick hair and a stain of ink, a snail's bed," Stephen thinks to himself:

Yet someone had loved him, borne him in her arms and in her heart. But for her the race of the world would have trampled him underfoot, a squashed boneless snail. She had loved his weak watery blood drained from her own. Was that then real? The only true thing in life? His mother's prostrate body the fiery Columbanus in holy zeal bestrode. She was no more: the trembling skeleton of a twig burnt in the fire, an odor of rosewood and wetted ashes. She had saved him from being trampled underfoot and gone, scarcely having been. A poor soul gone to heaven . . .

Amid such thoughts Stephen helps the boy with the first problem, asking at length:

– Do you understand now? Can you work the second by yourself?
– Yes, sir.

In long shaky strokes Sargent copied the data. Waiting always for a word of help his hand moved faithfully the unsteady symbols, a faint hue of shame flickering behind his dull skin. *Amor matris*: subjective and objective genitive. With her weak blood and wheysour milk she had fed him and hid from the sight of others his swaddlingbands.

"*Amor matris*: subjective and objective genitive." To such poignant thoughts that seem like messages from the depths of his soul Stephen responds by reducing them to grammatical categories. But this reaction extends to both poles of Joyce's Latinity. On the one hand, Latin is the deadest of all dead languages, an elaborate collection of fetishized rules to be lampooned or clung to as circumstances dictate. At the same time it is the language in which Stephen expresses, or tries to express, what matters most to him, a language that even in its hypertrophied taxonomy of grammatical and syntactic phenomena does not, finally, offer Joyce's gloomy hero the possibility of classifying and containing emotional unpleasantness, but

---

[43] Anderson (ed.), *A Portrait of the Artist as a Young Man*, p. 240.
[44] Gabler (ed.), *Ulysses*, pp. 123–67.

intensifies his discomfort by taking him to the very limit of dispassionate analysis and no farther. "*Amor matris*: subjective and objective genitive." A mother's love and love for one's mother. In the ambivalence of the Latin phrase a perfect reciprocity is expressed, a reciprocity in which Stephen knows he has been judged and found wanting.[45] Just as the beauty of *mulier cantat* cannot shield Stephen from the guilt of the betrayer, so his teacherly instinct to parse that guilt becomes itself a particularly exquisite and ineluctable form of self-reproach.

Joyce thus complicates the rather one-sided picture of Modernist attitudes towards Greek and Latin with which we began. He is not alone in doing so; and yet the picture remains in general. Why is this so? I have suggested that the cultural ascendancy of Greek over Latin in the twentieth century has its roots in both the Romantic and, in some ways even more importantly, in the Victorian period, but that this ascendancy comes to be expressed in terms that show a particular affinity with Modernist aesthetics; also that within one of the great temples of high Modernism, Joyce's *Ulysses*, evidence can be found to suggest that the situation might in theory have been reversed. It seems clear enough that the Greek and Latin languages themselves play important and very different roles in Modernist reception. I hope at least to have shown that the Modernist engagement with Latin involves not just antipathy, but elements of a profound and even mysterious attraction as well. The evidence suggests, I believe, that there is much more to this phenomenon than the occasional engagement of one Modernist writer with one or more ancient forebears. Instead, I would say that we are dealing with a subject that has to be approached from both directions: with attention to specific intertextual relations at the level of individual texts, but also in the knowledge that Latin and Greek themselves occupy quite specific and challengingly complex positions in the constellation of Modernist aesthetics.

In a more general sense, I hope to have shown why I believe that the phenomenon of literature is profoundly conditioned by both the writer's and the reader's personal circumstances, and also why a historically contingent response to literature need not be at odds with an aesthetic one.[46] But such a response obviously challenges the notion of the aesthetic as a

---

[45] Cf. the heartbreaking anecdote with which Schork (*Latin and Roman Culture in Joyce*, p. 13) opens his inquiry into Joyce's Latinity.

[46] The idea of "the aesthetic" as a transcendent category has gained a surprising amount of traction in recent years. In the context of the conference where these papers originated, Charles Martindale's recent work on Kant's *Critique of Judgment* as an appropriate frame of reference for the interpretation of Latin poetry (Martindale, *Latin Poetry and the Judgement of Taste*) stands as a particular salient example, and one that provocatively reverses what I have treated in this paper as the basic axioms of

transcendent category. Some Modernist writers did, it seems, regard Greek as a medium of literary and linguistic expression that was especially well-attuned to universal categories, and to have regarded Latin as quite unsuited or even antithetical to such purposes. Today, unless we share this belief, we can see that the identification of Greek with a universal aesthetic is a historically determined position, and one for which we can easily account. Indeed, from our (or perhaps I should say, from my) perspective, this belief looks a bit quaint or naïve. An appreciation of the capacity of Latin to serve similar purposes is no doubt equally contingent, depending on the intellectual and cultural formation of both artist and audience. Nor is the Arnoldian binary of "Hellenism" and Hebraism" itself more than an intellectual construct, useful under some circumstances, but inevitably limited by them. An appreciation of these facts does not mean that we (or even I!) cannot share a strong aesthetic response to some of the same Greek literature that inspired the Modernists. But it does, I think, call the universality of the responses into question. In my opinion, careful attention to those contextual factors that underlie the characteristic attitudes of literary Modernism, both in the reception of the classics and in other respects, can only improve our understanding of their aesthetic response and of our own.

literary Modernism. I do not find myself entirely in sympathy with Martindale's thesis (see Farrell, Review of Martindale, *Latin Poetry and the Judgement of Taste*), but I do welcome the book as, in some respects, a useful illustration of the points that I am making here about contingency in matters of reception.

CHAPTER 5

Lyricus vates: *musical settings of Horace's* Odes

Richard Tarrant

I first became aware of a connection between Horace's *Odes* and music as an undergraduate, when I read in Eduard Fraenkel's *Horace* that "not very long ago [i.e., from the perspective of the 1950s] it was the custom at many German schools to have the first stanza [of *Odes* 1.22, *Integer vitae*] sung at the funeral services in Hall, to a tune not distinguishable from that of an ordinary church hymn; the tempo, needless to say, was *molto adagio*."[1] Fraenkel was referring to a musical setting of the poem by F. F. Flemming (1778–1813), which gained wide circulation in both English- and German-speaking countries.[2]

Much more recently, in an amateur choral group, I performed a setting by Randall Thompson (1899–1984) of another solemn-sounding passage from the *Odes*, the final stanza of *Odes* 1.13, beginning *Felices ter* ("Three times happy").[3] While those two pieces represent a tiny and purely random sample of a large body of Horatian musical settings, they nevertheless share what we shall find to be several recurring features of the *Odes'* reception in music: they select a portion of an ode rather than setting the entire poem, they transform Horace's individual voice into a choral utterance, and they turn texts that are playful or ironic in their original context into morally uplifting statements.[4] In other words, they are in significant respects unfaithful to their Horatian originals. Those alterations in turn suggest that the *Odes*, although they have proven attractive to composers, are at the same time in some ways resistant to musical treatment.

The impact of Horace's *Odes* on Western music since the Renaissance cannot compare with that of, for example, the various episodes of Ovid's

---

[1] Fraenkel, *Horace*, p. 184. In a note he adds that the vocative *Fusce* in line 4 "very much puzzled me when I was a small boy."

[2] I return to Flemming and *Integer vitae* below, pp. 79–81.   [3] See below, pp. 82–3.

[4] A good parallel for the un-ironic use of originally humorous music is the performance of Handel's aria "Ombra mai fu" from *Serse*, a love song addressed to a plane tree, as part of a funeral or memorial service.

Metamorphoses, but Horace can claim the distinction of having had his own words, in Latin or in translation, set to music more often than any other classical author. The musical aspect of his reception has received little attention in recent companions and other works in English, a neglect that is sadly true of many studies of classical reception.[5] Fortunately, any investigation of the subject can draw on two indispensable guides: a splendid survey by Franco Piperno in the *Enciclopedia Oraziana*,[6] and an anthology of musical settings edited by Joachim Draheim and Günther Wille that brings together examples ranging from the Middle Ages to the 1970s.[7] The following discussion is of necessity highly selective; I have favored material that has not been treated in detail in earlier discussions, and I have often been guided in my choices by the availability of recordings.[8]

A link between the *Odes* and music would seem perfectly natural, given that the genre in which Horace was writing was in its Greek origins meant for musical performance and Horace himself employs the language of musical accompaniment to describe his poetry. (See, e.g., *Odes* 1.1.32–4 *si neque tibias / Euterpe cohibet nec Polyhymnia / Lesboum refugit tendere barbiton*; "if Euterpe does not withhold her flute and Polyhymnia does not refuse to tune the Lesbian lyre.") At least one lyric composition of Horace was intended for actual performance, the *Carmen Saeculare* commissioned by Augustus for the grand celebration of the Secular Games (*Ludi Saeculares*) of 17 BC and sung by twin choruses of twenty-seven boys and twenty-seven girls; it is inconceivable that the poem was performed without some form of musical accompaniment.[9] The *Carmen*, however, is clearly exceptional in its occasional and public character, and I know of no reliable evidence for musical performances in antiquity of Horace's collections of lyric poetry.[10]

Musical settings of the *Odes* are first attested in the Middle Ages, and are in fact as old as the Horatian manuscript tradition itself: the earliest extant manuscript, Vatican Reginensis latinus 1703, probably written in Alsace in the second quarter of the ninth century, marks the opening line

---

[5] For recent studies of Horatian reception see, e.g., Harrison (ed.), *The Cambridge Companion to Horace*, pp. 277–346 and Houghton and Wyke (eds.), *Perceptions of Horace*.

[6] Piperno, "Musica."

[7] Draheim and Wille (eds.), *Horaz-Vertonungen vom Mittelalter bis zum Gegenwart*. Thomas, "Musical settings of Horace's lyric poems" is also still useful. For information on individual composers, I am largely indebted to Sadie (ed.), *The New Grove Dictionary of Music and Musicians*.

[8] Details of recordings mentioned are given in the Discography (pp. 92–3 below).

[9] On the *Carmen Saeculare* in its original ritual setting, see Feeney, *Literature and Religion at Rome*, pp. 32–8.

[10] For the surprisingly eventful musical afterlife of the *Carmen Saeculare* in modern times, see below, pp. 88–92. The case for musical performance of the *Odes* in Horace's time has been argued most recently by Lyons, *Music in the Odes of Horace*.

of *Odes* 1.1 (*Maecenas atavis edite regibus*) and lines 5–8 of *Odes* 1.3 with
the medieval musical notation known as neumes; similar notation, either
of parts of odes or of entire odes, has been found in almost fifty Horatian
manuscripts from the ninth through the twelfth centuries.[11] Recent work
by the late Silvia Wälli and by Jan Ziolkowski has given us a much clearer,
but also more complex, picture of the phenomenon of neuming and its
possible motivations. As far as the *Odes* are concerned, the likeliest explanation for the practice is that the musical notation was meant to serve a
scholastic purpose, making Horace's complex and varied lyric meters easier
to analyze and remember. That function, however, would not account for
the frequent neuming of passages from works of Virgil, Lucan, and Statius
written in the more familiar dactylic hexameter; in such cases neuming
may have been intended to focus attention on passages of high emotion
(e.g., speeches) or on pivotal points in the narrative, perhaps as an aid to
effective declamation.[12]

One neumed manuscript of Horace can boast a connection (even if
probably a tangential one) with a momentous development in the history of Western music. In Montpellier, Ecole de Médecine 425H, written
in the eleventh century, *Odes* 4.11 (*Est mihi nonum superantis annum*) is
neumed with the same melody used by Guido of Arezzo shortly before as
a mnemonic device for teaching the ascending notes of the scale. Guido
connected the melody to the text of a famous hymn in honor of John the
Baptist attributed to Paul the Deacon (late eighth century), of which the
first stanza is as follows:

> *Ut queant laxis resonare fibris*
> *mira gestorum famuli tuorum,*
> *solve polluti labii reatum,*
>   *Sancte Ioannes.*

> So that your servants may sound forth
> the wonders of your deeds with loosened hearts,
> remove the guilt of our tainted lips,
>   Saint John.

Since each half-line of the first three verses begins on a progressively higher
note, Guido used the first syllable of each half-line to generate the series
ut–re–mi–fa–sol–la. With *ut* replaced by *do* and with the addition of *ti* and

---

[11] Details of all manuscripts with photographs and transcriptions in Wälli, *Melodien aus mittelalterlichen Horaz-Handschriften*; selected manuscripts in Lyons, *Music in the Odes of Horace*,
pp. 132–75.
[12] On the range of possible reasons for neuming see Ziolkowski, *Nota Bene*, pp. 109–72.

a second *do* to complete the octave, Guido's mnemonic forms the basis of the solfège or solmization system still in use today.[13] Most scholars believe that the melody in question was first used for *Ut queant laxis* and later transferred to the Horatian ode,[14] but in the absence of a neumed text of *Ut queant laxis* the question cannot be definitively resolved; there has even been wishful speculation that the tune originated with Horace himself.[15]

A desire to impart metrical instruction undoubtedly prompted some of the earliest post-medieval musical treatments of the *Odes*, produced in German humanist circles in the years around 1500 under the leadership of Conradus Celtis and his student the composer Petrus Tritonius (a name presumably bestowed before the tritone became stigmatized as the *diabolus in musica*). In these settings the musical line is clearly subordinate to the text and reproduces the metrical shape of the Latin, and since Latin prosody differentiates only between long and short syllables, the corresponding musical note values are limited to a single binary opposition (whole vs. half-notes, or half-notes vs. quarter-notes). The possibilities for musical expression are therefore severely limited; perhaps the most that could be accomplished within such a system is illustrated by some reharmonizations of Tritonius' settings by Ludwig Senfl (*c.* 1486–1542/3), one of the leading composers of the early sixteenth century.[16]

By the mid sixteenth century, metrically determined settings had largely given way to freer treatments in which the text was interpreted without regard for the quantitative values of the syllables. The middle decades of the sixteenth century arguably represent the high point of Horace's prestige among musicians: at this time various odes and epodes were set by several eminent masters, including Claude Goudimel (settings of nineteen odes, published 1555, unfortunately lost), Jacob Arcadelt (*Odes* 1.22 *Integer vitae*, 1.32 *Poscimus, si quid* and 3.22 *Montium custos*, all in Sapphic meter, published 1559),[17] Orlando di Lasso (setting of *Epode* 2, *Beatus ille*), and

---

[13] See Ziolkowski, *Nota Bene*, pp. 25–9. Photograph of *Odes* 4.11 in the Montpellier manuscript and transcription of the neumes in Wälli, *Melodien aus mittelalterlichen Horaz-Handschriften*, pp. 156–9.

[14] So, e.g., Draheim and Wille (eds.), *Horaz-Vertonungen vom Mittelalter bis zum Gegenwart*, p. 3. Lyons, *Horace's Odes and the Mystery of Do-re-mi*, pp. 26–40 argued instead that Guido found the inspiration for his mnemonic in the Montpellier manuscript, but that argument requires a pre-Guido dating of the manuscript that is unlikely on palaeographical grounds. Lyons, *Music in the Odes of Horace*, pp. 101–31 more cautiously suggests that Guido and the neumist of the Montpellier manuscript were drawing independently on a well-known melody of uncertain origin.

[15] A notion gently debunked by Thomas, "Musical settings of Horace's lyric poems," 78: "so at least people think who listen to it with the ear of faith."

[16] A specimen of Senfl's work can be heard in his setting of *Odes* 2.20 (*Non usitata nec tenui ferar*), recorded on the CD *Le Chant de Virgile*.

[17] The opening bars of Arcadelt's settings are given by Piperno, "Musica," pp. 668 and 672.

Cipriano de Rore (setting of *Odes* 3.9, to be discussed shortly). The musical form employed for most of these settings was the motet, a choral treatment of a text (usually fairly short) in a richly polyphonic style, scored for ensembles of between four and eight voices. The majority of motet texts were drawn from sacred scripture, and so the use of motet form for classical poetry was itself a sign of the high prestige enjoyed by canonical classical authors. The work most frequently represented is the *Aeneid*, and within that poem the passage most often chosen is Dido's last speech before her suicide, beginning *"Dulces exuviae,"* a text set by every significant choral composer of the century.[18]

Of the Horatian compositions from this time the most imposing is Cipriano de Rore's setting of *Odes* 3.9, *Donec gratus eram tibi*. The ode is unusual in presenting a dialogue between a woman (named Lydia) and a man (not named, and presumably Horace). They had been lovers but each is now involved with someone else; in a sequence of three paired stanzas in which the man speaks first and the woman responds, they recall their past happiness together, heap praise on their current partners, but in the end agree to resume their relationship. Rore's setting appears in a sumptuous choir-book commissioned by Duke Albrecht V of Bavaria and completed in 1559; the book is now Mus. MS B in the Bayerische Staatsbibliothek in Munich. The setting of *Odes* 3.9 occupies a place of honor near the opening of the book, following a Marian text and a setting of Dido's speech to Aeneas beginning *"Dissimulare etiam"* (*Aen.* 4.305–19).[19] It is scored for two four-voice choirs, one of low voices representing the male speaker and the other of high voices representing the female. As a close study by Jessie Ann Owens has shown, Rore's work is remarkable for its fidelity to Horace's text: the musical lines reflect the shape of the asclepiad rhythm (though with some liberties to permit more natural musical phrasing), the vocal writing is often homophonic (i.e., all voices sing the same words), allowing the words to be more clearly understood,[20] and the settings of the individual stanzas are subtly varied to convey both the parallelisms and movements of the characters' exchanges.[21] One detail may be singled

---

[18] *Aeneid* 4.651–8. The text was also frequently neumed in medieval manuscripts of Virgil; see Ziolkowski, *Nota Bene*, p. 149. The Boston-based early music group Convivium Musicum has recorded several settings of *"Dulces exuviae,"* and other versions are included in the collections *Le Chant de Virgile* and *Rome's Golden Poets*. See below, pp. 92–3.

[19] A facsimile of the first page of Rore's setting appears in Einstein, *The Italian Madrigal*, vol. II, following page 500.

[20] The largely homophonic treatment is very different from Rore's usual polyphonic style, as seen in his madrigals.

[21] Owens, "Music and meaning in Cipriano de Rore's setting of 'Donec gratus eram tibi.'" She also provides a score.

out to show how carefully Rore had studied the text: at the opening of the man's last stanza, where *quid si* ("what if") introduces his cautiously phrased proposal of a reconciliation, Rore gives *quid* a longer note value than the corresponding words carry in the previous stanzas, drawing attention to that crucial moment in the action.

In one important respect, though, Rore imposes an alien interpretation on the poem: after stanzas five and six have been sung by the respective male and female choirs, both groups join to repeat the woman's last words, *tecum vivere amem, tecum obeam libens* ("I would love to live with you and with you I would gladly die"). The writing also becomes exuberantly polyphonic at that point, to suggest a joyous release after the strictly controlled exchanges that have preceded. While this closural gesture is undeniably effective in musical terms, it sacrifices the emotional restraint and astringency that distinguish Horace's poem.[22]

My examples so far have all been choral in form, reflecting the Renaissance preference for choral music as the medium for serious expression. England in the late sixteenth and early seventeenth centuries produced a large body of solo song, to be accompanied either by lute or by a small consort of strings. The largest concentration of Horatian material from that period is in the work of John Wilson (1595–1674), who received his doctorate in music at Oxford in 1644 and was the first Heather Professor of Music there from 1656 to 1662. Wilson's songbook, a manuscript containing 226 items, is now in the Bodleian Library (Mus. B 1); it includes settings of eighteen Horatian odes (plus *Epodes* 2 and 7), along with other Latin texts by Petronius, Statius, Martial, Claudian, and Ausonius; the epilogue to Ovid's *Metamorphoses* (15.871–8) concludes the collection. Like his selection of Latin authors, Wilson's choice of odes is remarkable for its range: in addition to already established favorites such as 1.11, 1.22, and 3.9, he included such rarely set items as the hymn to Mercury (1.10), *Persicos odi* (1.38), *Diffugere nives* (4.7, the earliest musical setting I know of), and even one of the so-called Roman Odes (3.3), which have on the whole deterred composers because of their length and unremitting earnest tone; in fact Wilson's setting confines itself to the first two stanzas.[23] Wilson's

---

[22] In contriving a final *tutti* Rore was anticipated by a 1554 setting by Francisco Portinaro of an Italian translation of the ode; cf. Einstein, *The Italian Madrgial*, vol. ii, p. 474, Owens, "Music and meaning in Cipriano de Rore's setting of 'Donec gratus eram tibi,'" p. 99, n. 6. Rore's setting of *Donec gratus eram tibi* has been recorded in *Le Chant de Virgile*.

[23] As did a version for three-part male chorus by Zoltán Kodály from the 1930s, which I can only describe as glee-clubbish. (The piece can be heard on the CD *Rome's Golden Poets*.) Odes 3.3.1–8 exerted a powerful attraction on Latin poets after Horace; see Tarrant, "Ancient receptions of Horace," pp. 283–5 for discussion of related passages in Seneca, Prudentius, and Boethius.

straightforward musical treatments are not as varied as his choice of texts, and his versions do not capture the shifting tone of a poem such as *Diffugere nives*. His expressive devices are limited to placing emphasis on emotionally significant words, such as *interitura* ("doomed to die") and *pulvis et umbra sumus* ("we are dust and shadow") in 4.7.10 and 16. There is in general a stiffness about his settings that contrasts sharply with the freedom displayed in contemporary songs on English texts, e.g., those by Henry Lawes. The most persuasive case possible for Wilson's Horatian settings has been made in a recording by Emma Kirkby, long a leading figure in the British early music world, whom I recall meeting in one of Eduard Fraenkel's seminars, when she was an Oxford undergraduate reading Classics. Many years later, in recognition of her continuing interest in the Classics, the Classical Association of the UK elected her its Honorary President, and in lieu of the customary presidential address Dame Emma gave a presidential recital of works based on Greek and Latin texts – a practice that our own American Philological Association is, unfortunately, not likely to emulate.[24]

Horace's musical profile in the seventeenth and eighteenth centuries was less conspicuous than during the Renaissance, in part because of the growing popularity of opera, not a form hospitable to Horatian lyric – although Piperno does make a tantalizing reference to an 1868 Paris operetta by Montauby with Horace himself as its protagonist.[25] The more modest form of the cantata was more amenable to Horatian material, especially when presented in Italian translation. In England the composer–impresario Giovanni Gualberto Bottarelli, a prominent figure in the musical life of London in the decades following the death of Handel, organized two collections of cantatas based on the *Odes*, the first in 1757 containing twelve pieces and a sequel in 1775 containing six items. For each collection Bottarelli enlisted a sextet of composers, of whom the best known today were William Boyce and Thomas Arne in the first group and Johann Christian Bach in the second.[26] These works are notable for their emphasis

---

[24] For details of *Classical Kirkby* see below, p. 92.

[25] Piperno, "Musica," p. 672. Montauby is a figure of impenetrable obscurity, who has no entry in *The New Grove* and is not mentioned in Bruyas, *Histoire de l'opérette en France*, a work that refers to nearly 1,400 French operettas. As Piperno notes, Horace makes a brief appearance in Puccini's *La Bohème*: in Act II, set in a crowded Paris square on Christmas Eve, the philosopher Colline voices his scorn for the holiday crowd with the words "*Odio il profano volgo al par d'Orazio*" ("I detest the vulgar throng as much as Horace did"), an allusion to *Odes* 3.1.1 *Odi profanum vulgus*.

[26] Bottarelli's 1757 collection included versions of *Odes* 1.5, 1.8, 1.13, 1.19, 1.20, 1.22, 1.23, 1.26, 1.30, 1.32, 1.38, and 3.9. The composers represented were, in addition to Arne and Boyce, W. de Fesch, C. Heron, S. Howard, and J. Worgan. The 1775 collection comprised versions of *Odes* 1.13, 1.19, 1.22, 1.23, 1.30, and 1.32, and in addition to J. C. Bach contained compositions by G. Giordani, G. Boroni, M. Vento, I. Barthélemon, and I. Holzbauer.

on lighter, erotic themes, in contrast to much of Horace's earlier musical reception, in which he figures primarily as a moralist.[27] Some of these works should be considered as paraphrases or even looser treatments of Horatian material rather than settings in the strict sense: so, for example, J. C. Bach's "O Venere vezzosa" (based on *Odes* 1.30).[28]

The late eighteenth- and nineteenth-century development of the solo art song (the *Lied* in its German incarnation), based on poetic texts often in stanza form, might seem to be the ideal moment for a major musical exploration of the *Odes*. It is tempting to think what Mozart, for example, might have made of *Donec gratus eram tibi* (3.9), an ode sometimes described as "Mozartian" because of its graceful movement and its impression of serious feeling at work beneath a highly polished surface.[29] By that time, however, classical texts no longer enjoyed the currency of earlier periods; furthermore, the ostensibly simple and direct style found in most *Lieder* texts of the Romantic period is the polar opposite of Horace's highly wrought and verbally complex lyric manner. It is possible that some Horatian motifs appear in poems of, e.g., Goethe (a keen admirer of Horace) that were set to music, but I know of no *Lieder* that are settings of actual Horatian texts.[30]

Instead Horace's musical reception in nineteenth-century Germany is predominantly once more choral, in works composed for the many amateur choral societies established at the time. That is the context from which pieces such as F. F. Flemming's *Integer vitae* emerged.[31]

Flemming's hymn-like setting is a good match for the ode's first stanzas:

> *Integer vitae scelerisque purus*
> *non eget Mauris iaculis neque arcu*
> *nec venenatis gravida sagittis,*
> > *Fusce, pharetra,*
> *sive per Syrtis iter aestuosas*
> *sive facturus per inhospitalem*
> *Caucasum vel quae loca fabulosus*
> > *lambit Hydaspes.*

[27] The conception of Horace as a moral teacher is in part a holdover from his medieval persona, which was based more on the *Satires* and *Epistles* than on the *Odes*.

[28] Score in Draheim and Wille (eds.), *Horaz-Vertonungen vom Mittelalter bis zum Gegenwart*, pp. 52–97.

[29] Cf. the comment of Johann Gottfried Herder (cited by Draheim and Wille (eds.), *Horaz-Vertonungen vom Mittelalter bis zum Gegenwart*, p. 1): "wer wird nicht das unübertroffene 'Donec gratus eram tibi – Tecum vivere amem, tecum obeam libens' in einem Duett zu hören wünschen?" For the description "Mozartian" see Tarrant, "Da capo structure in some Odes of Horace," p. 49.

[30] Brahms's *Sapphische Ode* (published in 1884) sets a text by Hans Schmidt (1856–1923) whose form is that of the Sapphic stanza but whose content owes nothing to Horace (or Sappho).

[31] Flemming's setting may be found in Draheim and Wille (eds.), *Horaz-Vertonungen vom Mittelalter bis zum Gegenwart*, p. 102.

The man of upright life, devoid of crime, can do without Moroccan spears or a bow and quiver laden with poisoned arrows, my dear Fuscus, whether he makes his way through the scorching Syrtes or the forbidding Caucasus or the places washed by the Hydaspes, river of legend.

As the poem proceeds, however, the high moral tone of the opening is progressively undermined. In the middle two stanzas Horace supports his general statement with a purported piece of autobiography: one day as he was wandering unarmed in the woods singing of his girlfriend Lalage (whose name suggests "the Prattler"), a ferocious wolf ran from him. The closing pair of stanzas draws the moral: place him anywhere on earth, in arctic cold or equatorial heat, Horace will go on – not being *integer vitae*, but loving Lalage. The poem pokes gentle fun at the skewed logic of the besotted lover, while its concluding description of Lalage (*dulce ridentem . . . dulce loquentem* "sweetly smiling, sweetly talking") glances ironically at a famous poem of Catullus – in its turn a translation of an ode of Sappho – that presented a much more serious picture of a lover's obsession.[32]

At nearly the same time that the young Eduard Fraenkel was hearing Flemming's setting of *Integer vitae* sung at school funerals, the Harvard Sanskrit scholar C. R. Lanman remarked on the same practice in his own academic community. (Lanman cited it as a parallel to changes he believed had been made to Vedic texts for similarly incongruous ritual purposes.) His comments are worth quoting in full:

During the last twenty-four years, I have often been called to the University Chapel to pay the last tribute of respect to one or another departed colleague or friend. On such occasions, it frequently happens that the chapel choir sings the first two stanzas of the Horatian ode (i.22), *integer vitae scelerisque purus*, to the stately and solemn music of Friedrich Ferdinand Flemming. Indeed, so frequent is the employment of these words and this music, that one might almost call it a part of the "Funeral Office after the Harvard Use." The original occasion of the ode, and the relation of Horace to Aristius Fuscus to whom it is addressed, are fairly well known. The lofty moral sentiment of the first two stanzas, however seriously Horace may have entertained it, is doubtless uttered in this connection in a tone of mock-solemnity. Even this fact need not mar for us the tender associations made possible by the intrinsic appropriateness of these two pre-Christian stanzas for their employment in a Christian liturgy of the twentieth century. But suppose for a moment that the choir were to continue singing on to the end, even to *Lalagen amabo, dulce loquentem!* ["I will go on loving Lalage, with her sweet talk"] what

---

[32] *Dulce ridentem* comes from Catullus (51.4–5 *spectat et audit / dulce ridentem*), but Horace adds *dulce loquentem*, not in Catullus but in Catullus' source, Sappho (31.3 ἅδυ φωνείσας). On Horace's relation to Catullus here, cf. Putnam, *Poetic Interplay*, pp. 32–5. Putnam reads Horace's poem more seriously than I would, as "a hymn to Lalage, which is to say, to inspiration" (p. 34).

palpable, what monstrous ineptitude! If only the first two stanzas were extant, and not the remaining four also, we might never even suspect Horace of any arrière-pensée in writing them; and if we were to interpret them simply in the light of their modern ritual use, how far we should be from apprehending their original connection and motive![33]

Perhaps not surprisingly, Flemming's *Integer vitae* tune enjoyed another life as a hymn set to various English words. To a text by Elizabeth Charles (*c.* 1858) beginning "Praise ye the Father for his lovingkindness," it appeared in the *Congregational Psalmist* of 1875, and to a text by Charlotte Elliott (1789–1871) beginning "O holy Saviour, friend unseen," it occupied a place in the *Harvard University Hymn Book* from 1926 to 1964.[34]

In the realm of the French art song, among isolated settings by Jules Massenet and Camille Saint-Saëns, the most conspicuous use of Horace is the collection of ten songs entitled *Etudes latines*, written in Rome and published in 1900, by Reynaldo Hahn (1874–1947), a composer born in Caracas who spent almost the whole of his life in Paris and whose music is now enjoying a modest revival of interest, especially in Great Britain.[35] The texts of *Etudes latines* are drawn from a collection of the same name comprising eighteen poems by the Parnassian poet Leconte de Lisle (1818–1894), first published in 1852 as part of a larger collection of *Poèmes antiques*. The poems are not translations of Horace,[36] but reworkings of Horatian characters and themes, as is suggested by several of the titles: e.g., "Thaliarque" recalls the addressee of *Odes* 1.9, as "Pyrrha" does that of 1.5 and "Phyllis" that of 4.11.[37] Exhortations to drink and enjoy the moment are frequent, as in these lines from the opening poem, "Lydie": "ceignons nos cheveux blancs de couronnes de roses; / buvons,

---

[33] Lanman, *Atharva-veda Saṃhitā*, p. lxxvii.

[34] Hymn 252; the tune is named "Integer vitae" or "Flemming." Long before Flemming's time, a version of the Sapphic stanza – three lines of eleven syllables each, with word accent on the fourth, sixth and tenth syllables, followed by a line of five syllables with word accent on the first and fourth – had been used for Christian hymns, of which perhaps the best known is "Herzliebster Jesu," text by Johann Heermann (1630) and music by Johann Crüger (1640), harmonized by Bach in the *St. Matthew Passion*.

[35] In 1902 Hahn set a few lines of the Latin text of *Odes* 3.13 (*O fons Bandusiae*) as an independent composition; cf. Draheim and Wille (eds.), *Horaz-Vertonungen vom Mittelalter bis zum Gegenwart*, pp. 160–3. Sopranos and contraltos deliver lines 1 and 9–12 in a conspicuously plain manner, while a soprano solo performs elaborate melismas on the word "Ah!"

[36] Leconte de Lisle did translate Horace (1873), as well as the Greek tragedians, Homer, Hesiod, and Theocritus. His translation of Horace is in prose, and is surprisingly literal.

[37] There are also numerous verbal borrowings, as in the opening of "Phyllis": "*Depuis neuf ans et plus dans l'amphore scellée / mon vin des coteaux d'Albe a lentement mûri*" ~ *Odes* 4.11.1–2 *Est mihi nonum superantis annum / plenus Albani cadus* ("I have a jar filled with Alban wine, more than nine years in aging").

il en est temps encore, hâtons-nous!" Hahn's settings are in a style influenced by Gabriel Fauré and Henri Duparc;[38] one is dedicated to Fauré and another to Hahn's close friend Marcel Proust. Their mood is predominantly gentle and subdued, with frequent markings such as "calme," "tendre," "modéré" and "sérieux." Hahn's cycle has fared well on recordings: there are complete versions by Ian Bostridge and Stephen Varcoe[39] and by Bruno Laplante.[40]

Almost all musical settings of Horace prior to the twentieth century, whether based on the original Latin or a translation, aim at an effect that can be described as contemporary: they adapt Horace to the musical style of the period, whether that style is that of a sixteenth-century polyphonic motet or a nineteenth-century German *Männerchor*. In the twentieth century, by contrast, a number of composers have chosen to set Horace's Latin in conscious imitation of an earlier style, as a way of highlighting its otherness. (A similar use of Latin for its distancing effect can be seen in Stravinsky's *Oedipus Rex* and in Carl Orff's cantatas based on Catullus and the medieval *Carmina Burana*.) One exemplar of this deliberately archaizing approach is the American composer Randall Thompson, best known for his choral writing; his *Alleluia* (1940) is among the most often-performed choral works of the century.[41] Thompson cultivated a lifelong interest in the musical styles of earlier periods, especially sixteenth-century polyphony; in an informal set of reflections composed near the end of his life he wrote "my heart still leaps up when I see a cantus firmus."[42] Among his earliest published compositions are settings of five odes of Horace, written in 1924–1925 during his tenure of a Rome Prize at the American Academy.[43] They show the influence of Thompson's mentor Gian Francesco Malipiero, who at the time was immersing himself in the music of Monteverdi and his contemporaries. Almost thirty years later, in 1953, as a tribute to his Harvard teacher and colleague Archibald T. Davison on his retirement,

---

[38] One of the *Etudes latines*, "Lydie," had previously been set by Fauré and another, "Phidylé," by Duparc.

[39] A Hyperion CD (A 67141–2), issued in 1996.

[40] An Analekta CD (29402), a reissue of a recording made in 1974.

[41] I chose to focus on Thompson because of local circumstances as well as musical factors. He taught at Harvard for many years and was chair of the music department there from 1952–1957; in that capacity he was responsible for the building of the Eda Kuhn Loeb Music Library, where much of the research for this paper was carried out.

[42] Thompson, "On choral composition," p. 16.

[43] The odes in question are 1.5, 1.23, 1.30, 3.13, and 3.22. They are all relatively short poems (none longer than 16 lines), in keeping with Thompson's precept for choosing a text for musical treatment: "choose a good text and not too long a text" (Thompson, "On choral composition," p. 11). Performances of 1.23, 1.30, and 3.13 are included in *Rome's Golden Poets*.

Thompson returned to the *Odes* and composed a four-voice setting in the style of Palestrina of the final stanza (lines 17–20) of *Odes* 1.13:

> *Felices ter et amplius*
> *quos inrupta tenet copula nec malis*
> *divulsus querimoniis*
> *suprema citius solvet amor die.*

> Three times happy they, and more,
> who are held in an unbroken bond,
> whose love, divided by no bitter quarrels,
> will not loose them before their last day.[44]

For Thompson, the text must have seemed appropriate as a way to express his affection for the work's dedicatee;[45] he also recalled that he chose it because it appeared as an inscription on one of the gates leading into Harvard Yard.[46] In its original Horatian context, though, the stanza is considerably more problematic, and interesting. In the four stanzas that precede it, Horace details his jealous reactions when he hears Lydia (a former lover?) praising her boyfriend Telephus. His rage and despair are described in terms that strongly suggest parody of conventional love poetry. The swerve into apparent high seriousness in the closing lines thus presents the reader with a challenge of interpretation: is Horace setting an ideal vision of love against a foolishly romantic version, is he showing Lydia a kind of love she has no chance of enjoying with Telephus, or is he ruefully reflecting on what he himself had failed to achieve in his relationship with her?[47] This complexity disappears entirely when the final stanza is detached from its setting and read (or sung) in isolation.[48]

Even this highly selective discussion makes it clear that Horatian lyric has appealed to a wide range of composers over a long span of time. But surveying how the odes have been set also makes us more aware

---

[44] The piece has been recorded on the CD *Rome's Golden Poets*.

[45] Thompson had obviously forgiven Davison for denying him admission to the Harvard Glee Club during his undergraduate years.

[46] For those who know the area, it will be familiar as the Class of 1857 Gate, across from Holyoke Center and nearest the main entrance to the Harvard Square T stop. I have often wondered who was responsible for placing the Horatian inscription there and what relevance it was meant to have in its academic environment.

[47] One astute interpreter of Horace thought that the ending was deliberately ambiguous: "probably Horace intended the poem's close to leave us in uncertainty. He refuses, as he does so frequently, to allow us the satisfaction of restricting him to a single attitude" (Commager, *The Odes of Horace*, p. 155).

[48] The final stanza of *Odes* 1.13 had similarly been detached for musical treatment by the early Lutheran composer Johann Walther (1496–1570). Walther's piece was recorded on the CD *Rome's Golden Poets*.

of the difficulties they pose for musical treatment. The verbal density of Horace's writing is one obstacle; another is the awkwardness of his preferred line-lengths for modern musical styles. Many odes are too long to be comfortably set, especially if the musical handling is to have any complexity or richness. But perhaps the greatest challenge is posed by the variety of tone and content that Horace often encompasses within a single ode, a variety made all the more striking by the repetition of the same metrical patterns throughout a poem. One of Horace's best modern critics has written that "to cover ground is a merit in a poet,"[49] but music with a repeating stanzaic base does not readily express such differences of mood within a piece.[50] Those features, the last in particular, help to explain why so many settings have been made of parts of odes or even of individual stanzas, in which the musical treatment could evoke a single emotional mood, even if one not consistent with the Horatian text as a whole.[51] In this as in other respects, Horace's lyric poetry, which appears so direct and approachable, turns out to be stubbornly elusive.

Musicians are not the only readers of Horace who have plucked lines and stanzas out of their context in order to give them a more straightforward meaning. The same impulse lies behind the creation of anthologies of poetic excerpts, or *florilegia*, of which numerous examples survive from the Middle Ages and the early modern period. As it happens, both *Odes* 1.13.17–20 (*Felices ter*) and 1.22.1–8 (*Integer vitae*) appear in some manuscripts of the most widely circulated medieval anthology of excerpts from classical poetry, known as the *Florilegium Gallicum*; the former passage is listed under the heading *De concordia coniugali* ("On marital harmony") and the latter is headed *Que sunt commoda innocentie ad amicum* ("The advantages of innocence, to a friend").[52]

---

[49] Nisbet, "*Romanae fidicen lyrae*," p. 194.

[50] Rore's setting of *Donec gratus eram tibi* (above, pp. 76–7) is a significant exception.

[51] Among many examples is one of the only passages of Horace set to music by a composer unquestionably of the first rank, three lines (41–3) of *Odes* 3.29 arranged as a three-voice canon by Franz Joseph Haydn: *ille potens sui / laetusque deget, cui licet in diem / dixisse "vixi"* ("That man will live happy, his own master, who at the close of day can say 'I have lived'"); for the music see Deutsch (ed.), *Joseph Haydn*, p. 33. Haydn's tombstone bears a canonic treatment of a phrase of the following ode, *non omnis moriar* (3.30.6 "I will not wholly die"), apparently his favorite Horatian quotation.

[52] See Burton, *Classical Poets in the "Florilegium Gallicum*," pp. 278–9. The role of *florilegia* in guiding composers to isolated passages of Horace was acutely suggested by Philip Barnes in his notes to the CD *Rome's Golden Poets*. For example, a *florilegium* is very probably the source of the single hexameter *principibus placuisse viris non ultima laus est* ("to have pleased the leading men is not the worst grounds for praise," *Epist.* 1.17.35), set to music by Jacob Handl (1550–1591), with a decidedly unclassical pentameter added to create an elegiac couplet: *summa Deo laus est qui placuisse studet* ("the highest praise belongs to the one who strives to please God").

Perhaps because of the difficulties that Horace's Latin lyrics pose for musical setting, a closer approach in music to the spirit of the *Odes* can sometimes be achieved by a less immediate relationship to their text. That is to say, the Horatian ethos may be better reflected in musical settings of texts that are either inspired by Horace or compatible with his lyric voice, but whose form offers composers a more accessible basis for their music.

One example is provided by the poetry of A. E. Housman (1859–1936). Although Housman's famous translation of *Odes* 4.7, *Diffugere nives* ("The snows are fled away"), first published in 1897 and included in *More Poems* (1936), does not yet seem to have attracted any composer's attention, the brevity and verbal directness of Housman's own poems have prompted musical settings by the hundreds.[53] Among the most successful of Housman settings are the cycle *On Wenlock Edge* by Ralph Vaughan Williams (1872–1958), consisting of six poems from *A Shropshire Lad*, composed in 1908–09, and the two collections by George Butterworth (1885–1916), *Six Songs from A Shropshire Lad* (1909–11) and *Bredon Hill and Other Songs* (1912). In contrast to the liberties that many musical settings of Horace have taken with the poems, Housman settings are remarkable for their fidelity to the text – in part, to be sure, because of the poet's well-known sensitivity on that point.[54]

Housman's *faux-naif* diction has little in common with Horace's style, but he often deals with Horatian themes, such as the use of images from nature to reflect human mortality. In the opening of "On Wenlock Edge" that motif is combined with a direct allusion to Horace: "On Wenlock Edge the wood's in trouble" points to the opening stanza of *Odes* 1.9 (*Vides ut alta*), describing the snow on Mt. Soracte, and specifically the phrase *nec iam sustineant onus / silvae laborantes* (1.9.2–3), "the toiling woods no longer bear the weight." After that opening gesture, it cannot be coincidental that the poem goes on to connect the speaker with a nameless Roman who

---

[53] Nearly 400 musical settings of poems by Housman are listed by Gooch and Thatcher, *Musical Settings of Late Victorian and Modern British Literature*; they include thirty-five separate settings each of "Loveliest of trees, the cherry now" and "When I was one-and-twenty." There is apparently a more recent catalog by Bill Lewis that lists almost 500 settings (referred to by Venables, "A composer's approach to setting A. E. Housman," pp. 72, 74), but I have not yet been able to locate it.

[54] When Vaughan Williams dropped the two stanzas of "Is my team ploughing" referring to football, the poet was not pleased. He wrote his publisher, Grant Richards, "I am told that composers in some cases have mutilated my poems, – that Vaughan Williams cut two verses [*sic*] out of *Is my team ploughing* (I wonder how he would like me to cut two bars out of his music)." See Burnett (ed.), *The Letters of A. E. Housman*, vol. 1, p. 458. Housman even took offense when Butterworth, who had been given permission to set poems from *A Shropshire Lad*, thought he was therefore entitled to print the texts of the poems in a concert program. See Burnett (ed.), *The Letters of A. E. Housman*, vol. 1, p. 279.

looked upon the same woods in ancient times. In the lines "The tree of man was never quiet: / Then 'twas the Roman, now 'tis I," Housman seems almost to be advertising the Horatian pedigree of his thought.

Housman's manipulation of stanza form sometimes shows similarities to Horatian practice. "Is my team ploughing" resembles *Donec gratus eram tibi* (*Odes* 3.9) in representing a dialogue in which each pair of stanzas is divided between speaker and respondent. The speaker is a dead man who wishes to know how life is proceeding now that he is gone; in the first three pairs of stanzas he is told (by whom is not immediately clear) that all those to whom he was close have quite forgotten him. As in Horace's ode, the final pair of stanzas introduces an unexpected twist:

> "Is my friend hearty,
>   Now I am thin and pine,
> And has he found to sleep in
>   A better bed than mine?"
> Yes, lad, I lie easy,
>   I lie as lads would choose;
> I cheer a dead man's sweetheart,
>   Never ask me whose.[55]

Butterworth's setting is for a single voice; the speakers are distinguished by tempo and dynamic markings, *molto moderato* and *pianissimo* for the ghostly questioner and *poco più mosso* ("a little faster") and *forte* for the robust survivor. As is his usual practice, Butterworth employs the same melodic material for each pair of stanzas; in this case the musical repetition suits the similar question-and-answer structure of the verses. Only in the final phrase, "never ask me whose," does Butterworth vary the vocal line, mirroring the sharp turn taken by the text at that point.

Another aspect of Horatian structural composition occasionally seen in Housman is what I have elsewhere described, borrowing a term from musical structure, as a *da capo* effect, an ABA arrangement of themes in which the concluding section of a poem seems to announce a return to the opening while introducing a significant new element.[56] A powerful example in Housman is "Bredon Hill," which opens with the sound of church bells ringing:

> In summertime on Bredon
>   The bells they sound so clear;
> Round both the shires they ring them,
>   In steeples far and near,
>   A happy noise to hear.

---

[55] I cite the text from Burnett (ed.), *The Poems of A. E. Housman*, p. 29.
[56] On Horace's use of such a structure see Tarrant, "Da capo structure in some Odes of Horace."

The speaker recalls how he and his sweetheart would hear the bells as they lay together, and how he looked forward to having them peal at their wedding; instead his lover died and "went to church alone ... and would not wait for me." The last stanza begins with a compressed echo of the first:

> The bells they sound on Bredon,
>   And still the steeples hum.
> "Come all to church, good people,"–

But at that point the speaker bursts out with a cry of exasperation:

> Oh, noisy bells, be dumb;
> I hear you, I will come.[57]

Vaughan Williams brings out the *da capo* character of the last stanza by his tempo marking (*tempo alla prima*, "tempo as at the beginning") and repeats the vocal part of the first stanza almost unchanged for the first three lines, making the impassioned outcry that follows even more shocking.[58]

An example from another poet and composer that provides an even more compelling illustration is the first of Benjamin Britten's *Five Flower Songs* (op. 47, from 1950), to a text by Robert Herrick, "To Daffadills." The content of the poem parallels that of Horace's ode to Leuconoe (1.11 *Tu ne quaesieris*), the source of what is today Horace's most familiar phrase, *carpe diem.* The form of Horace's poem corresponds mimetically to its theme: it is noticeably short (11 lines) and is composed in a meter remarkable for a succession of three choriambs (a metrical unit with the shape long/short/short/long), which creates an impression of almost breathless speed. Herrick develops the underlying metaphor in *carpe diem*, of the day figured as a flower that soon withers and dies, while his short phrases capture the rapidity of Horace's metrical scheme.

> Faire Daffadills, we weep to see
>   You haste away so soone:
> As yet the early-rising Sun
>   Has not attain'd his Noone.
>   Stay, stay
> Untill the hasting day
>   Has run
>   But to the Even-song.

---

[57] Text from Burnett (ed.), *The Poems of A. E. Housman*, pp. 22–4. I understand the last line to mean that the speaker has no more reason to live and so can heed the summons of the bells to his own death.

[58] Butterworth also begins the last stanza with the same vocal line as the first, but since that line, or a slight variation of it, introduces each stanza, the *da capo* effect is much diminished.

And, having pray'd together, we
    Will goe with you along.

We have short time to stay, as you,
    We have as short a Spring;
As quick a growth to meet Decay,
    As you, or any thing.
            We die
        As your hours doe, and drie
            Away,
    Like to the Summers raine;
Or as the pearles of Mornings dew
    Ne'r to be found againe.

Britten's setting conveys the sense of swiftly passing time primarily through the choice of tempo. He marks the first stanza "Allegro Impetuoso," a rare (and possibly *ad hoc*) tempo indicator that highlights the quickly moving setting of the words. The second stanza bears the marking "Sempre Allegro," and the pace does not slacken until the last four bars, with a "rall[entando]" that corresponds to the final word, "againe," which is repeated several times. In a performance that gives Britten's tempo markings their full weight, the song is over almost before the listener knows it has begun – an effect that produces in music an effect comparable to what Horace expresses in words: *dum loquimur, fugerit invida / aetas* ("while we speak, spiteful time has fled").[59] Here for once a Horatian sentiment has found a fully appropriate musical equivalent.[60]

THE *CARMEN SAECULARE*

The musical fortunes of the *Carmen Saeculare* in modern times are themselves a rewarding object of study. For such a quintessentially occasional poem, the *Carmen* has proven remarkably adaptable to a variety of contexts

[59] I know of no recording that takes the piece quite as quickly as Britten's markings suggest. John Eliot Gardiner establishes a brisk opening tempo, but loses momentum at the end of the first verse by introducing a ritardando not called for in the score.

[60] A possible contemporary instance is "The instant gathers," a piano trio by Joan Panetti (a longtime member of the Yale music faculty), which premiered in New York in June 2006. According to the review by Anthony Tommasini in *The New York Times* of June 5, 2006, "Ms. Panetti said that the title was taken from a Theodore Roethke poem in which the poet warns us that time, the instant, is passing so we had best make the most of it." Tommasini went on to write that "she has put the poet's advice to good use in this eventful, intense yet impressively economical 13-minute, three-movement work." The sentiment is authentically Roethkean as well as Horatian, but I have not yet been able to locate the phrase itself in Roethke's work, although I have noted two occurrences of "the instant ages" ("but now the instant ages" in "Give way, ye gates" and "the instant ages on the living eye" in "Infirmity"). A query to the composer was not answered.

and purposes.[61] The composers who are said to have set it, in whole or in part, include François-André Danican Philidor, Carl Loewe,[62] Georges Bizet, Max Reger,[63] Gian Francesco Malipiero, and (at one remove) Giacomo Puccini.

The setting by Philidor, which received its first performance in London in 1779, remains by far the most ambitious musical composition ever based on Horace's poetry; in its pomp it may well have exceeded the original performance of the *Carmen*, at the *Ludi Saeculares* of 17 BC.[64]

The moving spirit behind the enterprise was Joseph (né Giuseppe) Baretti (1719–1789), a writer and critic with close ties to Samuel Johnson and other prominent literary and artistic figures of the time: when Baretti was tried for murder in 1769, he was able to enlist Johnson, Edmund Burke, Oliver Goldsmith, Joshua Reynolds, and David Garrick as character witnesses for his (successful) defense. Baretti's introductory pamphlet to his translation of the *Carmen* laments the neglect of Horace by contemporary composers:

whenever I happened to look into those Odes, I have wondered at the inattention of our Composers, who ever since the invention of modern Musick, have been hunting every where for harmonious verses, yet never bethought themselves of Horace's, which in point of harmony, as well as other excellence, are, by universal confession, superiour to any thing of the kind produced these two thousand years.[65]

---

[61] It continues to be invoked in non-musical contexts as well: when in April 2010 the London-based Society for the Promotion of Hellenic Studies wished to celebrate the centenary of its sister organization, the Society for the Promotion of Roman Studies, it did so in the form of a Latin ode in sapphic stanzas composed by Armand D'Angour that makes an explicit reference to the *Carmen*. (Text and translation were published in the *Times Literary Supplement* for May 28, 2010.)

[62] Carl Loewe (1796–1869) was a prolific composer of songs and choral music. In 1836 he published settings of five odes, or parts thereof (Op. 57 = *Odes* 3.3.1–12, 3.12, 3.29.29–56, 3.13, and 2.16.1–8, 13–16, 25–28), arranged for four-part men's chorus. His setting of the *Carmen Saeculare* followed in 1845; Piperno, "Musica," p. 675 states that it was composed in honor of Friedrich Wilhelm IV of Prussia, but the only work by Loewe that I can find with that dedication is his 1848 *Festkantate zur Feier der silbernen Hochzeit des Königs Friedrich Wilhelm IV und der Königin Elisabeth*; Fleischhauer, "Carl Loewes Horaz-Vertonungen op. 57," p. 425 suggests instead that the *Carmen* setting was composed for a celebration at the Gymnasium in Stettin where Loewe was a professor of music. Scores of Loewe's ode settings and of the *Carmen* are in Draheim and Wille (eds.), *Horaz-Vertonungen vom Mittelalter bis zum Gegenwart*, pp. 106–24.

[63] A setting by Reger dating to 1900 is mentioned by Piperno, "Musica," p. 673, but I have found no trace of it in Reger's collected works.

[64] On the genesis and performance history of this remarkable work, see Carroll, "A classical setting for a classical poem."

[65] Baretti, *The Introduction to the Carmen Saeculare*, pp. 3–4. That statement probably constitutes an implicit polemic against Bottarelli's two cycles of Horatian cantatas (1757 and 1775), with which Baretti must have been familiar. (See above, pp. 78–9.) A similar complaint was made by Johann Gottfried Herder, in his *Briefe über das Lesen des Horaz, an einen jungen Freund* of 1803: "auch

Determined to give the *Carmen Saeculare* a suitable modern musical treatment, Baretti went in search of a composer: "I wanted a man of sense, a man of taste, a man of enthusiasm, fertile in ideas and expedients, and able to temper alternately the solemnity of church-musick with the brilliancy of the theatrical."[66] He thought he had found his man in Philidor (1726–1795), a frequent visitor to London whose previous compositions included a comic opera based on Fielding's *Tom Jones*.[67]

Philidor's *Carmen Saeculare* is a full-length oratorio, only the last section of which is a setting of the *Carmen* proper. It is preceded by several other texts from the *Odes* with related themes, arranged to produce a quasi-narrative sequence. The main sections are as follows: Prologue, "The Poet bespeaks the attention of the hearers by the greatness of his subject" (*Odes* 3.1.1–4 *Odi profanum vulgus et arceo* etc.); Part I, "The Poet exhorts the young Singers of both sexes to sing his verses well" (*Odes* 4.6.29–44); Part II, "Both Choirs implore of Apollo to approve and protect the Secular Song" (*Odes* 4.6.1–28); Part III, "The Boys and Maidens, forming two choirs, encourage each other to sing the praises of Apollo and Diana" (*Odes* 1.21); Part IV, "Prayers for the prosperity of the Empire and the Emperour" (*Carm. Saec.*).[68]

Aiming to avoid the potential for monotony in setting thirty-five stanzas of verse, Philidor divided the text into twenty-five musical numbers, allocating the Prologue and most of Part I to a tenor soloist representing the poet and in the remaining parts interspersing choral segments with solo arias, duets and quartets.[69] As a result, while a performance of the entire work takes up about ninety minutes, no single number much exceeds five

---

wundert es mich wirklich, daß Horaz von unsern Musikmeistern, die doch an guten Texten oft Mangel leiden, so wenig componirt ist" (cited by Draheim and Wille (eds.), *Horaz-Vertonungen vom Mittelalter bis zum Gegenwart*, p. 1).

[66] Baretti, *The Introduction to the Carmen Saeculare*, p. 12.

[67] Philidor was also an internationally recognized authority on chess, whose treatise *L'Analyse du jeu des échecs* went through numerous printings in French, English, and German between 1750 and 1900.

[68] The credit (if that is the right word) for assembling the texts in that way belongs to the Jesuit Noël-Etienne Sanadon, who called the result the *Polymetrum Saturnium in Ludos Saeculares*; it first appeared as part of Sanadon's translation of Horace in 1728. The version set by Philidor reflects a slight revision of Sanadon's order introduced by Philip Francis in his Dublin, 1742 edition of Horace; cf. Carroll, "A classical setting for a classical poem," pp. 98–9. The headings to the various sections are cited from the translation of the *Polymetrum* by Baretti distributed at the first performance. In his *Life of Johnson* (entry for March 16, 1779), Boswell recalls an occasion on which Johnson was pressed for his opinion of Baretti's translation of the *Carmen*. Unable honestly to commend it but not wishing to give offense, he made the diplomatic reply, "Sir, I do not say that it may not be made a very good translation" (Boswell, *The Life of Samuel Johnson*, vol. III, p. 400).

[69] See the outline in Carroll, "A classical setting for a classical poem," pp. 108–9.

minutes, and most are significantly shorter. The sequence of musical numbers, ending with a choral fugue, resembles the structure of Haydn's late oratorios (*The Creation* [1798], *The Seasons* [1801]), but Philidor operates at a much lower level of inspiration: instead of combining solemnity and flair, as Baretti had hoped, much of his music falls into a bland middle ground, graceful and well made, but instantly forgettable.[70]

After initial success in London and Paris, and keen interest taken in the work by Empress Catherine the Great of Russia, Philidor's *Carmen Saeculare* fell into near-total oblivion. A recent recording[71] has made the work once more accessible, but live performances will in all likelihood remain rare.

In the nineteenth and twentieth centuries, the *Carmen Saeculare* was often understood in a wider sense as a timeless celebration of Rome and its glories. That may explain its appeal for the youthful Bizet, since he embarked on setting it during his tenure in 1857–1860 of the Prix de Rome awarded by the Paris Conservatoire. The music is lost, and it is not clear if the work was even completed.

Malipiero's setting is the most ingenious in the use to which it puts Horace's poem. It forms the conclusion of his opera *Giulio Cesare* (1935, first performed 1936), loosely based on Shakespeare's play. In the final scene, following the battle of Philippi and the suicide of Brutus, the victorious armies of Antony and Octavian march onto the stage while the chorus declaims selected stanzas of the *Carmen Saeculare*.[72] Whether or not Malipiero dedicated the work to Mussolini, as has been reported,[73] its conclusion certainly reflects a pride in *Romanità* that is characteristic of the period.

The celebration of *Romanità* is also the motivating theme of Puccini's "Hymn to Rome" (*Inno a Roma*), composed in 1919 as part of post-World War I patriotic observances, and later enthusiastically adopted by the Fascist régime. (Puccini himself was candid about the work's shortcomings, describing it in a letter to his wife as "una bella porcheria," "a real piece of garbage.")[74] Puccini's hymn is set to a text by Fausto Salvatori (1870–1929)

---

[70] The double fugue for chorus on the stanza beginning *Certus undenos* (*Carm. Saec.* 21–4), though strongly suggestive of an academic exercise in counterpoint, is still one of the work's most distinctive movements.

[71] See below, p. 93. The recording was made in 1998 but not released until 2007.

[72] The passages set are lines 9–12, 25–8, 37–40, 45–8, and 61–8. The first stanza is marked "*maestoso*," and the tempo slows to "*molto solenne*" before the concluding two stanzas.

[73] There is no such dedication in the piano–vocal score published by Ricordi; Piperno "Musica," p. 676 plausibly suggests that Malipiero added a handwritten dedication to a copy of the score presented to Mussolini.

[74] See Marchetti, "Tutta la verità sull 'Inno a Roma' di Puccini," p. 402.

that is only loosely connected to the *Carmen Saeculare*: it uses as a refrain the phrase "in all the world you [i.e., the Sun] will see nothing greater than Rome" ("Tu non vedrai nessuna cosa al mondo / maggior di Roma" = *C. S.* 11–12 *possis nihil urbe Roma / visere maius*) and has other less explicit echoes, but it is essentially an independent composition – though one that closely parallels the ethos of the *Carmen*.[75] Puccini planned for it to be performed by several thousand singers (schoolchildren, soldiers, teachers, etc.) with several brass bands accompanying, but on the scheduled day, April 21 (the traditional birthday of Rome), the performance had to be cancelled because of a sudden rainstorm. The only recording I know of is not by a chorus but by Plácido Domingo accompanied by Julius Rudel on the piano, and in fact the writing (particularly the *energico* opening and the optional high A in the final phrase) seems to me better suited to a soloist than to a chorus, especially a large amateur group. Although it antedates the Fascist era, Salvatori's hymn could easily be mistaken for a product of that period, which shows how much Mussolini appealed to already potent nationalistic sentiments and to an idealized image of Italy as warlike but peace-bringing, harmonious, fertile and morally sound. That image is remarkably similar to the Augustan Italy evoked in Horace's poem, and Puccini's *Inno* may therefore serve as another example of a musical work at some remove from Horace that comes closer to the Horatian spirit than many works based more directly on his words.

DISCOGRAPHY OF RECORDINGS CITED

Collections of works by various composers are listed first, followed by recordings of works by individual composers.

Classical Kirkby. BIS CD 1435. 2002. Performed by Emma Kirkby (soprano) and Anthony Rooley (lute). Includes John Wilson, *Diffugere nives* (*Odes* 4.7) and *Integer vitae* (*Odes* 1.22).

Dido's Lament. CD produced by Convivium Musicum. 2006. Performed by Convivium Musicum, Scott Metcalfe (dir.). Includes settings of *"Dulces exuviae"* by Adrian Willaert, Marbriano de Orto, Josquin Desprez, and Jehan Mouton.

Le Chant de Virgile. Harmonia Mundi CD 901739. 2001. Performed by the Huelgas-Ensemble, Paul van Nevel (dir.). Includes Ludwig Senfl, *Non usitata* (*Odes* 2.20), *Mollis inertia* (*Epode* 14), and *Petti, nihil me* (*Epode* 11), Cipriano de Rore, *Donec gratus eram tibi* (*Odes* 3.9), and settings of *"Dulces*

---

[75] Salvatori appears to have been an equal opportunity panegyrist: he also composed a hymn to Trieste (*Inno a Trieste*, also referred to as the *Canto del tricolore*), set to music by Luigi Mancinelli (1848–1921) and premiered on March 9, 1919; see Mariani, *Epistolario Luigi Mancinelli*, p. 341.

exuviae" by Josquin Desprez, Jehan Mouton, Marbriano de Orto, Jakob Vaet, Theodoricus Gerarde, and Orlando di Lasso.

Rome's Golden Poets. CD produced by the chorus in conjunction with Bolchazy-Carducci Publishers. 1999. Performed by the St. Louis Chamber Chorus, Philip Barnes (dir.). Includes Johann Walther, *Felices ter* (*Odes* 1.13.17–20), Jacob Handl, *Principibus placuisse* (*Epist.* 1.17.35) and *Oderunt hilarem* (*Epist.* 1.18.89–90), Peter Cornelius, *O Venus* (*Odes* 1.30), Zoltán Kodály, *Iustum et tenacem* (*Odes* 3.3.1–8) and (arr.) *Rectius vives* (*Odes* 2.10.1–12), Randall Thompson, *Felices ter* (*Odes* 1.13.17–20), *Vitas hinnuleo* (*Odes* 1.23), *Montium custos* (*Odes* 3.22), and *O fons Bandusiae* (*Odes* 3.13), Antonín Tučapsky, *Ne forte credas* (*Odes* 4.9.1–4), *Iam satis terris* (*Odes* 1.2.1–5), *Nunc est bibendum* (*Odes* 1.37.1–4), *Eheu fugaces* (*Odes* 2.14.1–4), and *Tu ne quaesieris* (*Odes* 1.11), and settings of "*Dulces exuviae*" by Adrian Willaert, Jacob Handl, and Josquin Desprez.

Benjamin Britten, *Five Flower Songs*, Op. 47. DG CD 453 433–2. 1997. Performed by the Monteverdi Choir, John Eliot Gardiner (dir.).

George Butterworth, *"Bredon Hill" and Other Songs* and *Six Songs from "A Shropshire Lad."* Hyperion CD A67378. 2003. Performed by Christopher Maltman (baritone) and Roger Vignoles (piano).

Reynaldo Hahn, *Etudes latines*. Analekta CD 29402, a reissue of a recording made in 1974. Performed by Bruno Laplante (baritone) and Janine Lachance (piano).

Hyperion. CD A67141–2. 1996. Performed by Ian Bostridge (tenor), Stephen Varcoe (baritone), and Graham Johnson (piano).

André-François Danican Philidor, *Carmen Saeculare*. Naxos CD 8.557593–94. 2007. Performed by the orchestra and chorus of Radio Svizzera, Jean-Claude Malgoire (dir.).

Giacomo Puccini, *Inno a Roma*. Columbia CD MK 44981. 1989. Performed by Plácido Domingo (tenor) and Julius Rudel (piano).

Ralph Vaughan Williams, *On Wenlock Edge*. Chandos CD 10465. 2008. Performed by Mark Padmore (tenor) and the Schubert Ensemble.

PART II

Reception as Self-Fashioning

CHAPTER 6

Petrarch's epistolary epic: Letters on Familiar Matters (Rerum familiarum libri)

Giuseppe Mazzotta

The 350 letters composing the *Rerum familiarum libri* were written between 1325 and 1366.[1] The event that led Petrarch to think of assembling them in one volume occurred in 1345, when he rediscovered in the Cathedral Library of Verona the corpus of letters Cicero had written to Atticus, Quintus, and Brutus. These letters, along with Seneca's *Epistle to Lucilius*, gave him the impulse to compose the *Familiares* in a volume. It was meant to be taken mainly as a book of instruction for daily living.

Much like Cicero and Seneca, Petrarch throughout dispenses prescriptions about questions of ethics: the value of moderation and chastity, the rewards of friendship, rules for dining, care about the condition of far-away friends, tranquillity of mind, how to contain feelings of anxiety about the flight of time, praise of the solitary life, cultivation of body and soul, appeals to peace, on how to bear grief, how to exercise virtue in the face of fortune's adversity, avoid suffering, offer consolation for death, and so forth. But because a book of ethics, a term to be understood as the art of living, can only emerge out of the texture of one's life, Petrarch includes in his collection accounts of what he himself has actually lived through. The slices of his life range from an experience such as mountain climbing, or taking walks among the ruins of the Roman Forum, to countering malevolent gossip about his personal reputation (especially the general suspicions about his purported envy toward Dante). On occasion he treats subjects that belong to the arena of politics or public discourse, such as Cola di Rienzo's quest for power that ended tragically, defenses of poetry and oratory, the need

---

[1] "Petrarch's epistolary epic: *Letters on Familiar Matters (Rerum familiarum libri)*" by Giuseppe F. Mazzotta was first published in *Petrarch: A Critical Guide to the Complete Works*, edited by Victoria Kirkham and Armando Maggi. Copyright © 2009 by The University of Chicago. All rights reserved. I have used Rossi (ed.), *Le Familiari*. The Latin quotations from *Fam.* I.I are taken from Dotti (trans.), *Petrarca, Libro Primo*. The number in each quotation refers to the paragraph of the letter. The English translations are taken from Bernardo (trans.), *Rerum familiarum libri* I–VIII. The other letters are to be found in Bernardo (trans.), *Letters on Familiar Matters. Rerum familiarum libri*.

for reform of the papal curia, or even reflections on time-honored themes, such as the desirable form of the education of the prince.

Such a fluid multiplicity of topics may produce the effect of an organized incoherence, a sort of deliberate reflection of the randomness of the concerns of daily life, but it does not really forfeit the volume's rhetorical unity. For all his ramblings, Petrarch's thoughts are so intimately woven together that it is difficult to remember where one letter ends and the next begins. Several of them are stitched around a rubric (for example, the educational practices of his time, the value of eloquence or grammar). Over time, Petrarch freely re-arranged many of them (by putting in the last book, say, the letter to Cicero he had written on discovering his manuscript in 1345) in order to generate connections or relationships that are not simply fortuitous or contingent. And he counters the digressiveness or apparent disconnectedness of the volume by giving it an epic framework or design. We know that originally Petrarch had conceived of writing twelve books of letters. In 1359, however, after reading through the partial translation of the *Odyssey* by Leontio Pilato, he settled on twenty-four books. With that discovery, an epistolary epic is born, and, as such, it is marked by a number of peculiar stylistic and thematic features.

In the dedicatory letter (1.1) to the *Familiares*, which he sends to his friend Socrates (the pseudonym for Ludwig Van Kempen, a Flemish musician he had met in Avignon), Petrarch admits to a stylistic pluralism as the dominant trait of his letters. The reason for the lack of unification or for the inconsistencies of style, he says, is to be attributed to the variety of his correspondents. They are dead or alive, drawn from antiquity or contemporary life, and they include Socrates, Cicero, Seneca, Homer, Cardinal Giovanni Colonna, Robert, king of Sicily, the Emperor Charles IV, Boccaccio, the Doge of Venice (Andrea Dandolo), the grammarian Zanobi, the archbishops of Genoa and Prague, Guido Sette, the Seneschal for the kingdom of Sicily, his brother Gherardo, etc. They constitute a panoply or elite corps of impressive individuals, though unequal in rank. "Indeed," Petrarch writes,

the primary concern of a writer is to consider the identity of the person to whom he is writing. Only in this way can he know what and how to write, as well as other pertinent circumstances. The strong man must be addressed in one way, the spiritless one in another, and finally, yet in another manner must be addressed the man of letters renowned for his talents and the ignoramus who would not understand anything you said if you spoke in even a slightly polished fashion (*Fam.*, Bernardo (trans.), 1:9).

This self-conscious commonplace from what sounds like a primer of the rhetoric of letter-writing sheds light on the economy of the whole volume. Petrarch draws attention to the mixed styles he deploys and urges us not to dismiss them as a mere idiosyncrasy. They do not fit together in one over-arching style, and the multifariousness of the styles he exhibits makes him appear "inconsistent" and even "self-contradictory." Inconsistency, however, turns into a virtue. For one thing, it signals that his styles entail a careful evaluation of or perspective on the character, power, and status of his many correspondents. By addressing them and drawing them into his confidence, they are bound to feel that they are his privileged interlocutors to whom he seems to open up the intimate recesses of his mind. To be sure, they are never given a voice in the text, and yet Petrarch coaxes them and co-opts them as agents or co-players in the epic battles he fights – and they are to fight with him – against his own personal detractors, his "hostile critics," and, more generally, against the cultural and spiritual decadence of their times. Together, they are to join forces against their common enemies.

Petrarch calls his "inconsistency" an "expedient" that allows him to come to terms with the "infinite . . . varietates hominum" and their minds (Dotti, *Petrarca*, par. 29). The inconsistency he claims for himself in dealing with all sorts of people leads to a carefully calculated writing posture. His (self-consciously) ambiguous posture – a mixture of candor, need for complicity, and careful distance, which is appropriate to self-confessions – involves even his Socrates. Petrarch asks him not to share with anybody else the letters he sends him. They are to be kept hidden from the intrusive, "lynx-like eyes" of his other friends. Each friend is to have access to a part or fragment and not to the whole. By keeping letters and friends separate from one another, Petrarch achieves one aim: none can claim to know or to understand him completely. Only he is to enjoy an omniscient, transcendent viewpoint encompassing all styles, as well as his cohorts' partial perspectives. The outcome resembles a musical orchestration where all players are assigned specific roles under his sole direction. He ranks and arrays them in an epochal war that largely takes place in his mind (in every sense of the phrase).

As befits an epic, the *Familiares* recounts a war in which the author's arguments are nothing less than weapons, and his ruses of styles are strategies against the enemy and friends alike. Life on earth, as Petrarch says, is "not only a military service but like actual warfare" (*Fam.*, Bernardo (trans.), 1:8–9). Rhetoricians, when they are at their most skilful, act like military leaders, who, in their rhetorical strategies, know how to fight and when to retreat or conceal themselves. The overt analogy between rhetoric and war (that goes back to the *Phaedrus* and its claim that Ulysses was the inventor of rhetoric during the leisure hours of the Trojan war) surfaces, but is quickly submerged as Petrarch accounts for the design of his letter collection: "as the rhetoricians and military leaders are wont to place their weakest parts in the middle, so I shall give the work both a beginning and an end consisting of the most manly advice" (*Fam.*, Bernardo (trans.), 1:13–14).

It may well be that the reason for such highly controlled tactics in the letters has to do with Petrarch's generalized and particular sense of danger. It prevents him from really opening himself up even to his trusted friends, especially, as he adds in one apparently self-ironic aside that may betray his real thinking, when one is "unsure of how many true ones" there are. His predicament highlights his conviction that he is the lonely, beleaguered hero in a war he wages on many fronts. His heroic life, worthy of an epic hero, will be warmly recalled like both an old man's distant war memories and dark presages of new storms lying in ambush on his life.

One war, common to him and his reader, is fought against time, which, as if it were sand flowing in the hourglass, "has slipped through our fingers" (*Fam.*, Bernardo (trans.), 1:3). Another war must be seen as a triumph against death. The starting point of the dedicatory letter is 1348, the year of the plague, which, of course, also triggered the writing of the *Decameron*. Against this tragic background, "which subjected us to irreparable losses" (*Fam.*, Bernardo (trans.), 1:3), Petrarch longs to begin anew, to dispel the shadow of death, and to free himself from the tyranny of his own past. He tosses to the fire a pile of these writings in which he can no longer recognize himself. Like the plague, the fire destroys and yet purifies his purposes, and both show him that to destroy is the pre-condition for producing a new work, or, to say it with his own image, to embark on a new voyage.

The voyage, which is the central figure organizing the movement of the *Familiares*, can be called more an adventure than a project. Petrarch has not settled on a clear course nor does he journey "home." He has no home. If anything, the collection closes, as if in a circle, with a letter to his friend Socrates (*Fam.* 24.13), and the circular structure he imparts to the work suggests that "home" is identified by Petrarch as the ideal realm of a friendship enduring across time and space. In his intellectual biography, this last letter is not a "conclusion": it preludes the *Seniles* (*Letters of Old Age*). In point of fact, he lives in perpetual exile, displaced, as his father was displaced from Florence, along with Dante, in 1302 and neither was ever allowed to return. His birth in exile (Arezzo), his continual travels among many people and through many towns (Pisa, Avignon, Bologna, Verona, etc.) and the present impossibility of reaching land, cast him as the epic hero Ulysses:

I have spent all my life, to this moment, in almost constant travel. Compare my wanderings to those of Ulysses. If the reputation of our names and of our achievements were the same, he indeed traveled neither more nor farther than I. He went beyond the borders of his fatherland when already old... I experienced danger even before being born and I approached the very threshold of life under the auspices of death... my father, expelled from his native city, fled with a large number of good men. From there, in my seventh month of life I was taken and carried through Tuscany. Our Tuscan wanderings ended in Pisa, whence I was once again snatched, this time at the age of seven, and transported by sea into France. We were almost shipwrecked by winter winds not far from Marseilles and once again, I was not very far from being denied a new life on its very threshold... As for how many kinds of dangers and fears I have encountered on my trips no one knows better than you except myself... I have enjoyed recalling some of this for you... provided I have now grown old and that even more painful things are not reserved for me in my old age. (*Fam.*, Bernardo (trans.), 1:8)

This autobiographical account, the journey of life ranging from birth to the present, signals that the *Familiares* aims at telling a coherent story of Petrarch's life and ordeals as they mirror the life of his mind. In this sense, the letters' underlying purpose is to bring literature as close to life as possible, to contain and document it. More to the point, this autobiography is couched as an epic journey or quest: just as St. Augustine casts his autobiographical *Confessions* as the *Aeneid* of the heart, so Petrarch's experience of homelessness comes through as an existential *Odyssey*. Like Ulysses, he visits the land of the dead (the shades of Homer, Cicero, Seneca) who turn out to be the oracles of history. Like Ulysses, who ends being without companions, he faces inner demons and monsters. One term, *"errores,"* joins the two of them. The word conveys the sense of the circuitousness and aimlessness of their shared misadventures, the iterative and random patterns of their minds.

Petrarch's Ulysses in the *Familiares* is the hero neither of the Neoplatonists' *nostos* (return home) nor of the Neoplatonic Christian fathers (St. Ambrose, St. Augustine's *De Beata Vita* [*On the Blessed Life*]) for whom the Greek hero's round-trip to Ithaca figures the allegory of the flight of the soul back to its homeland. It resembles somewhat Seneca's version of Ulysses as the emblem of the troubled mind tossed around by the winds and ills of life (*Epistle* 78.7). In addition, in Petrarch's version, Ulysses sets out from his homeland in his old age ("*Ille patriae fines iam senior excessit,*"

Dotti, *Petrarca*, par. 22) and, in this sense, he recalls the errors of Dante's representation of the hero.

There are two reasons, one extra-textual and one textual, for this suggestion. In 1352 Boccaccio writes his biography of Dante, *Trattatello in laude di Dante*, which he dedicates to Petrarch. Boccaccio even hand-delivers a copy to him in Padua as well as another one to Dante's daughter, Sister Beatrice, in Ravenna. He had met both of them in 1350, when he went to Ravenna to give ten gold florins to the nun and when, in the month of October of the same year, Petrarch visited Florence. Boccaccio paid special attention to both Petrarch and Sister Beatrice because he had something of a dream. He wanted to bring back to Florence the children of the exiles of 1302 and, to this end, he even argued that reparations be paid for the property confiscated from their parents. In the biography, Dante's peregrinations are described as if they re-enact those of Ulysses.[2] Petrarch appropriates the emblem to himself. He recalls his personal odyssey and the dangers he experienced "even before being born" (*Fam.*, Bernardo (trans.), 8). As he also recalls his father's exile from Florence (which "he fled with a large number of good men," *Fam.*, Bernardo (trans.), 1:8), he raises a pointed objection to Boccaccio's version of the myth of Ulysses. Petrarch moves in the wake of Dante's representation of the Greek hero, and in the process he gives a complex, more equivocal conception than either Dante or Boccaccio did.

Like Dante, Petrarch casts Ulysses' quest as if it were Aeneas' open journey toward the unknown. As in Dante's version, Ulysses went beyond the borders of his fatherland when already old. The conjunction between Ulysses and Aeneas (as well as Virgil and Homer) can be traced to other texts by Petrarch. See, for instance, sonnet 186 in the *Rime Sparse* or *Familiares* 9.13 to Philippe de Vitry: "You who are now the sole French poet, have pity on this Ulysses or Aeneas of yours" (*Fam.*, Bernardo (trans.), 2:40). And if Dante makes Ulysses a rhetorician supremely aware of style, one who speaks both eloquently and covertly, but at the same time distances himself from the viciousness of the hero, Petrarch displays his own polytropic

---

[2] "*Uscito adunque in cotale maniera Dante di quella città, della quale egli non solamente era cittadino, ma n'erano li suoi maggiori stati redificatori, e lasciatevi la sua donna, insieme con l'altra famiglia, male per picciola età alla fuga disposta . . . Non potendo gli amorosi disiri, né le dolente lagrime, né la sollecitudine casalinga, né la lusinghevole Gloria dei pubblici office, né il miserabile esilio, né la intollerabile povertà giammai con le loro forze rimuovere il nostro Dante dal principale intento, cioè dai sacri studii; perciò che, sì come si vederà dove appresso partitamente dell'opere da lui fatte si farà menzione, egli, nel mezzo di qualunque fu più fiera delle passioni sopra dette, si troverà componendo essersi esercitato.*" Ricci (ed.), *Trattatello in Laude di Dante*, pp. 455–7. Cf. *Inferno* 26, which, after the attack against Florence, features Ulysses' speech: "*Nè dolcezza di figlio, nè la pieta / del vecchio padre, nè il debito amore, / lo qual dovea Penelope far lieta . . .*" (vv. 94–6).

powers as he brings to the forefront of his reflections the question of style's simulations in the way the Greek hero addresses his companions. Yet, unlike Dante, for whom Ulysses dies tragically, Petrarch silences this central feature of the Dantesque myth. He gives no hint that Ulysses dies after traveling beyond the Pillars of Hercules.

Does Petrarch's silence about the deadly outcome of Ulysses' journey toward "virtue and knowledge" constitute a morality of hypocrisy or is it ignorance or just an outright rejection of Dante's reading of Ulysses? When Boccaccio equates Dante and Ulysses he knows what he is doing: he condemns both. He makes no bones that Dante, from a political perspective, was a tragic failure in that he was an exile and not a citizen. The same question can be stated differently in this manner: grandiloquence or epic narcissism about oneself aside, why does Petrarch choose to view Ulysses as the emblem of his own life?

The most direct answer is that Petrarch, for whom literature is the prism through which he looks at and understands the world, likes Ulysses because he is a literary figure. Above all, he likes him because, as a literary figure, Ulysses appears steadily in the most contradictory, shifty light. Ulysses is, at one and the same time, the multifarious, polytropic hero: both a sage under the protection of Athena and a crafty dissimulator in words and deeds. As Dante's representation in *Inferno* 26 shows, Ulysses speaks covertly, forever hidden in the tongues of fire, and yet his language attains sublime heights of rhetoric; he is the bearer of a secret knowledge (the secret of self-knowledge) but remains unknown to others, and, in the Homeric version, he keeps his identity concealed even from his wife Penelope.[3] The tradition – from Homer to St. Augustine, from the Neoplatonists to Seneca and Cicero (*De finibus*), to Dante and Boccaccio – has appropriately represented him in ever-inconsistent ways, each account at odds with another, and each account often at odds with itself. For his part, Petrarch in his *Familiares*, where he is engaged in a literary creation of his own self in the form of a confessional self-revelation, has chosen Ulysses as a figure of himself exactly because he is both a recognizable hero and yet he remains a stubbornly enigmatic, elusive character. He is forever on his way, forever displaced, never to be fixed in time or space.

This rhetorical move is bound to puzzle us. For, in spite of his openly staged inability to live according to his best judgment and in spite of his divided will, Petrarch wants to come through, indeed he must appear to

[3] For a reading of Dante's rhetorical and philosophical ambiguities in the representation of Ulysses see Mazzotta, *Dante, Poet of the Desert*, pp. 66–106.

his friends, as an ethical, morally reliable character. It is his only way to give credibility to his role as a moral and spiritual counselor. After all, the strong disapproval he voices of Cicero and Seneca is developed around the question of their moral inconsistencies. On the one hand, Petrarch acknowledges their moral precepts and rhetorical exemplarity for the *Familiares*. On the other hand, Cicero's letters to Atticus allow Petrarch to peek into the moods of his soul and into the unprincipled political conduct whereby he is led to disapprove of Cicero's lack of commitment to either the Roman republic or to Octavian. By the same token, the letter Petrarch writes to Seneca (24.5) praises him for his philosophical pedagogy of Lucilius and for turning philosophy into a daily practice of Stoic self-governance. At the same time, he points out that Seneca's cultivation of self never gets out of the exclusive, narrow circle of vain self-centeredness. His tragedies (*pace* the earlier Paduan humanists' cult of Seneca and Mussato's *Ecerenis*, who are deliberately Petrarch's polemical target) stage the failure of Senecan philosophy to lead Nero on the same path of Stoic self-knowledge trod by Lucilius. Petrarch sees in both his authors, Cicero and Seneca, an inconsistency between the way they lead their lives and the moral claims they advance in their literature.

All the models – philosophical, rhetorical, and literary – Petrarch deploys in the *Familiares* share the self-same fate, one on which, however, he does not dwell. Dante's Ulysses leads himself and his companions to disaster; Cicero died a death unworthy of a philosopher – his tongue and arms were cut off by Mark Antony's henchmen in his villa at Formia; Seneca was forced to commit suicide by the passions of his disciple, the tyrant Nero. Dante, as a man, is pitied for his radical political failures culminating in exile, while in the *Trionfi* these failures are retrieved as a form of visionariness and power as a love poet.

The dissimulated knowledge (or feigned ignorance) of the tragic fate of these fictional and real figures is flanked by the explicit acknowledgement of exile as the harsh punishment arbitrarily inflicted by Florence's democratic government on his own father and on himself even before being born. It expresses itself as fear of the tyrants who rule the cities. It comes through openly as a "war" to be waged against his critics, and even as a fear that his own friends may not be altogether trusted with his shadowy secrets. Such a historical background – of future fears and memory of wrongs he has suffered – triggers in Petrarch the need for a politics of writing, which is dramatized as a care in subjecting his letters to a prudent rhetorical discipline whereby he both reveals and veils his deeper purposes.

From this point of view, the *Familiares* marks the birth of what later will be known as a practice of simulations and dissimulations.[4] One image from an Ovidian fable in *Familiares* bends the intrinsically double discourse of literature into the horizon of a hazy, intellectually ambivalent political discourse. Letter 1.1 dramatizes Petrarch's strategy through the image of the spider. This is the context of the reference. In a mock-epic tone, Petrarch describes how, while searching through his dusty writings, "a spider, enemy of Pallas, attacked me for doing the work of Pallas" (*Fam.*, Bernardo (trans.), 1:3). The reference is clear. In Book 6.5–145 of the *Metamorphoses*, Ovid tells the artistic contest between Minerva and Arachne. Arachne rejects the tyrannical rule of the gods and weaves on her tapestry the stories of their impieties (especially Jupiter's disguises and trickeries). Pallas Minerva (or Athena), the goddess of weaving and of the mighty intellect, first, disguises herself as an old woman to appeal to Arachne's piety and, later, punishes Arachne's transgression, which consists in her undermining the authority of the gods. Minerva turns Arachne into a spider doomed forever to spin its fragile threads. For Petrarch, Ovid's narrative weaves an esthetic–political tale that he keeps in mind (though, ironically in terms of his own safety from Augustus and future exile on the Black Sea, Ovid himself did not).

Petrarch begins by siding with the tyrannical goddess Pallas against the enemy-spider. By the end of the letter (which is predictably described as a coming ashore) he wishes farewell to his Socrates and recalls once again the fable of Arachne. He shifts his perspective and expresses the desire that he were Arachne: "these letters, therefore, woven with multi-colored threads, if I may say so, are for you. However, if I were to enjoy a steady abode . . . I would weave on your behalf a much more noble and certainly a unified web or tapestry" (*Fam.*, Bernardo (trans.), 1:14).[5] No doubt, the myth of Penelope, the artful weaver and the stable center of the *Odyssey*, looms behind the myth of Arachne. Penelope is the object of Ulysses' quest, and so, her oblique recall gives a formal coherence to the epic structure of the *Familiares*. One might add that the figure catches the distinctive trait of Petrarch's voice: he casts himself as simultaneously the subject and the object of his own quest, simultaneously as Ulysses and as Penelope. He is both the starting point and the point of arrival of his reflections.

---

[4] For the historical development of this practice see Simonetta, *Il Rinascimento segreto*. The issue of Petrarch's ambiguities has recently been treated with historical precision by Fubini, "Pubblicità e controllo del libro nella cultura del Rinascimento," pp. 207–10.

[5] Dotti (trans.), *Petrarca,. Libro Primo*, p. 48: "*hec igitur tibi, frater, diversicoloribus, ut sic dicam, liciis texta dicaverim; ceterum, si stabilis sedes . . . contigerit . . . nobiliorem et certe uniformem telam tuo nomine meditor ordiri.*"

But because Petrarch highlights the tragic fate of Arachne (and silences Penelope), the passage also shows Petrarch's genuine concerns, his sense of the necessity to speak with a double voice. The issue for him is not, as it was for Ulysses, to come home. It is to take cover from the possible violence of the gods of the city, be they popes or the despots and the tyrants who are his patrons and who are likely to have the principles of their own authority violated by the poet's sovereign claims.

The desire to speak with one voice, to live a coherent life, and to weave a seamless story lingers on even as he ends up acknowledging that tyrannical gods and artists alike disguise themselves. They speak the truth, as it were, by lying. The gods hide their misdeeds. The artist, such as Arachne, tells the truth about the gods through art and, unlike the goddess, she loses her life but retains her art. By the end of the letter, Petrarch, who began by siding with Pallas, ends up in Arachne's camp. He will lie to protect his life, his status, and his power, and his power fantasies from the gods of the city – and he knows that only by creating himself as a character in fiction will he really survive in every sense.

All this talk about simulation and lies does not mean that Petrarch is not an authentic artist. To be authentic, we might say by a spin on Dante's etymology of *auctor* from "*autentin*" (to be worthy of faith) (*Convivio* 4.6.3–6), is to be the author of one's own acts.[6] The *Familiares* is an authentic work, a way for Petrarch to imagine the possibility that kings, lords, teachers, poets, chancellors, and cardinals will heed his advice; that he, like an epic hero, could throw his very friends to the fire; and that his subterfuges, like Penelope's secret steady weaving and unweaving to hold at bay her suitors, will circumvent the harassment of his patrons. Petrarch is authentic in that he can imagine a world alternate to the existing one, and he can conceive a grand project of culture, such as the one dreamed up by his real model, Varro, who was Caesar's librarian.

The empire of culture Petrarch envisions is, in its universalizing impulse, Roman but it is not Rome. The final book of the collection takes us to the familiar territory of the classical Roman tradition. Introduced by a letter to Philippe, Bishop of Cavaillon (*Fam.* 24.1), which is made of distant echoes and aphorisms on the existential sense of time, on time and mortality as inward dimensions of life, the book shifts its focus and records letters

---

6 "*È dunque da sapere che 'autoritate' non è altro che 'atto d'autore.' Questo vocabulo, cioè 'autore,' senza quella terza lettera C, può discendere da due principi . . . L'altro principio onde 'autore' discende, sì come testimonia Uguiccione nel principio de le sue Derivazioni, è uno vocabulo Greco che dice 'autentin,' che tanto vale in latino quanto 'degno di fede e obedienza.'*" *Convivio* in Vasoli and de Robertis (eds.), *Opere Minori*, Vol. 1, Part 2.

to Cicero, Seneca, Varro, Quintilian, Livy, Asinius Pollio, Horace, Virgil, and Homer (which contains a quick reference to Penelope and Ulysses and, more importantly, a quite traditional comparison between Virgil and Homer in favor of Virgil). The book ends, as stated above, with a letter to Petrarch's friend, Socrates. Taken in its entirety, the book, which contains an eloquent summing-up of his understanding of the deeper elements of the classical tradition, is governed by its own inner logic.

Against the background of time as a subjective experience of ruptures (and the casting of the self through Horace's self-transparent figure of Postumus), the classical tradition, toward which he acknowledges his indebtedness, provides the framework of a continuity transcending and countering the radically time-bound limitations of the self. Roman culture was established and founded by this series of thinkers as much as by the power of Rome's armies. But this history of Roman culture is never idealized. It is now damned to a ghostlike existence. And it is marked by tensions and rifts: such as the one between Quintilian and Seneca, who, in spite of their common origin, hate each other; or the one between Caesar and Varro, respectively the figure of political power and the intellectual; or the relation between poets (Virgil and Homer), in which the successor fails to acknowledge the decisive import of his predecessor. Seen in this light, the final letter to Socrates clarifies Petrarch's strategy: it defines him in his existential solipsism, inexorably part of the world of devouring time. The idea of time's rifts triggers in him the conviction that the fate of present culture depends on him.

The empire of culture he conceives, incarnated in the classical and Christian branches of the tradition, needs no geographical boundaries and yet is run in his name by his cronies/guards or international intellectual elites. It is the empire of culture as he articulates it in his *Collatio Laureationis*. From this standpoint, the *Familiares* remains the key text in Petrarch's canon because it introduces us to his extraordinarily lucid and self-conscious plan and yet shadowy, secretive project of cultural politics. This cultural project comes through by necessity under the cover of an ethical text. But the veil is subtle. It is so subtle that it did not keep Machiavelli from seeing with his sharp lynx-like eyes the politics underlying Petrarch's ostensible discourse. Like a true kindred spirit, he does not fail to acknowledge Petrarch's poetry as he closes off *Prince*.

CHAPTER 7

The first British Aeneid: a case study in reception

Emily Wilson

The *Aeneid* is a special case in the reception of classical literature. It is the classical poem that has had the greatest and most continuous influence over post-classical literature in the West. Almost every European country has tried, at some time or another, to claim the story of the *Aeneid* for itself. We are all descended from the Trojans. There are many reasons for the dominance of Virgil's poem over the tradition, most of which I can only hint at in this paper.[1] I am going to focus on just one reason why the *Aeneid* played such an important role in the tradition, namely that the poem is itself concerned with the reception of the classical past. The earliest translators of the *Aeneid* into vernacular European languages were highly conscious of the fact that this is a poem about translation, and about reception.[2] I will concentrate on Gavin Douglas, who wrote one of the first complete translations of the *Aeneid* into a vernacular language.

Douglas' *Eneados* was the first complete British version of any work of Greek or Latin literature. Douglas, who was not English, but Scottish, was the Roman Catholic provost of St. Giles' church, Edinburgh. He finished the poem in 1513, but the translation was not published until after his death – it appeared in 1553.[3]

---

[1] For more detailed discussion of the reception of Virgil, and the special status of the *Aeneid* in the classical tradition, important recent studies and collections include: Ziolkowski and Putnam, *The Virgilian Tradition*; Thomas, *Virgil and the Augustan Reception*; Putnam, *Virgil's Aeneid*; Ziolkowski, *Virgil and the Moderns*; Bernard, *Vergil at 2000*. A short overview of translations of Virgil is given by Burrow, "Virgil in English translation."

[2] Patterson (*Negotiating the Past*, pp. 157–95) discusses this factor in the reception of the *Aeneid* in the twelfth century, noting that the poem itself includes a strong thread of ambivalence about the idea of *translatio imperii*. Frost ("Translating Virgil, Douglas to Dryden") associates the large number of British translations of the poem in the sixteenth and seventeenth centuries with the development of British national identity.

[3] For the *Eneados*, I have used Coldwell's edition. For the *Aeneid*, I have used the Oxford Classical Text. Douglas' text of Virgil differed in various important respects from modern texts, but these differences are not directly relevant to my essay, so it seemed more useful to use a readily available modern text.

The reception of the *Eneados* has been somewhat mixed.[4] Douglas was highly regarded as a poet among his contemporaries, and his work as a translator has had various enthusiastic admirers in later times. The *Eneados* was never the standard vernacular British version, perhaps largely because it is in Scottish dialect: instead, the plodding Twyne and Phaer translation became the standard English Virgil until Dryden (1688). Probably Douglas' language – not merely his use of Middle Scots, but his individual verbal inventiveness – quickly made his work seem difficult or obscure. But Douglas had an important impact on other translators of Virgil, as well as on later Scottish writers.[5] In the twentieth century, literary interest in Douglas revived: Ezra Pound claimed that Douglas' version of the *Aeneid* was better than Virgil "whenever the text touches the sea or the elements," and C. S. Lewis argued that Douglas' "medievalism" allowed him a liveliness of expression that was closer to the original than the statelier neo-classical version of Dryden.[6] More recent critics have generally agreed that, as Alistair Fowler says, "Douglas was a brilliant translator."[7] It has been convincingly demonstrated that – *pace* Pound – Douglas is often particularly good at echoing stylistic or conceptual features of his original.[8]

Many modern critics have challenged the claim that Douglas is an essentially medieval writer and translator, arguing that his translation anticipates the early modern period in several important ways.[9] The period distinction is, of course, a scholarly fiction, which relies on a caricature of the two contiguous time periods. In this case, the medieval is associated with courtly love and spirituality, whereas the early modern is associated with secular political questions about the duties of princes, and with the development of a new national identity in vernacular literature. Those who say it is medieval point to the fact that Douglas calls his style "knightly," and argue that he presents Aeneas as a chivalric hero on a quest, or on a spiritual journey through suffering to redemption.[10] Those who say it is early modern point out that Douglas makes Aeneas as a good *king*, as well as a

---

[4] For a survey of the reception of Douglas' work, see Bawcutt, *Gavin Douglas*, pp. 192–206, with bibliography.

[5] Ridley, "Surrey's debt to Gawin Douglas"; Rutledge "Gavin Douglas and John Bellenden."

[6] Pound, *Selected Prose*, p. 386 (from "The art of poetry;" further remarks in "The ABC of reading," in Pound, *Selected Prose*); Lewis, *English Literature in the Sixteenth Century*: see, especially, pp. 79–89.

[7] Fowler, "Gavin Douglas," p. 84. Further modern appreciations of Douglas as a writer and translator include: Baswell, *Virgil in Medieval England*; Canitz, "'In our Awyn Langage.'"

[8] See Fowler, "Gavin Douglas," pp. 91–4.

[9] The case is first made by Dearing, "Gavin Douglas's *Eneados*"; see also Singerman, *Under Clouds of Poesy*. An important exception to this scholarly trend is Blyth, *The Knychtlyke Stile* (in a dissertation first submitted in 1963).

[10] See, especially, Blyth, *The Knychtlyke Stile*.

pious, compassionate and admirable man, and therefore a reflection and model for Scotland's own monarch, James IV – it is, then, a forerunner in the *Mirror for Magistrates* tradition.[11]

But readings which take the *Eneados* as either primarily a spiritual poem, or primarily a political one, seem motivated by an unwarranted desire to fit this original translation into a pre-ordained mould. In fact, the translation is hard to fit precisely into the terms of either period. Douglas is far less interested in religious interpretation of Virgil than some earlier medieval commentators had been; and he explicitly distinguishes his own work from the medieval Virgil of Chaucer. Moreover, it is misleading to exaggerate the political elements in the *Eneados*;[12] as has recently been pointed out, an admirer and follower of Douglas, John Bellenden, used classical translation for far more explicit political purposes than Douglas himself ever did.[13]

A danger in reading literature in terms of historical progression from one period to another is that it may lead one to neglect or even not see the features of a particular work which were new, but which did not have an obvious impact on later writers in the same tradition or subgenre. Most later translators of the *Aeneid*, at least up to Dryden, interpreted it primarily as an imperial epic, and therefore "modernity," his distance from the medieval tradition, is defined in terms of his anticipation of that later reading: Douglas is more "modern" the more he presents Aeneas as an ideal king.

More convincing accounts of Douglas' position within literary history take a more nuanced approach, recognizing that his work contains elements which look both forwards and back. Priscilla Bawcutt helpfully suggests that Douglas, although he was not a learned "humanist" on the model of Erasmus, in the sense that he did not edit classical texts or translate Greek classics into Latin, nevertheless had important affinities with European humanism, especially in his secularizing and critical attitudes towards the classical text.[14] Alistair Fowler has recently read Douglas as a "romantic humanist," an oxymoronic term which rightly emphasizes his poetic originality.[15]

The issue of periodization overlaps with another, perhaps even more contentious, issue in the critical reception of the *Eneados*, namely its identity within the Scottish literary canon. The choice of the *Aeneid* as the work of classical literature to translate is itself clearly a political choice, which might imply that Scotland will be at the center of a new Europe – the

[11] Singerman, *Under Clouds of Poesy.*   [12] As rightly noted by Bawcutt, *Gavin Douglas.*
[13] Rutledge, "Gavin Douglas and John Bellenden."   [14] Bawcutt, *Gavin Douglas*, pp. 31–6.
[15] Fowler, "Gavin Douglas."

equivalent of Rome within the Roman Empire. The fact that the *Eneados* is the earliest British translation of this acclaimed work of classical literature has also been taken as evidence for the Scottish Renaissance.

Scottish nationalists have been particularly interested in this approach to Douglas: the translation was republished in 1972 by the Scottish Text Society, with an introduction which guides the reader to take the translation as a sign of Scotland's advanced culture, and a monument to the greatness the country might have had, if the flower of the age had not been cut down in the disastrous battle of Flodden Field, only two months after the completion of Douglas' poem.[16] More recent critics have taken up the idea that vernacular translations in general, as well as Douglas' decision to translate Virgil in particular, should be seen in terms of early modern patriotism and nation-building.[17]

But there are various difficulties with a reading of the *Eneados* purely in terms of Scottish national and political pride. For one thing, as Colin Burrow has rightly pointed out, Douglas – like many other early modern translators from classical literature – was set apart in several ways from the mainstream of national identity.[18] He was, after all, a Roman Catholic. Moreover, in his various attempts to gain extra power for himself, he colluded with the English court, and was condemned as a traitor in Scotland.[19] Douglas clearly had ambitions for his work to be read and admired south of the border. Margaret Tudeau-Clayton has suggested that reading Douglas in terms of patriotism, and democratization, is misleading: rather, we should see a kind of "strategic duplicity" in Douglas' use of language, which is, like his political activities, designed to help his social climbing.[20] He creates a vernacular dialect which appeals to the elite of both Scotland and England.

I would like to propose a different approach, focusing on the ways that Douglas writes his own task as a translator into the story of the *Aeneid*. The Prologues to the various books of the translation have sometimes been read (and anthologized) as if they were entirely separable from the translation

---

[16] Coldwell, *Virgil's Aeneid, translated by Gavin Douglas.*

[17] On the idea that translating the classics was an important element in the construction of national identity in early modern Scotland and England, see Conley, *The First English Translators of the Classics*; Hill, *Intellectual Origins of the English Revolution*, pp. 27–31; and Helgerson, *Forms of Nationhood*. On Douglas' translation as a contribution to Scottish nationalism, see Frost, "Translating Virgil, Douglas to Dryden"; Canitz, "'In our Awyn Langage.'"

[18] Burrow, "Virgil in English translation."

[19] For further biographical details, see Bawcutt, *Gavin Douglas.*

[20] Tudeau-Clayton, "Richard Carew, William Shakespeare, and the politics of translating Virgil in early modern England and Scotland," p. 516.

itself.[21] But Douglas uses the prologues as an invitation to make an analogy between the journey of Aeneas and Douglas' own poetic and scholarly task. The *Eneados* offers a striking example of how a translator can meditate on the whole process of the reception of classical culture in a new and alien environment. Douglas reinvents himself, the translator, as a new Aeneas, and rediscovers the *Aeneid* as a poem which itself deals with the process of re-writing a Latin poem in the Scottish language.

The narrative Douglas has to tell includes and is framed by the story of how he came to write it. The technique is reminiscent of Dante's presence as a character in the *Divine Comedy*, but it also anticipates later uses of the first person in epic (think of Milton's invocations to Books 3 and 7 of *Paradise Lost*), or even in other genres, such as lyric and prose fiction. Douglas moves well beyond the commentators he used, in seeing the journey of Aeneas not only as an allegory of the spiritual life of man in general,[22] but also as parallel to his own life – and not only to his religious and moral life, but to his literary life, as the translator of Virgil. Readings of the *Eneados* as a gesture of Scottish nationalism are misleading, insofar as they imply that the *Aeneid* was a fixed symbol of Roman imperialism, understood in advance, which Douglas wanted to claim for his own country. Rather, it is through the process of translation that Douglas discovers an interpretation of Virgil. His own struggles to understand Virgil's true meaning become associated with Aeneas' bewilderment about the will of the gods; his own task, of bringing Roman words into the Scottish vernacular, is analogous to Aeneas' duty to bring Troy to Italy.

Through translating the *Aeneid*, Douglas discovers that translation is also Virgil's subject – and, conversely, that his own achievement as a translator is, as it were, celebrated in the *Aeneid*, or at least in the *Eneados*. The *Aeneid* is about transferring the culture of one country to another. Douglas may not have been fully aware of how much Virgil imitates from Homer: despite a bold or brazen claim that he could have translated either Homer or Virgil into his native language, he probably knew no Greek. But he is highly conscious that the subject of the *Aeneid* is cultural translation. The parallel between the narrative of the *Aeneid*, and the narrative of its re-telling, works to valorize the duty of the scholarly translator as he labours to unveil Virgil's meaning, and carry it dutifully to his own far-distant

---

[21] See Parkinson, "Orpheus and the translator," with bibliography, for a sensitive reading of the narrator's self-identification as Orpheus in the twelfth Prologue – which, however, does little to relate the prologue to the rest of the translation.

[22] On medieval allegorical readings of the *Aeneid*, see Desmond, "Bernard Silvestris and the *Corpus* of the *Aeneid*."

country. The *Aeneid* itself guides and informs his own work as a poet and as a scholar.

Douglas sees it as his duty to provide the first responsible interpretation of Virgil for the British people. In the Prologue to the first book, he unites many of the usual *sententiae* surrounding translation. It had been conventional, since at least Lucretius, to deprecate the *egestas patriae linguae*, the poverty of one's own native language, and to exalt the original author; both these tropes appear in Douglas' first prologue, when he invokes "Maist reverend Virgill, of Latyn poetis prynce" and regrets that "Besyde Latyn our langage is imperfite." He says he had to use "sum bastard Latyn, French or Inglys oyss / Quhar scant was Scottis – I had nane other choys."[23]

But Douglas also asserts that Scottish is not, after all, an inferior or "scant" language compared to other vernaculars, although it may be so in relation to Virgil's Latin. It is a sign not of Scottish inferiority, but of Douglas' personal integrity as a translator. He insists on the importance of retaining Virgil's "sentence," a word he repeats again and again.[24] It means, primarily, "sense" as opposed to expression: Douglas must preserve Virgil's meaning, although obviously a translation cannot preserve the actual Latin words. But the term "sentence" is also close to the Latin *sententia*: Douglas wants to bring the goodness of Virgil's opinions or pronouncements, particularly on moral or spiritual questions, to those who cannot read him in the original. "Sentence" may also connote a passage of writing, or a saying. Douglas wants to maintain Virgil's "sentence" in all these senses.[25]

He is aware of the old saw that one must translate not word for word, but sense for sense. What makes Douglas the first *translator* of Virgil, as opposed to those who had adapted the *Aeneid* before him, is that he insists that the sense of the poet can be brought out only through meditation on every word – a point that has often been emphasized in discussions of Douglas' modern, non-medieval sensibility.[26] He rages against previous adaptations of the *Aeneid* story, in particular Caxton's *Eneados*, saying it is "na mair lyke than the devill and Sanct Austyne" (1.Prologue.143). He also condemns Chaucer as a reader of Virgil, despite admiring him as a poet: he remarks that "My mastir Chaser greatly Virgill offendit" (1.Prologue.410).

[23] For further discussion of this passage, see Tudeau-Clayton, "Richard Carew, William Shakespeare, and the politics of translating Virgil in early modern England and Scotland."

[24] 1.Prologue.133, 147, 289, 309, 352, 356, 365.

[25] For the multiple meanings of "sentence" in Middle Scots, see Skretkowicz and Rennie, *Dictionary of the Scots Language*, s.v.

[26] See Dearing, "Gavin Douglas's *Eneados*."

Caxton and Chaucer adapted Virgil too loosely for Douglas' tastes. Neither provides anything like a complete translation of the *Aeneid*, instead re-telling only a very select part of the story. Douglas insists that one can understand Virgil only if one reads him more than twice; he demands the same close attention for his own work. His book stands or falls by its fidelity to the master: if he has failed to pay him due "honour and reverens", he says wildly, "warp it in the see, / Thraw it in the fyre or rent it every crum" (1.Prologue.280–1).

But Douglas' insistence on philological fidelity is only part of the story. Equally striking is the deeply personal relationship with Virgil suggested by Douglas' imagery. He presents himself as Virgil's competitor, as well as his defender. It is his responsibility not only to "follow Virgillis lantern" (1.Prologue.413) as Chaucer claimed to do, but to "follow hym fut hait." The phrase suggests a race, in which Douglas must stay always at Virgil's heels, line by line or even foot by foot.

Douglas' method has important interpretative implications. He suggests that only devoted study of the whole poem will prevent such mistakes as Chaucer's idea that "Eneas to Dydo was forsworn." Caxton and Chaucer both concentrate almost exclusively on the story of Dido, and, in common with most medieval readers, they present her as a noble and sympathetic queen, treacherously abandoned by a caddish Aeneas.[27] Chaucer, in particular, emphasizes Aeneas' lack of mercy to the wretched Dido. She says, in the *Legend of Fair Women*,

> "I am with childe, and yeve my child his lyf!
> Mercy, lord! have pite in youre thought!"
> But al this thing avayleth hire ryght nought,
> For on a nyght, slepynge he let hire lye,
> And stal away unto his companye.
> And as a traytour forth he gan to sayle
> Toward the large contre of Ytayle.[28]

Douglas challenges this view of Aeneas as a merciless traitor, relying on what he presents as a closer, more accurate reading of Virgil's poem, and in particular, of the word *pietas*, which, he thinks, implies both pity and piety.[29] Chaucer's passage alludes to the moment in the *Aeneid* where

---

[27] On the shift in perceptions of Dido in early modern readings see Watkins, *The Specter of Dido* with Stevenson, "Aeneas in fourteenth-century England" on the representation of Aeneas as a traitor in fourteenth-century literature.

[28] Chaucer, *Legend of Fair Women*, 1323–9.

[29] The wordplay is discussed by Blyth, *The Knychtlyke Stile* and Singerman, *Under Clouds of Poesy*.

Dido, exhausted with cursing and wailing, collapses, and Aeneas, instead of comforting her, goes off to his ships.

> *at pius Aeneas, quamquam lenire dolentem*
> *solando cupit et dictis auertere curas,*
> *multa gemens magnoque animum labefactus amore*
> *iussa tamen diuum exsequitur classemque reuisit.*
>
> (*Aeneid* 4.392–5)

Chaucer ignores the fact that Aeneas wants to comfort Dido, and is shaken by great love, and he skips the word *pius*. Douglas gives a reading of this passage, and in particular of the word *pius*, which is a direct challenge to Chaucer's suggestion that Aeneas has no mercy.

> Bot 3yt, althoucht the *reuthful* Eneas
> The dolorus quyn to meyss ful bissy was,
> To do hir comfort, and hir dyseyss asswage,
> And with hys wordis return hir sad curage,
> Bewalyng mekill hyr sorow and distress,
> Proplexte in mynd by gret lufe; netheless,
> The command of the goddis, by and by,
> He execut, and vysseys hys navy.
>
> (VII.vii.63–70)

Douglas, like Chaucer, suggests Aeneas has a duty to Dido, but unlike Chaucer he implies he satisfies that duty. Douglas makes Aeneas explicitly "reuthfull" where Chaucer makes him deny Dido's appeal for mercy, and where Virgil is ambiguous about his emotional state. When Virgil's Aeneas goes back to his fleet he is *multa gemens*: it is an open question whether he is grieving for Dido or for himself, or both. Douglas makes him unambiguously generous, thinking only of her pain and "Bewalyng mekill hyr sorow and distress." He is moved not by his own loss, but by her suffering. This is an Aeneas who is *pius* in both Douglas' senses of the word: he is capable both of pity for Dido, and also of piety and obedience to the gods' command.

Chaucer and Caxton were interested in Aeneas' infidelity to Dido, whereas Douglas is interested in his own fidelity to Virgil – which means, fidelity to the whole of Virgil. For Douglas, it is a dereliction of duty to imitate or to read only part of the *Aeneid*: he has to do it all. For Douglas, unlike earlier writers, Book 4 is not really the center of the poem. If there is one book that matters more than the others, it is not Book 4 but Book 6, in which the pagan Virgil shows most clearly that he has things to teach a Christian reader.

In the Prologue to this book, Douglas inveighs against those who accuse Virgil of paganism, saying, "O hald your pace, ye verray goddis apis!" (vi.Prologue.11). He defends the book on the grounds that it is, he suggests, almost entirely compatible with Roman Catholic Christianity, complete with Limbo. Douglas suggests that Aeneas' journey into the underworld provides an accurate account of what we can expect after death, although one which is described in mysterious, poetic terms. Pluto is Satan; the Elysian fields with heavenly rewards for the just. Those who take the trouble to read the book properly will realize that Virgil has given as good an account as any pagan could of the truth about the afterlife.

But Douglas goes even further than this, finding in Virgil's Sibyl a type of the Virgin Mary – another maiden overpowered by the divine. Douglas appeals to his own superhuman female guide to help him through the task of translation, saying, "Thow art our Sibill, Crystis moder deir" (vi.Prologue.145–6). Here, Douglas makes an explicit analogy between the Sibyl who led Aeneas through the mysteries of the underworld, and Mary, who leads Douglas himself. The comparison of the two guides implies that there are also two comparable journeys here. Douglas' own attempt to understand Virgil, and to see through him to the truth about life after death, is parallel to Aeneas' descent into the underworld. He prays, "The dym dongeoun of Ditis till assailȝe, / Or in the lyknes this mysty poetry, / Help me, Mare" (vi.Prologue.165–7). "This mysty poetry" is Virgil's poetry, and in particular, the mysterious pagan names which Virgil gives to underlying Christian truths. Douglas suggests that his own process of discovery or interpretation, guided by Mary, is like Aeneas' journey into the underworld. The struggle to understand the truth beneath "mysty poetry" resembles Aeneas' struggle to interpret divine purpose and find his way to his new home.

But the primary ways in which Douglas suggests that his task resembles that of Aeneas are not connected to the interpretation of divine mysteries. Rather, Douglas and Aeneas are similar because they both have to struggle to preserve an ancient culture, in a new and inhospitable environment. In both cases, the task requires heroic self-discipline and enormous amounts of *labor*. For example, in Book 3, Aeneas tells the story of how the exhausted Trojans drop anchor on the island of Leucas. They celebrate their escape from the Odyssean dangers of the journey, they work out, and they stay till winter comes. When they leave, Aeneas sets up a trophy in the temple. In Virgil, we are told,

aere cauo clipeum, magni gestamen Abantis,
postibus aduersis figo et rem carmine signo:
AENEAS HAEC DE DANAIS VICTORIBVS ARMA.

(286–8)

Douglas' version runs:

> Apon a post in the tempyl I hang
> A bow and scheild of plait, quhilk Abas strang
> Bair vmquhile, and, the maner to reherss,
> I notyfy and tytillis with this verss:
> "Eneas hec de Danais victoribus arma,"
> That is to say, "Eneas festnyt thus
> This armour of the Grekis victorius."

(iii.v.5–11)

Aeneas, having escaped from the dangers of battles with Greeks, from monstrous Harpies and from storms by sea, hangs up the shield of Abas. Servius notes that Virgil seems to be drawing on a story about a mythical king of Argos, Abas, who had a shield, possibly made by his grandfather Danaus.[30] Abas himself dies, and a mob tries to take over the city; but the shield is given to a young man, who rushes with it against the enemy; as soon as the enemy see the shield of Abas, they are terrified and run away. It is not at all clear how Aeneas has got hold of this shield from ancient Argos, but it is very appropriate that Aeneas has a weapon which is apparently only defensive (a shield) but which is also offensive. It is a good image for the idea that survival can become a kind of victory.

Douglas quotes Aeneas' Latin line, in Latin, in the middle of his own translation. He draws attention to the process of translation, by offering first the Latin, and then his own interpretation. The fact that this happens at precisely this moment suggests a connection between the process of translation, and the hanging up of the shield. The Latin *carmen*, echoed by the Scottish "verse," perhaps guided Douglas to see this as a metapoetic moment, a moment of linguistic as well as military triumph. Aeneas hangs up the shield he has won from the victorious Greeks; Douglas hangs up the verse that he has won from Virgil. Like the Argives over the Trojans, Virgil is apparently the winner over Douglas. But Douglas creates a sense of a greater triumph than that of Aeneas, by the positioning of the word "victorious": "Eneas festnyt thus / This armour of the Grekis victorius." In the Latin, it is obvious that those who are victorious, for now, are the

---

[30] Thilo and Hagen (eds.), *Servii Grammatici*, vol. 1, p. 392.

Danai. But in Douglas's version, it is ambiguous: the line could imply that
Aeneas himself is victorious over the Danai. The ambiguity suggests that
Douglas himself may also be finally victorious in his struggle to capture
lines from Virgil.

The connections between Douglas' own task, and that of Aeneas, are
made most obvious in the interplay between the prologues and the main
text of the poem. There is an intimate relationship between the two strands
of the text, which points to the analogies between Aeneas' quest, as founder
of Rome, and Douglas' own quest, as translator of Virgil. Douglas begins
the prologue to Book 7 with a description of winter. The language he uses
echoes that Virgilian winter in Book 3. Douglas assimilates this winter
with the Virgilian one, by recycling the same phrase he had used before
for *Aquilonibus* in Book 3: the "blastis of the northyn art" occurs in both
passages (III.v.3; VII.Prologue.15). It is hard, for the first ninety lines of
the prologue, to work out where all this iciness is taking place: it could
almost be Italy, except that it seems too cold and too mountainous. Then
the narrator is introduced, and he is clearly Douglas himself, at home in
Scotland. During this cold snap, he tells us he lay down in bed, and "I
crosyt me." As he lies in bed, he listens to the "the wild geiss claking eik by
nightis tyde" (VII.Prologue.109), and eventually falls asleep. He is woken
by more birds, and he gets up to shut the window. As he huddles by the
fire to ward off the cold, he sees his Virgil, and knows he must go on with
the task of translation.

> And seand Virgill on a lettron stand,
> To write onone I hynt a pen in hand,
> Fortil perform the poet grave and sad,
> Quham sa fer furth or than begun I had,
> And wolx ennoyt sum deill in my hart
> thar restit oncompletit sa gret a part.
> And to my self I said: "In gud effect
> Thou mon draw furth, the ʒok lyis on thy nek."
>
> (vii.Prologue.143–50)

The language emphasizes that Douglas now feels an intimate personal
connection with Virgil. He sees not the book of Virgil, but "Virgil," as
if the ancient poet has come into his house. He must complete not the
translation, but the poet. In translating Virgil, Douglas must in some sense
become him.

But he is depressed and overwhelmed at the prospect. The "poet grave
and sad" is going to get more and more grave and sad, in the following

books. The trouble, for Douglas, is partly that the *Aeneid* is so long – there remains "so great a part" – and yet he is committed to doing the whole thing. The yoke lies on his neck, an image which emphasizes the brutal hard work involved in rendering every part of Virgil into Scottish.

But this story is not only a lament for the sorrows of translators. It is also part of Douglas' interpretation of the poem itself. He incorporates his own task into the Virgilian narrative. The transition between Books 6 and 7 marks a great turning point in the *Aeneid*. The second half charts the Trojans' struggle to create peace and a homeland in Italy. The Sibyl told Aeneas that the hard thing is not to enter hell – *facilis descensus Averno* – but to find a way back up and out: *hoc opus, hic labor est* (*Aeneid* 6.129). The whole of the following six books can be read as the story of a confusing and violent quest to find a way out of Hades. In moving from Book 6 to Book 7, we turn from the promise of the future glory that Rome will be, to the outbreak of war and the reminder that if peace is coming, it is still a long way off. It is appropriate, then, to Aeneas' situation as well as his own, that Douglas should here be full of doubt and sadness over how much remains to do. The connection between the prologue and the main text is that, like Aeneas emerging from Hades, the translator must move out of this cold bleak landscape, towards the final triumph which he finds in Book 12.

The prologue to Book 12 is a counterpart to the Book 7 prologue; the description of winter is answered by a virtuosic description of spring.[31] The sense of unmitigated joy created by this prologue may be puzzling to modern readers of Book 12, which seems a pretty bloody and unspringlike affair – even for those who think that Aeneas does the right thing in killing Turnus. Douglas is celebrating partly his own triumph, in finally defeating Virgil: he is at last almost at the end of his work, "the latter buke of Dan Virgill," "Quhilk me had tareit al to lang a quhile." When Aeneas finds the opportunity for single combat with Turnus, Virgil describes him as *laetitia exsultans* (*Aeneid* 12.700); Douglas tells us that "he hoppit up for ioy, he was so glad," which maintains the leaping inherent in *exsultans*, but sounds if anything even more bouncy (*Eneados* XII.xii.6). Juno's joy at getting her own way about the name of the Trojans is also rendered in a particularly reassuring and happy fashion: where in Virgil, we are told that Juno has changed, or rather, twisted, her mind (*mentem laetata retorsit, Aeneid* 12.841), Douglas, retaining the metaphor of twisting, tells us explicitly that Juno's wrath is now over – he introduces a characteristically alliterative play

---

[31] For a sensitive reading of the Book 12 prologue in terms of the story of Orpheus and his difficult return from the underworld, see Parkinson, "Orpheus and the translator."

on words, "Hir wraith hess writhit" (xii.xiii.120). He emphasizes that she was delighted, "ful blith and ioyus" for the single word *laetata*, and adds that she said goodbye to Turnus, which is not in the Latin at all (xii.xiii.119; xii.xiii.121). Douglas does all he can to read Virgil's last book as a happy ending, and as one which leaves no loose ends still trailing.

It might seem, then, that he would have no need of the extra happy ending and the extra tying up of ends provided by Book 13. There were several attempts in this period to "finish" the *Aeneid*, but the most successful, and the one Douglas does translate was written in 1428, in sub-Virgilian Latin by an Italian humanist called Maphaeus Vegius. It wraps up all Virgil's loose ends, and resolves or corrects some of the disturbing suggestions left by the end of the *Aeneid*. Turnus was to blame, Vegius insists, for all passionate excess, anger and *furor*; the book re-invents Aeneas as a character who has never lost his temper or his head. With the bad guy Turnus safely out of the way, the Rutuli surrender, and there is universal peace. Aeneas marries Lavinia, founds a city, and lives happily until he dies and is granted apotheosis among the stars. The new ending makes it much easier to read the *Aeneid* as a sort of pilgrim's progress, in which after worldly sorrow and tribulation, the true Christian hero achieves his heavenly reward. It suggests that the end of Aeneas' journey lies not in the worldly city of Rome, but in the city of God.[32]

Douglas' prologue to the thirteenth book suggests that he was very much in two minds about including this later addition to the text. He is well aware that it is not by Virgil, and he is devoted enough to his Mantuan master to feel vaguely ashamed of tacking on this inferior modern ending. Douglas suggests, in honour of the Christian religion, and to please the vulgar, who will not even know the difference, he will include the book.

Douglas' doubts about including Vegius are a good indicator both of his taste, and of his commitment as a scholar. He knows that the thirteenth book sits oddly with the rest of Virgil, and that his task of translating the whole *Aeneid* is already complete. The addition of Mapheus also undermines the point which Douglas has worked hard to make clear, that Virgil alone is not unprofitable for a Christian reader. But what else could he do? Douglas reveals at the end of Book 13 that the addition was made not, as in his fictional dream sequence, at the behest of Mapheus, but because his patron asked for it.

---

[32] For discussion of Mapheus' continuation, see Brinton, *Mapheus Vegius and his Thirteenth Book of the Aeneid*; Hijmans, "*Aeneia Virtus*." For a recent text and translation, accompanied by a full introduction, see Putnam and Hankins (eds.), *Maffeo Vegio*.

But Douglas ends his book on a note of triumph which transforms the
work of Mapheus Vegius. The thirteenth book describes the apotheosis of
Aeneas into heaven; Venus carries up his soul and sets it amid the stars. After
his translation of this ending, Douglas provides an epilogue which is like
an alternative ending, an alternative kind of final triumph and apotheosis.
He declares the glorious end of his own literary journey:

> The bettir part of me salbe vpheld
> Abufe the starnys perpetualy to ryng,
> And heir my naym remane, but enparyng;
> Throw owt the ile yclepit Albyon
> Red sall I be, and sung with mony one.
> Thus vp my pen and instrumentis full ʒor
> On Virgillis post I fix for evirmor.[33]

The echo of the end of Ovid's *Metamorphoses* shows Douglas' awareness that
he has succeeded in transforming Virgil's *Aeneid* into a Scottish poem.[34]
But the position of this conclusion, immediately after Aeneas' apotheosis,
invites comparison between Douglas' triumph and that of Aeneas. Douglas,
like Aeneas, has been lifted into the sky. Very similar language was used,
only a few lines earlier, to describe how Venus lifted Aeneas' soul:

> And bair it vp abuf the ayr full hie
> Onto the hevyn, quhar reuthfull Eneas
> Amyd the starnys chosyn hass his place.
>
> (XIII.xi.74–6)

Douglas lays claim to an apotheosis in the stars, just like that of Aeneas.

He also uses the language of military victory, which again suggests an
analogy with what Aeneas achieved. The imagery of the final lines, where
Douglas fixes his "pen and instruments full yor / On Virgil's post", associates
the act of translation with Aeneas' victory over Turnus in Book 12, and
especially with Aeneas' hanging up of his arms in Book 3. The pen is the
weapon Douglas has used to meet the challenge posed by the *Aeneid*, and
he has won a permanent triumph.

Douglas invites a further analogy between his own work and the story
of Aeneas, in yet another epilogue or conclusion. He invokes the image of
a dangerous sea voyage, to describe the act of translation – a voyage which,
as he tells potential detractors, is at last complete. Douglas has achieved
something which will benefit his people, especially those without Latin,

---

[33] Coldwell, *Virgil's Aeneid, translated by Gavin Douglas*, vol. IV, p. 187.
[34] See Parkinson, "Orpheus and the translator."

for years to come. Guided by God, he has brought his ship through the storm, and performed a great act of public benefit. The simile invites a comparison between the process of translation, and the process of *translatio imperii*: Douglas has, like Aeneas, carried a precious cargo through stormy seas, and brought it to a new homeland. The work of translation becomes associated with the struggles of Aeneas to reach Italy.

But for Aeneas, the arrival in Italy is not the end of the journey. Douglas is also aware on some level that the fortunes of his book are not necessarily over. He has not one, but four separate conclusions at the end of Book 13 – an obvious mark of anxiety about whether his work really is finished. Douglas has his own kind of difficulty about ending the *Aeneid*. He knows that the process of interpretation and even translation of Virgil has not ended with his own work. People may still criticize what he has done; some may say that he has misinterpreted Virgil, in this place or the other. They will crow over his mistakes, saying, "Lo, heir he failȝeis, se thar he leys, luyk!"[35] Douglas' response is a further challenge: those who think they can do better are welcome to try. Douglas knows that the founding of the first British *Aeneid* is not the end of the story of translation. But he rightly demands respect for what he has accomplished, in making Virgil available for the first time in the "wlgar tong" of the British Isles.

Is the *Eneados* by Douglas, or is it by Virgil? The second may seem at first like the more modest claim, but in a way, it is even more ambitious. It is a mark of Douglas' achievement that he manages to obscure the difference between his own work and that of Virgil, and to see in the *Aeneid* a reflection of his own achievement as a translator. The translation of heroic epic is itself, Douglas suggests, a heroic enterprise.

I would like to end by sketching a few more general conclusions to be drawn from the study of Douglas' *Eneados*. This text provides a good example of the ways in which the translation of a classical text may be bound up with contemporary issues of national, political, and personal identity. Virgil's *Aeneid*, which has so often been seen as the most "classical" of classical texts,[36] can itself provide a lens through which to explore the position of modern writers and translators as they re-make antiquity for their own age. The *Eneados* illustrates the complexity of transferring classical literature to a post-classical culture – or cultures. It shows how the choice to translate a classical text may imply some kind of subservience to antiquity, but may also represent an attempt to gain new cultural authority

---

[35] Coldwell, *Virgil's Aeneid, Translated by Gavin Douglas*, vol. IV, p. 192.
[36] See Eliot, *What is a Classic?*; Kermode, *The Classic*.

for the vernacular, or to re-invent the vernacular itself for a newly defined readership. But it also shows that the story, for each text and for each writer, artist or thinker, is a personal one: poets and translators are not merely the representatives of their age. Rather, each act of recreation (or creation) of a classical text, within a new vernacular tradition and culture, is its own heroic accomplishment.

CHAPTER 8

Ovid's witchcraft

Gordon Braden

Ovid's influence on Shakespeare has been an active topic at least since Richard Farmer's *Essay on the Learning of Shakespeare* in 1767. Robert Kilburn Root made an attempt to treat the matter systematically and comprehensively in 1904; his conclusion that over 80 per cent of Shakespeare's very numerous references to classical mythology are specifically Ovidian in their provenance[1] still stands, and helped establish the study of Ovid's role in Shakespeare's creative process as a more or less permanent scholarly and critical franchise. A fresh and newly sophisticated round of activity in that franchise begins in the mid-1980s, with William Carroll's *The Metamorphoses of Shakespearean Comedy* (1985), the lengthy last chapter of Leonard Barkan's *The Gods Made Flesh* (1986), and various shorter publications; it culminates in a capstone work, Jonathan Bate's *Shakespeare and Ovid* (1993), which, like Barkan's book, remains in print. This work is marked by a desire to conceptualize "Ovidianism" at a new pitch of subtlety, to search for it in ways that go beyond more or less direct references to particular myths or imitations of particular passages. The results have been copious and impressive, and subtend some broader affirmations about Ovid's centrality to Shakespeare's imagination: "by reading Shakespeare's reading of Ovid we may come to a remarkably full . . . picture of the sort of artist that Shakespeare was."[2] That sort is a somewhat contrary humanist:

his sceptical, dynamic temperament would have had a certain resistance to the humanist implication that "the essential nature of human beings" does not change; what Ovid taught him was that everything changes . . . and this accorded with his desire as a dramatist to examine human beings at key moments of change in their lives, such as when they fall in love or make a renunciation or, most drastically, decide to kill themselves. Ovid's philosophy of instability modified the "essentialist" premiss of humanism even as his exemplary force sustained it.[3]

---

[1] Root, *Classical Mythology in Shakespeare*, p. 3. [2] Bate, *Shakespeare and Ovid*, p. vii.
[3] Bate, *Shakespeare and Ovid*, p. 6.

Such claims have been welcome ones, and Bate's discussion and its kin have found widespread acceptance. There are nevertheless risks with the approach, as Bate himself is clear-headed enough to acknowledge even as he defends his method. He is careful to call many of the connections that he makes "affinities" rather than, say, "allusions":

Allusion and affinity may, but do not necessarily, coexist: an allusion may signal a more far-reaching correspondence, but it may be merely incidental or ornamental; an affinity may be made apparent on the surface of the text, but it may operate at the level of the imagination . . . Paradoxically, the most profound affinities may be the least demonstrable precisely because they go deeper than the explicit local parallel.[4]

Bate goes on to admit, engagingly, "The problem with affinities is that if you're looking for them they're easy to find, but if you're not they cease to exist." It is hard to know where to draw the line, or whether there is a line to be drawn. Ovid's big idea can certainly become too big to mean anything in particular; as John Velz puts it, stating the more or less obvious, "The risk of an analysis of 'metamorphosis' in Shakespeare is that one may be tempted to discuss changes that are not really matters of morphosis. Since all traditional drama is about change through action . . . the net catches everything in the action, making metamorphosis mean too much and (*ergo*) too little."[5] Bate's book has been the object of a particular critique by Charles Martindale, who finds its purportedly historicist methodology "open to challenge," is unpersuaded by some of the individual readings, and thinks that Bate "tends to foreground sameness (partly from a 'humanist' belief in the continuity of human nature and concerns)," whereas "what we need now is an alternative analysis that *rigorously* foregrounds difference."[6] Martindale gestures toward a "very different" picture from Bate's: "Bate sees Shakespeare as consistently sceptical and 'Ovidian' (as Ovid is now seen), imitating Ovid in a consistent manner . . . My story was, and remains, that the relationship between Shakespeare and his sources is always more discontinuous and opportunistic than that."[7]

Put it that way, and my sympathies, methodologically speaking, would be with Martindale, but I am not really convinced by the line of distinction that he is trying to draw; I think the rhetoric of academic disputation exaggerates the distance between his and Bate's respective views on the

---

[4] Bate, *Shakespeare and Ovid*, p. 190.
[5] Velz, "Shakespeare's Ovid in the twentieth century," p. 190.
[6] Martindale, "Shakespeare's Ovid, Ovid's Shakespeare," pp. 199, 210.
[7] Martindale, "Shakespeare's Ovid, Ovid's Shakespeare," p. 211.

subject at hand. Martindale's own narrative of Shakespeare's commerce with Ovid's big poem takes some curves, but its destination is comparable to Bate's:

My view is that [Shakespeare's] sense of [the *Metamorphoses*] deepened and changed as he grew – though maybe that is another way of saying that three of his late plays, *Cymbeline*, *A Winter's Tale*, and *The Tempest*, construct what is, from my perspective, a peculiarly rich "Ovid." Many of the earlier plays are lavishly decked out with Ovidian mythological references in Meres' sweet witty style. In the great tragedies Ovid goes underground, though traces may remain. In general in the three romances there is less superficial Ovidianism, but the plays can be read *inter alia* as profound meditations on the character of Ovid's greatest poem.[8]

Martindale himself is interested in getting beyond the "superficial Ovidianism" of explicit reference and borrowing, and, indeed, in the end is willing to ignore its relative absence in a desire to affirm a profound merger of these two literary imaginations. His Shakespeare just takes longer to get there than Bate's.

I want to make my own argument about the centrality of Ovid to Shakespeare's work, and about the underappreciated inclusiveness of that debt: with due awareness of the dangers of overstating the case, though the conclusion I come to is in its way extreme and by no means commonsensical. Any serious attempt to decenter Ovid within the Shakespearean cosmos would need to get around some important pieces of evidence, and I want to focus on one of the best known. What Bate accurately calls "Shakespeare's most sustained Ovidian borrowing"[9] also has a uniquely resonant placement in Shakespeare's last great play, which itself has great summarizing force within his work as a whole. At the beginning of the last act of *The Tempest*, Prospero enters "*in his Magicke robes*" and readies himself for the last phase of his great plan for regaining his dukedom from his enemies and securing his daughter's place as the future queen of Naples; when alone on stage, he "*drawes a circle with his staffe*" and speaks:

> Ye Elves of hils, brooks, standing lakes & groves,
> And ye, that on the sands with printlesse foote
> Doe chase the ebbing-*Neptune*, and doe flie him
> When he comes backe: you demy-Puppets, that
> By Moone-shine doe the greene sowre Ringlets make,
> Whereof the Ewe not bites: and you, whose pastime
> Is to make midnight-Mushrumps, that rejoyce
> To heare the solemne Curfewe...
>
> (5.1.33–40 original emphasis)

---

[8] Martindale, "Shakespeare's Ovid, Ovid's Shakespeare," p. 212.
[9] Bate, *Shakespeare and Ovid*, p. 249.

Playful miniature agents from the natural world, only faintly mischievous, much like the lower-ranking fairies in *A Midsummer Night's Dream* – but their power can be incongruously great and fearsome:

> by whose ayde
> (Weake Masters though ye be) I have bedymn'd
> The Noone-tide Sun, call'd forth the mutenous windes,
> And twixt the greene Sea, and the azur'd vault
> Set roaring warre: To the dread ratling Thunder
> Have I given fire, and rifted *Joves* stowt Oke
> With his owne Bolt: The strong bass'd promontorie
> Have I made shake, and by the spurs pluckt up
> The Pyne, and Cedar. Graves at my command
> Have wak'd their sleepers, op'd, and let 'em forth
> By my so potent Art.   (40–50 original emphasis)

Building to one of the darkest of arts, the speech becomes a boast and a threat – though at just that point, it takes the turn that defines Prospero's character and the course of the play:

> But this rough Magicke
> I heere abjure: and when I have requir'd
> Some heavenly Musicke (which even now I do)
> To worke mine end upon their Sences, that
> This Ayrie-charme is for, I'le breake my staffe,
> Bury it certaine fadomes in the earth,
> And deeper then did ever Plummet sound
> Ile drowne my booke.   (50–7)

The long-planned perfection of Prospero's power is also, and by intention, the moment at which he will divest himself of it. He has stated his wish, against a good deal of human and theatrical convention, not to take revenge on his enemies once they are in his power: "with my nobler reason, gainst my furie / Doe I take part: the rarer Action is / In vertue, then in vengeance" (26–8). Exercising that virtue is simultaneous with a renunciation of his supernatural authority and a return to mortal weakness; afterwards, "Every third thought shall be my grave" (314).

    The opening line and middle section of Prospero's soliloquy are taken, at points with great specificity, from Ovid (*Metamorphoses* 7.197–209). We are also at this point in the presence of some of the strongest evidence of Shakespeare's interest in Arthur Golding's fourteener translation of the *Metamorphoses*,[10] completed in time for sufficiently prescient parents to have given Shakespeare a copy of it for his third birthday:

---

[10] Golding, *Shakespeare's Ovid*.

> ye Elves of Hilles, of Brookes, of Woods alone,
> Of standing Lakes, and of the Night approche ye everychone.
> Through helpe of whom (the crooked bankes much wondring at the thing)
> I have compelled streames to run cleane backward to their spring.
> By charmes I make the calme Seas rough, and make the rough Seas plaine
> And cover all the Skie with Cloudes, and chase them thence againe.
> By charmes I rayse and lay the windes, and burst the Vipers jaw,
> And from the bowels of the Earth both stones and trees doe drawe.
> Whole woods and Forestes I remove: I make the Mountaines shake,
> And even the Earth it selfe to grone and fearfully to quake.
> I call up dead men from their graves: and thee O lightsome Moone
> I darken oft, though beaten brasse abate thy perill soone.
> Our Sorcerie dimmes the Morning faire, and darkes the Sun at Noone.
>   (Golding 7.265–77)

Golding's translation of *di* as "Elves" fits the un-Ovidian tone for the first part of Prospero's speech, and "this rough Magicke" seems to owe its famous adjective to its double appearance in a line of Golding. This passage was the occasion of one of the first bits of Shakespearean *Quellenforschung* to be publicly announced, brandished by Farmer as proof that Shakespeare did not read his classics in the original.[11] In fact, as later scholars have been prompt to note,[12] there are places where Golding is not in the loop – he turns Ovid's *robora* into generic "trees," but Prospero specifically speaks of assaulting "*Joves* stowt Oke" – and the passage is actually one of the strongest and most economical demonstrations of what we now take to be the case, Shakespeare's recourse to both Ovid's Latin and his English intermediary.

The confluence of texts here has been the object of a number of recent discussions, all of them appreciative of its special resonance. As Barkan points out, there are not many books on the prop lists for Shakespeare's plays;[13] in three of the cases that do occur, the object in question is identifiably a text of Ovid, and it is all but impossible to resist the implication that Prospero's fabulous book, the font of his power, is on some level of implication – certainly the level on which the character grades into the playwright who creates him and whose first published work carried two lines of Ovid's Latin on the title page – a copy of the *Metamorphoses*.[14] The farewells of *The Tempest* are among other things a farewell to that poem and its author.

---

[11] Farmer, *An Essay on the Learning of Shakespeare*, pp. 54–5.
[12] Baldwin, *William Shakspere's Small Latine and Lesse Greeke*, vol. II, pp. 443–551.
[13] Barkan, *The Gods Made Flesh*, p. 243.
[14] Barkan, *The Gods Made Flesh*, p. 288; Brown, *The Metamorphosis of Ovid from Chaucer to Ted Hughes*, p. 84; Lyne, "Ovid, Golding, and the 'Rough Magic' of *The Tempest*," p. 161.

The Ovidian passage that Prospero quotes is in its original context not a farewell. It is from Medea's summoning of her own magic powers to rejuvenate Jason's aged father Aeson. That rejuvenation is successful – the last we hear of Aeson, he is delighted at the disappearance of 40 years – but it is also the setup for the first of Medea's great crimes, when she tricks the daughters of Pelias into murdering their own father; and her whole shocking career is in her own awareness one of the wrong end knowingly and perversely pursued: *uideo meliora proboque, / deteriora sequor* (*Metamorphoses* 7.20–1; "I see and approve the better, I follow the worse"). That moral self-arraignment on her part, with its uncanny echo of Saint Paul (Romans 7:15), resonated strongly in Renaissance literature,[15] and her incantation was repeatedly cited in connection with black magic.[16] Cornelius Agrippa quotes nine lines of the incantation in his compendious *De Occulta Philosophia* (1533), in the context of numerous citations of Ovid, from almost all of his extant works. Agrippa's attention to Ovid is mirrored in more pointed form in England by Reginald Scot's *Discoverie of Witchcraft* (1584). Scot adverts to the incantation no fewer than five times, in one case quoting several lines of it in Latin and in verse translation (presumably his own), and cites Ovid's other works with a range comparable to Agrippa's; Scot indeed, in a work predictably rich in biblical references, finds Ovid perhaps the prime classical source to cite (the fullest study of the connection is Fox).[17] Such interest suggests, among other things, a distinctive perspective on Ovid's *oeuvre* as a whole. What if we thought of him as the great poet of witchcraft?

The invitation is particularly worth entertaining because of Scot's availability to Shakespeare. Two different, more familiar versions of Ovid figured significantly in the late sixteenth century. Golding's translation came packaged as an updated *Ovide moralisé*, with two prefatory poems giving instructions on how to read the stories as "pithye, apt and pleyne / Instructions which import the prayse of vertues, and the shame / Of vices, with the due rewardes of eyther of the same" (ll.64–6 in Golding's *Epistle to the Earl of Leicester* [*Shakespeare's Ovid*, p. 2]). Nothing is said of Ovid's exile; parallels between the Promethean creation of man and Genesis even suggest that Ovid "perchaunce" had read the Bible. In the 1590s the first English translation of the *Amores*, by fellow playwright Christopher

---

[15] Braden, "Shakespeare's Petrarchism," pp. 177–8.
[16] Carroll, *The Metamorphoses of Shakespearean Comedy*, pp. 237–8, Bate, *Shakespeare and Ovid*, pp. 252–4; to the references given by Carroll, add Bodin, *Colloquium Heptaplomeres de Rerum Sublimium Arcanis Abditis*, p. 18.
[17] Fox, "Authorizing the metamorphic witch."

Marlowe, foregrounded an immoral Ovid, the shameless poet of sexual license, and this would seem to be his main reputation in the theatrical world; both George Chapman and Ben Jonson compose new personations of him (in *Ovid's Banquet of Sense* [1595] and *Poetaster* [1601] respectively) as the supposed lover of the Emperor's daughter Julia, an indiscretion generally supposed to have been the cause of his banishment. Scot evinces no concern with Ovid's personal life, but otherwise offers what can be considered a more complete image of Ovid's interests, though also one that links him to another and potentially more serious kind of disreputability. Beyond Medea's overt practice of pharmaceutical magic, the main prompt for Ovid's presence in a book on witchcraft is the great theme of his great poem; all those transformations of human beings into other forms match many of the stories told of what witches do with their devilish powers. But Scot's rubric also takes in the erotic. Medea's story itself is of course one of unmastered sexual passion on her part; Scot goes to the *Ars Amatoria* and *Remedia Amoris* for passages about love charms and poisons, and includes in his discussion the "naturall witchcraft for love," whereby "fascination or witchcraft" can "be brought to passe or provoked by the desire, by the wishing and coveting of anie beautifull shape or favor."[18] Antiquity, where the category "witchcraft" did not have the same contours or urgency that it does for Scot, would not have readily seen Ovid this way; a recent scholarly collection of Greek and Roman texts on magic[19] barely mentions Ovid, and finds no occasion to quote him. But within the culture of early modern Europe the notion of Ovid as the poet of witchcraft could acquire real cogency; and as a possible key to what Ovid might have meant for Shakespeare it has the advantage of being – unlike anti-essentialist humanism – a term that Shakespeare himself would have known and used. Certainly, the equation of sexual desire and black magic was a ready part of his repertoire: "You have Witch-craft in your Lippes" (*Henry V* 5.2.274).

As a take on Ovid, that is not an implausible one, and this is arguably one of those cases where a changing cultural context makes it possible to see something in an author that would not have been visible to his contemporaries, or at least not have seemed as significant as it later would. The most interesting thing about Scot's book, however, is not its view of Ovid but its perspective on witchcraft generally. His title makes modern readers expect a witch-hunting manual, but that is exactly not what it is; instead it is a rare and bracing polemic against the deluded and destructive belief in the dark arts. What Scot "discovers" about witchcraft is that it

---

[18] Scot, *The Discoverie of Witchcraft*, p. 407.   [19] Luck, *Arcana Mundi*.

by and large does not exist, and witch-hunting is an ugly fraud. His book is one of the targets of attack in King James' *Daemonologie*, where Scot is denounced as one who "is not ashamed in publike print to deny that ther can be such a thing as Witch-craft: and so mainteines the old error of the Sadducees, in denying of spirits."[20] Scot himself is not actually attacking Ovid; Ovid is at one point congratulated on his skepticism about erotic pharmaceuticals, and in any case is just doing what poets do. The outrage is directed at malignly gullible readers, especially Scot's main target among his contemporaries, Jean Bodin, whose *Démonomanie* had been published in 1580: "least some poets fables might be thought lies (whereby the witchmongers arguments should quaile) he maintaineth for true the most part of *Ovids Metamorphôsis*, and the greatest absurdities and impossibilities in all that booke."[21] Scot twice quotes with approval from the so-called *Canon Episcopi*, an early medieval church document (probably from the ninth century) which aligns such credulousness with heresy: "Whosoever beleeveth, that anie creature can be made or changed into better or woorsse, or transformed into anie other shape, or into anie other similitude, by anie other than by God himselfe the creator of all things, without all doubt is an infidell, and woorsse than a pagan."[22] Such was the official church position until the fourteenth century; the Inquisition was not given jurisdiction in accusations of witchcraft until 1398. Scot regards the whole business of witch-hunting as yet another instance of the papist corruption of the church in its latter days.

The principal evidence for Shakespeare's familiarity with Scot's book relates to *A Midsummer Night's Dream*; Scot presents some of the lore about Robin Goodfellow, and tells the Apuleian story about a man changed into an ass. Shakespeare could of course have gotten both from other sources, and the evidence is not decisive; but the connection once proposed ramifies in significant ways. Scot's attitude toward his topic is given a less angry representation in Shakespeare's play in the words of Theseus: "I never may beleeve / These antique fables, nor these Fairy toyes" (5.1.2–3) – this in what is by common consent Shakespeare's most overtly Ovidian play, indeed "the most magical tribute that Ovid was ever paid."[23] The audience is not in the best position to endorse Theseus' rationality; two acts earlier it witnessed a literal (if not total) human-to-animal transformation – the only one in a Shakespearean play. But the play's concluding speech invites us to imagine

[20] James VI, *Daemonologie*, [A]2ʳ. [21] Scot, *The Discoverie of Witchcraft*, p. 92.
[22] Scot, *The Discoverie of Witchcraft*, p. 97; for a modern translation of the whole text, see Kors and Peters, *Witchcraft in Europe 400–1700*, pp. 60–3.
[23] Rudd, "Pyramus and Thisbe in Shakespeare and Ovid," p. 125.

that none of what we thought we saw was, as they say, real – "this weake and idle theame, / No more yielding than a dreame" (Epilogue 5–6) – and Richard Strier has compellingly argued that Shakespeare's perspective here is ultimately to be identified with Scot's.[24] Scot's acerbic unbelief is in any case worth recalling when we come to Prospero's commerce with Medea's witchcraft in *The Tempest*.

The question of how black Prospero's magic is has been something of a crux in the critical tradition. Frank Kermode insisted that it is not black at all;[25] a more recent willingness to detect menace wherever possible has tended at the very least to stress the dark potential of the powers that Prospero commands. A certain amount hinges on how far we pursue the allusion to Medea. Bate characteristically takes it very seriously; the allusion specifically motivates the abjuration with which Prospero's speech ends: his magic "must be rejected because it is, for all its apparent whiteness, the selfsame black magic as that of Medea."[26] This in turn is a point on which Charles Martindale, writing in collaboration with Michelle Martindale, thinks that invoking the original context would be to consider too curiously: "In this instance it should be plain that the use Shakespeare is making of Ovid is imitative, not allusive."[27] Yet this very demur is immediately followed by an affirmation – "educated members of the audience would recognize the presence of Ovid" – that gestures toward another path to the same end: Medea is to Prospero as Medea's author is to Prospero's author.

The tradition of seeing in Prospero an unusually direct Shakespearean self-portrait and valedictory comment on his whole career is almost two centuries old. It continues to annoy scholars, but not all scholars, and shows no signs of going away. To the specific tradition of seeing Prospero's book as a book of Ovid, and his drowning of that book as a comment on nearly a lifetime's involvement with that author, I have perhaps two things to add. One is that the abjuration of magic is also at work in the play's handling of the everyday genre of witchcraft of which Ovid wrote so memorably and influentially. The love story of Miranda and Ferdinand is part of Prospero's great plan, but his nurturing of it comes with a jarring fear that their desire will break its legal bounds. He threatens Ferdinand with a heart-stopping curse on their marriage if that happens:

[24] Strier, *Shakespeare and the Skeptics*, pp. 176–80.   [25] Kermode (ed.), *The Tempest*, p. 149.
[26] Bate, *Shakespeare and Ovid*, p. 252.
[27] Martindale and Martindale, *Shakespeare and the Uses of Antiquity*, p. 23.

> If thou do'st breake her Virgin-knot, before
> All sanctimonious ceremonies may
> With full and holy right, be ministred,
> No sweet aspersion shall the heavens let fall
> To make this contract grow; but barraine hate,
> Sower-ey'd disdaine, and discord shall bestrew
> The union of your bed, with weedes so loathly
> That you shall hate it both.   (4.1.15–22)

Prospero then proceeds to stage a wedding masque whose main plot point is the absence of Venus and Cupid, who meant "to have done / Some wanton charme, upon this Man and Maide" (94–5). This is not to be a sexless marriage, obviously, since progeny are to be expected, but Prospero does seem to want one in which sexual excitement is to be sharply disciplined. The dangers of fleshly lust make an Ovidian pair with those of black magic, and both require severe restraint. Yet moral righteousness is not the only intonation in Prospero's pronouncements, and it is not I think ultimately the dominant one. It is quickly trumped when the wedding masque itself is interrupted for Prospero's most famous speech. It is a speech about the dispersing of illusion – initially the illusion of theatrical performance, but expanding as he talks to include "the great Globe it selfe, / Yea, all which it inherit" (153–4). He is beset, as Borges has it in "Everything and Nothing,"[28] with "the tedium and the terror" of having so long inhabited a "controlled hallucination": "we are such stuffe / As dreames are made on, and our little life / Is rounded with a sleepe: Sir, I am vext, / Beare with my weakenesse, my old braine is troubled" (156–9). Alongside anxieties about the morality of his magic is the simpler thing about it that so upset Scot: it is a fraud, it does not really exist outside of the confidence game of which it is part. For Scot that confidence game is papistry; for Shakespeare it is his life's work. In the twin valedictions to Ovid and the theater he takes his leave of overwhelming unrealities that used to look like everything.

[28] Borges, *Labyrinths*, p. 249.

CHAPTER 9

The streets of Rome: the classical Dylan

Richard F. Thomas

Immature poets imitate; mature poets steal; bad poets deface what they take, and good poets make it into something better, or at least something different. The good poet welds his theft into a whole of feeling which is unique, utterly different from that from which it is torn; the bad poet throws it into something which has no cohesion. A good poet will usually borrow from authors remote in time, or alien in language, or diverse in interest.

T. S. Eliot, from "Philip Massinger" (1920)

TAMING THE PROUD: THE CASE OF VIRGIL

For those of us – and there are a few of us in my neck of the woods – interested in the Roman poet Virgil and in the art of Bob Dylan, the strange days that followed September 11, 2001 were particularly memorable. Dylan's two-year stint in the Hibbing High Latin Club was at that point unknown to me. In the summer of 2005 a trip to the Seattle Music Experience revealed his early interest, set out on the page of the Hibbing High School yearbook, the Hematite, as it is called. The page is also featured in Scorsese's *No Direction Home*. But even on the first time through *"Love and Theft"*, even before we had noted the quotes around the title that drew attention to the theft of Eric Lott's title, before we had been handed the snippets of *Confessions of a Yakuza*, transformed into Appalachian and other vignettes, there was Virgil, loud and clear, in the tenth verse of "Lonesome Day Blues" (itself a Blind Willie McTell title):

"Lonesome Day Blues": I'm gonna spare the defeated – I'm gonna speak to the crowd / I'm gonna spare the defeated, boys, I'm going to speak to the crowd / I am goin' to teach peace to the conquered / I'm gonna tame the proud

This chapter is a revised and occasionally augmented version of Mason and Thomas (eds.), *The Performance Tradition of Bob Dylan*, 30–56.

Virgil, *Aeneid* 6.851–3 (trans. Mandelbaum): but yours will be the rulership of nations, / remember Roman, these will be your arts: / to teach the ways of peace to those you conquer, / to spare defeated peoples, tame the proud.

Teaching peace, sparing the defeated and taming the proud. Too much precision there for accident, even without the album's title or Junichi Saga's presence. Now Virgil's Latin is close to the translation I give, but Latin it is, with the three Roman arts spread over a line and a half:

> *tu regere imperio populos, Romane, memento*
> *(hae tibi erunt artes) pacique imponere morem*
> *parcere subiectis et debellare superbos.*

The Latin in fact has four Roman qualities: "to rule over people with empire, to institute law in addition to peace, to spare the subjected, and to war down the proud." If I had given that translation, and it is more "faithful" to the Latin though less poetically put, there might be doubt as to whether Dylan was alluding at all. But that is the point: Dylan's intertext is not the Latin of Virgil – though Hibbing High's Robert Zimmerman may possibly have gotten far enough in his Latin to have read some Virgil back then. Rather, Dylan read, as I have given it, the 1971 English translation of Allen Mandelbaum,[1] the best contemporary translation until 2005, when Stanley Lombardo's excellent new version arrived on the field.[2]

The cover of Lombardo's *Aeneid* translation shows a section of the Vietnam Veterans Memorial Wall, fragments of names of those killed in the war. This reflects recent readings of Virgil's poem that see it as, among other things, a questioning of the worth of the imperial enterprise. Already, Mandelbaum's 1970 preface let the wrongs of that war into the Roman world of the Virgil he was translating:

And place, which for me at least had always been the last mode through which I heard a poet, after twelve years lived in the landscapes of Virgil, finally began, even as I was leaving Italy, to reinforce the voice of Virgil. That happened to me at a time of much personal discontent. I had long contemned any use of the poetic word for purposes of consolation. But pride lessens with the years, and Virgil consoled. The years of my work on this translation have widened that personal discontent; this state (no longer, with the Vietnam war, that innocuous word "society") has wrought the unthinkable, the abominable. Virgil is not free of the taint of the proconsular; but he speaks from a time of peace achieved, and no man ever felt more deeply the part of the defeated and the lost. (p. xiv)

---

[1] Mandelbaum, *The Aeneid of Virgil.*
[2] The Virgil quote has been noted by many blogs. Østrem, "A day above ground is a good day," cites Mandelbaum's translation without comment.

Mandelbaum's preface also quotes (p. xii) the lines Dylan used, and that context – connecting Roman war to American – may explain how Dylan saw the uses of the Virgilian text.

What does it *mean* that Dylan incorporated these lines from a 2000-year-old poem into his 2001 song? That depends on the reader. For me the verse activates the Roman poet's conflict about empire: Aeneas fails to live up to his father's urging that he tame the proud but spare the defeated, when at the end of the *Aeneid* he kills his wounded and suppliant enemy. Further, the war in "Lonesome Day Blues" becomes – again, for me – not just the war of the *Aeneid*'s mythological frame, set 1000 years before Virgil's time, but also the Roman civil wars, and the wars against Antony and others on which the empire of Augustus would be founded. Before the intertext emerges and as long as the singer of Dylan's song seems to belong in the time of Robert Zimmerman, the war that has brought desolation to the singer is most naturally the Vietnam War, the defining war of ethically failed imperial aspiration of the last century. The two contexts – Rome and America – merge and make the song about no war and every war, as happens so often with time and place generally in Dylan.

But this doubling of the temporal frame is of course too simple, once we add the ingredient of Junichi Saga's *Confessions of a Yakuza*, from which Dylan disperses some twelve undeniable passages across five songs, including two in "Lonesome Day Blues":[3]

"Lonesome Day Blues": Samantha Brown lived in my house for about four or five months. / Don't know how it looked to other people, I never slept with her even once.

Confessions of a Yakuza, p. 208: Just because she was in the same house didn't mean we were living together as man and wife, so it wasn't any business of mine what she did. I don't know how it looked to other people, but I never even slept with her – not once.

"Lonesome Day Blues": Well my captain he's decorated – he's well schooled and he's skilled / My captain, he's decorated – he's well schooled and he's skilled / He's not sentimental – don't bother him at all / How many of his pals have been killed.

Confessions of a Yakuza, p. 243: There was nothing sentimental about him – it didn't bother him at all that some of his pals had been killed. He said he'd been given any number of decorations, and I expect it was true.

It is not difficult to see the appeal of Saga's work, which blurs the genres of novel and biography, fiction and non-fiction, and whose narrative

---

[3] The "theft" was first noted in *The Wall Street Journal*, on July 8, 2003.

complexity and shifts, along with its lively use of colloquial language (at least in John Bester's translation), clearly appealed to Dylan's literary sensibility. *Confessions* recounts the life of an early to mid-twentieth-century gangster, Ijichi Eiji (born 1904), narrated in his own voice but as "quoted" by the novelist Saga who portrays himself as the late twentieth-century doctor of the dying Eiji. The two passages in question come from late in the novel. The first (p. 208) has to do with Osei (= Samantha Brown) whose stay with Eiji happened during World War II, soon before the American defeat of Japan's "imperial empire," to quote from "Honest With Me," another song that would quote from *Confessions*. The second (p. 243) comes from Eiji's final narrative chapter, as he recollects Osei turning up in 1951 (p. 238): "The Korean War was going strong, and my new gambling place in Tokyo was doing really well" – why does this sound so much like a line from "Brownsville Girl" or some other Dylan narrative? The unsentimental source for Dylan's decorated captain is one Nagano Seiji, encountered while Eiji is in prison, and a man who had sliced off a fellow prisoner's arm. The pals whose death didn't bother him were the about-to-be arch-enemies of the clearly American singer of "Lonesome Day Blues," Japanese soldiers who died in the Chinese–Japanese War (1937–1945).

So the war that is the backdrop of "Lonesome Day Blues" ("Well, my pa he died and left me, my brother got killed in the war") is further and utterly mystified, but not finally so. Eyolf Østrem notes Dylan's use of two passages (uncovered by "Nick") from Twain's *The Adventures of Huckleberry Finn*:[4]

"Lonesome Day Blues": My sister, she ran off and got married / Never was heard of any more.

Huck Finn (ch. 17): . . . and my sister Mary Ann run off and got married and never was heard of no more . . .

"Lonesome Day Blues": Last night the wind was whisperin', I was trying to make out what it was / Last night the wind was whisperin' somethin' – I / was trying to make out what it was / I tell myself something's comin' / But it never does

Huck Finn (ch. 1): I felt so lonesome I most wished I was dead. The stars was shining, and the leaves rustled in the woods ever so mournful; . . . and the wind was trying to whisper something to me and I couldn't make out what it was.

The first of these quotes comes from the Grangerford-Shepherdson episode of the novel, which has itself been seen as Twain's metaphor for the broader

----

4 http://dylanchords.nfshost.com/41_lat/lonesome_day_blues.htm.

Civil War. It is also noteworthy that the tale Huck is here spinning is just that, a fiction. If Dylan's Twain reference complicates our identification of the singer's "my brother got killed in the war," making us move from Vietnam back to the American Civil War, the Virgilian lines which immediately follow the reworking of *Huck Finn* force us back even further, to the wars of Virgil's youth, the civil wars that tore the Roman republic apart and led to the establishment of the Roman empire, the paradigmatic empire of the West. The singer is an American from the twentieth century ("I'm forty miles from the mill – I'm droppin' it into overdrive"), but he is also Aeneas, also the Japanese warrior speaking within the narrative of a 1989 Japanese gangster, and, perhaps closest to home for Dylan/Zimmerman, he is Huck Finn. Dylan was wearing a Huck Finn hat before he became Dylan, more or less, but the creative renaissance that has been going on since *Time Out Of Mind* (and before it in terms of performance) has brought Twain's world into focus with Dylan's. Mississippi, Missouri, the river flooding or not, from its source in the Highlands, "Cold Irons" or North Country, north of Hibbing or north of anywhere and nowhere, down to New Orleans, a place that still defies identification other than as a place of loss and trouble – these have always been the places of Dylan's creative exploration, as they were of Twain's. US Route 61, "Highway 61," was how the blues came north, from its beginning in New Orleans to Duluth MN, city of Dylan's birth, and beyond.[5] As it follows the Mississippi it also passes through Hannibal MO, where Twain grew up.

Back to Virgil and the Classics. The examples of *Huck Finn* and *Confessions of a Yakuza* show that Dylan is quite freewheeling in his intertextuality, and is unbounded by song, or even by album in the case of *Time Out Of Mind*, "*Love and Theft*", and *Modern Times*, the third part of a trilogy. As with the voice of Ijichi Eiji, so that of Aeneas, and the Aeneas who will bring empire, spare the defeated and tame the proud, may legitimately be seen elsewhere in these songs. On December 22, 2001 *Rolling Stone* published Mikal Gilmore's post-"*Love and Theft*" interview of Dylan, who said, as the topic turned to the chronological range of the songs on his new album, "I mean, you're talking to a person that feels like he's walking around in the ruins of Pompeii all the time."[6] A little later he says of it

---

[5] See Gray, *The Bob Dylan Encyclopedia*, pp. 318–21 for the historical and cultural importance of US Route 61, and its significance for the 1964 album, *Highway 61 Revisited*.

[6] Cott, *Bob Dylan: The Essential Interviews*, p. 425. There are two other classical mentions in the interview, "Achilles heel," and "Socrates." Perhaps Dylan visited Pompeii the year before the interview (when the songs of the album will have been taking shape) on June 1, 2000, between concerts in Ancona (31 May) and Cagliari (2 June). In Cagliari, the songs were all old, the only post-1960s song being "Tangled Up In Blue," most of which is about the 1960s.

"The whole album deals with power...[T]he album deals with power, wealth, knowledge and salvation"; and then "It speaks in a noble language [including Latin perhaps?]. It speaks of the issues or the ideals of an age in some nation, and hopefully, it would also speak across the ages."[7] *Some nation?* That obviously includes imperial Rome and imperial Japan. If so, we can invoke not just the pure intertexts of Saga and Virgil, but other reflections as well. The ending of "Bye and Bye," whose lyrics suggest the interchangeability of time ("Well the future for me is already a thing of the past"), may also work for the world of Rome, the world in which Virgil saw Augustus, descendant of Aeneas in his own propaganda, turn republic into empire: "I'm gonna establish my rule through civil war / Gonna make you see just how loyal and true a man can be." And in "Honest With Me" empire comes up again: "I'm here to create the new imperial empire / I'm going to do whatever circumstances require." From Aeneas and Augustus to Bush, this works with any empire, with the issues of "some nation" "across the ages" as Dylan said of the album containing these allusions to Rome's epic poet.

INTO EXILE WITH OVID

One of the immediate classical resonances on *Modern Times* (2006) comes in the first song, "Thunder on the Mountain." Particularly in the wake of "Lonesome Day Blues" with its Virgilian intertext, the sixth verse of the new song pointed straight to Ovid, and his *Ars Amatoria*: "I've been sittin' down studyin' the art of love / I think it will fit me like a glove." But that was just the beginning. On October 10, 2006, Cliff Fell, a New Zealand poet and teacher of creative writing, wrote in the *Nelson Mail* (Nelson, New Zealand) of a striking discovery. He happened to be reading Peter Green's Penguin translation of Ovid's exile poetry, the *Tristia* and the *Epistulae ex Ponto* (*Black Sea Letters*), while listening to *Modern Times*:

and then this uncanny thing happened – it was like I was suddenly reading with my ears. I heard this line from the song "Workingman's Blues 2", "No-one can ever claim / That I took up arms against you." But there it was singing on the page, from Book 2.52 of *Tristia*: "My cause is better: no-one can claim that I ever took up arms against you."

Fell experienced what many of us experienced, though in an inverted way, when we heard in "Lonesome Day Blues" the familiar lines from *Aeneid* 6: as he read on in Ovid he came across further lines that were entering his consciousness from listening to *Modern Times*:

[7] Cott, *Bob Dylan: The Essential Interviews*, p. 426.

Bob Dylan, "Ain't Talkin'"	Ovid, *Black Sea Letters*, 2.7.66
Heart burnin', still yearnin' / In the last outback at the world's end.	I'm in the last outback, at the world's end.
Bob Dylan, "Workingman's Blues #2"	Ovid, *Tristia*, 5.12.8
To lead me off in a cheerful dance.	or Niobe, bereaved, lead off some cheerful dance.
Bob Dylan, "Workingman's Blues #2"	Ovid, *Tristia*, 5.13.18
Tell me now, am I wrong in thinking / That you have forgotten me?	May the gods grant . . . /that I'm wrong in thinking you've forgotten me!
Bob Dylan, "Workingman's Blues #2"	Ovid, *Tristia*, 2.179:
My cruel weapons have been put on shelf/Come sit down on my knee/You are dearer to me than myself/As you yourself can see[8]	Show mercy, I beg you, shelve your cruel weapons.
	Ovid, *Tristia* 5.14.2
	wife, dearer to me than myself, you yourself can see.

I emailed Cliff Fell, who then mentioned our conversation, and the current article which I had mentioned to him, in a radio show that made it onto the best and most thorough Dylan website, expectingrain.com. This in turn led to an email to me from Scott Warmuth, Albuquerque DJ and Dylan aficionado, who had followed up on Fell's discovery and added further Ovidian intertexts:

Bob Dylan, "Ain't Talkin'"	Ovid, *Tristia* 1.3.24:
Every nook and cranny has its tears.	every nook and corner had its tears.
Bob Dylan, "Ain't Talkin'"	Ovid, *Tristia* 1.3.65:
all my loyal and my much-loved companions.	loyal and much loved companions, bonded in brotherhood.
Bob Dylan, "Ain't Talkin'"	Ovid, *Tristia* 1.3.68
I'll make the most of one last extra hour.	let me make the most of one last extra hour.
Bob Dylan, "The Levee's Gonna Break"	Ovid, *Tristia* 4.7.51
Some people got barely enough skin to cover their bones.	there's barely enough skin to cover my bones.
Bob Dylan, "Ain't Talkin'"	Ovid, *Tristia* 5.7.63–4
I practice a faith that's been long abandoned.	I practice / terms long abandoned.
Bob Dylan, "Ain't Talkin'"	Ovid, *Tristia* 5.7.66
They will tear your mind away from contemplation.	tear my mind from the contemplation of my woes.
Bob Dylan, "Ain't Talkin'"	Ovid, *Black Sea Letters* 3.2.38
They approve of me and share my code.	who approve, and share, your code.

---

[8] Dylan's brilliant conflation of two disparate Ovidian poems creates an exquisite verse, based on both intertexts, but achieving its own lyrical heights in ways that take the verse to a high literary and pathetic level.

At this point I ordered from amazon.com one of the two available used copies of Peter Green's out-of-print 1994 Penguin translation of Ovid's exile poems – it is currently back in print. I can now add the following further intertexts from my own reading:

Bob Dylan, "Ain't Talkin'":	Ovid, *Tristia* 1.2.12–13
Who says I can't get heavenly aid?	Who says *I* can't get heavenly aid when a god's angry with me? (original emphasis)
Bob Dylan, "Spirit on the Water":	Ovid, *Tristia* 5.1.80
I want to be with you any way I can.	I want to be with you any way I can.
Bob Dylan, "Ain't Talkin'"	Ovid, *Tristia* 5.8.3–5
They will jump on your misfortune when you're down.	Why jump / on misfortunes that you may well suffer yourself? / I'm down.
Bob Dylan, "Workingman's Blues #2"	Ovid, *Tristia* 5.12.19–20
Now the place is ringed with countless foes.	I'm barred from relaxation / in a place ringed by countless foes.
Bob Dylan, "Spirit on the Water":	Ovid, *Black Sea Letters* 2.4.24:
Can't believe these things would ever fade from your mind.	I cannot believe these things could fade from your mind.
Bob Dylan, "Workingman's Blues #2"	Ovid, *Black Sea Letters* 4.6.42–3
Them I will forget / But you I'll remember always.	*Them* I'll forget, / but *you* I'll remember always. (original emphasis)

There is much else on the album beyond these nineteen undeniable correspondences that shows Dylan identifying his singer with the exiled and aging Ovid. Where Ovid wrote (*Black Sea Letters* 4.9.95–6) "No man, no child, no woman has had grounds to complain on my account," Dylan followed with ("Workingman's Blues # 2") "No man, no woman knows / The hour that sorrow will come." And Ovid's (*Black Sea Letters* 4.14.7) "I don't give a damn about where I'm posted from this country" becomes in Dylan's "Thunder on the Mountain" "I don't give a damn about your dreams." And finally we have a sense from Dylan of marvel at the extent of the world, also of the debatability of its being round: "Ain't Talkin'": "The whole wide world which people say is round." The phrase "whole wide world" is common in Green's translation (*Tristia* 3.10.77, 4.8.38, 5.7.44, 5.8.24–5; *Black Sea Letters* 4.9.126). The culture and age behind Dylan's sentiment "the whole wide world which people say is round" points right to a world (third-century Greece and Rome following) that had proven, in theory and practice, but maybe didn't quite believe, that the world was indeed round.

Fell noted the appropriateness of the intertexts: Dylan, 65 years old, in the inner exile he has created for his own protection, invokes the Ovidian exile poetry, coming at the end of the career of Ovid. Indeed the last words of the last song, "Ain't Talking," and therefore the last words of the third album of the trilogy, suggest a finality, a closing of the book, and they are straight from Ovid (see above), as Dylan puts himself "in the last outback, at the world's end." At the same time it needs to be noted that Dylan's borrowings – or thefts – are all transposed into new situations which have little to do with, but evoke comparison with, those of the Ovidian models, the essence of creative intertextuality.

THE *LA REPUBBLICA* INTERVIEW

Dylan rarely gives interviews, but he tends to do so around the time of new releases. Soon before that fateful day, September 11, 2001, in fact three days before the release of *"Love and Theft"*, on 8 September, the Italian newspaper *La repubblica* published an Italian version of such an interview. The interview itself took place earlier in the year, in July of 2001. An English version of it (translated by David Flynn) turned up on the website expectingrain.com, where it was joined by an English translation of a Swedish summary, and other bits of furniture.[9] On May 22, 2006, two days before Dylan's 65th birthday, the actual interview, consisting of seven mp3 files, was posted on the website whitemanstew.com.[10] Where it had been all these years it is hard to say, and one has to conclude that the release was somehow deliberate.

Whether or not that is so, the interview shows that the Dylan of *"Love and Theft"* even without the evidence of "Lonesome Day Blues," had been thinking about Greek and Roman literature and his place in it. Already in "When I Paint My Masterpiece," which came out on *Bob Dylan's Greatest Hits, vol. 2* (1971), there was a turning back to those who came before: "Oh, the streets of Rome are filled with rubble, / Ancient footprints are everywhere." The song moves from the Colosseum, where Dylan imagines himself "Dodging lions and wastin' time," and goes back through time to a story he perhaps picked up in his Latin Club days: "Train wheels runnin' through the back of my memory, / When I ran on the hilltop following a pack of wild geese." The wild goose chase surely alludes to one of Rome's most famous myths of its early history, one of the scenes on Aeneas' shield in Book 8 of the *Aeneid*, that is the geese of Rome's Capitoline Hill, whose

---

[9] www.expectingrain.com/dok/cd/2001/loveandtheft.html.
[10] The website no longer exists. Quotes from the review are of my own transcriptions of the audio of the interview, which is not to be found in Cott, *Bob Dylan: The Essential Interviews*.

honking alerted the Romans to the invading Gauls. Thirty years later the Rome interview goes back to those days:

My songs [on *"Love and Theft"*] are all singable. They're current. Something doesn't have to just drop out of the air yesterday to be current. This is the Iron Age, you know we're living in the iron age. What was the last age, the age of bronze or something? You know we can still feel that age. We can still feel that age. I mean if you walk around in this city, people today can't build what you see out there. You know when you walk around a town like this, you know that people were here before you and they were probably on a much higher, grander level than any of us are. I mean it would just have to be. We couldn't conceive of building these kind of things. America doesn't really have stuff like this.

The "current" can be a long time before yesterday, as the Virgilian and Ovidian lines show. Dylan then deflected a question that might have taken the interview deeper. Asked whether he reads books on history, he responded "Not any more than would be natural to do." A similar deflection occurs a few minutes later when he is asked whether he is "still eagerly looking for poets that you may not have heard of or read yet?" The reply comes after a long pause: "You know I don't really study poetry." More importantly Dylan in this interview also shows he has become familiar with the major Greco-Roman metaphor of mythical–religious cultural change. At first sight it looks as if Dylan is simply including us in the actual Iron Age (following the various Stone Ages and Bronze Age) that began in Europe at the beginning of the first millennium BCE. But some minutes later in the discussion the subject comes up again, when he is asked about a reference he had made on the liner notes of *World Gone Wrong*:

Interviewer: In the same liner notes you talk about the new Dark Ages in the contemporary world.

Dylan: Well, the Stone Age, put it that way. We've talked about these ages before. You've got the Golden Age which I guess would be the Age of Homer, then we've got the Silver Age, then you've got the Bronze Age. I think you have the Heroic Age some place in there. Then we're living in what people call the Iron Age, but it could really be the Stone Age. We could be living in the Stone Ages.

Unfortunately none of the interviewers saw where he had been headed, or what he was really talking about, and one cracks a joke ("Maybe in the Silicone Ages?"), to which Dylan replies with a laugh "Exactly." And the topic shifts to the internet, the mask back on.

From a scientific point of view Homer (c. 750 BCE) in fact belongs to the Iron Age, while the Trojan War (c. 1200 BCE) belonged to the Bronze Age. The system Dylan refers to is not that one, however, but rather the myth of the ages found in Hesiod (c. 700 BCE), in whose poem the *Works and Days* (109–201) is our first record of the five ages of the world, seen from the perspective of the present, the debased Iron Age, as Dylan noted. The progression is as Dylan has it, from ideal Gold (Eden) through Silver then Bronze, with the Age of Heroes preceding the Iron Age. Hesiod puts the Trojan War in the Age of Heroes, doubtless motivated by the existence, in pre-publication form, of oral versions of the *Iliad* and *Odyssey*. Ovid has a version of it, without the Bronze Age, at the beginning of his *Metamorphoses*, "the scary horror tale, . . . next to the autobiography of Davy Crockett" in Ray Gooch's library, if we care to believe *Chronicles: Volume One* (p. 37), to which we soon turn.

Dylan's thinking about and use of classical texts and images seems to be somewhat recent, as compared for instance to his relationship with the Bible, which has been there from very early on. The idea of Eden and the fall, and his use of the story, make it likely that he would in his reading eventually encounter the Hesiodic version or some variant of it. "Gates of Eden" itself (from *Bringing It All Back Home*, 1965) seems devoid of anything classical, but "Changing of the Guards" (from *Street Legal* 1978) may be another matter. In an interview for *SongTalk* in 1991 Paul Zollo put it to Dylan:[11]

Your songs often bring us back to other times, and are filled with mythic, magical images. A song like "Changing Of The Guard" seems to take place centuries ago, with lines like "They shaved her head / she was torn between Jupiter and Apollo / a messenger arrived with a black nightingale . . . " How do you connect with a song like that?

Dylan pauses before replying, enigmatically, "A song like that, there's no way of knowing, after the fact, unless somebody's there to take it down in chronological order, what the motivation was behind it." And later "To me, it's old. [Laughs] It's old." In part it too is as old as Hesiod, where the cultural change away from Golden Age towards Iron is also figured at the divine level as the father-slaying that happens when the son Jupiter/Zeus takes over not from Apollo, but from Saturn/Kronos. We therefore have an intimation of that system, with the woman torn between the old and the new, with conflicting loyalties in the changing of the guard. As with the war of "Lonesome Day Blues" the cultural change is not quite that of Genesis (though "Eden is burning"), not quite that of Hesiod (though we have Greco-Roman gods), but quintessentially Dylan's own hybrid which

---

[11] See Cott, *Bob Dylan: The Essential Interviews*, p. 371.

embraces both and much else besides. Generally, then, Dylan's contact with Greece and Rome is a more recent phenomenon, though in his own creative fictions it is already a thing of the past, as we shall see.

What to make of this remarkable scene from the second chapter of Dylan's 2004 masterpiece *Chronicles: Volume One* (pp. 35–9)? "The Lost Land" suggests myth and fiction, a world outside of history, but one that in the setting of Dylan's "autobiography" is around 1961. Dylan is recently arrived in New York City, and staying at this moment with Ray Gooch and Chloe Kiel, a colorful couple whose reality has been suspected by some readers and reviewers. The description of the two on pp. 26–7 is virtuoso descriptive writing, not just of Ray, who "was like a character out of some of the songs I'd been singing" – or maybe memoirs he was writing? Dylan finds himself "looking for the part of my education that I never got," and so takes us on a tour of Ray's books. The reading he does is the reading we know he did at some stage, and presumably already in high school, "the poetry books, mostly. Byron and Shelley and Longfellow and Poe." It is the other books he seems to have just browsed rather than read: "I would have had to have been in a rest home or something in order to do that." Some he started, such as *The Sound and the Fury*: "didn't quite get it, but Faulkner was powerful." Of Albertus Magnus, St. Albert the Great, the German friar and encyclopedic writer from the thirteenth century, he says "Magnus seemed like a guy who couldn't sleep, writing this stuff late at night, clothes stuck to his clammy body." He adds, "a lot of these books were too big to read, like giant shoes fitted for large-footed people." Is Dylan letting his Latin in (*magnus* = big, large)?

However big the book of Magnus, "it was lightweight compared to Thucydides." The great Athenian historian of the Peloponnesian War seems to be at the peak of Dylan's Parnassus, receiving three mentions in two pages. Dylan gets the title of the work wrong (*The Athenian General*), not necessarily a mistake, but no matter, for he captures the relevance of the Greek historian (p. 36):

It was written four hundred years before Christ and it talks about how human nature is always the enemy of anything superior. Thucydides talks about how words in his time have changed from their ordinary meaning, how actions and opinions can be changed in the blink of an eye. It's like nothing has changed from his time to mine.

The Penguin translation of Rex Warner gives the following for one of the most famous passages of Thucydides' *History of the Peloponnesian War* (1.22):

It will be enough for me, however, if these words of mine are judged useful by those who want to understand clearly the events which happened in the past and which (human nature being what it is) will, at some time or other and in much the same ways, be repeated in the future. My work is not a piece of writing designed to meet the taste of an immediate public, but was done to last for ever.

Nothing has changed from Thucydides' time to mine, says Dylan. What is his time? Somewhere in 1961, if we can bring ourselves to imagine his book is straight autobiography. But the comment works better for 2004, when Dylan was writing the book and when many of us were connecting events of our present years, including imperial adventures, with similar events from classical antiquity. Not least of these is the Athenian expedition against Sicily (415–413 BCE). Thucydides' narrative "would give you the chills" says Dylan. Certainly some of us got the chills in 2003 when we recalled Thucydides 6.24, of the unwise decision of the Athenians to invade Sicily: "The result of this excessive enthusiasm of the majority was that the few who were opposed to the expedition were afraid of being thought unpatriotic if they voted against it, and therefore kept quiet."

Other classical works encountered in the "library" of Ray Gooch include "*The Twelve Caesars*" (presumably the work of Suetonius), "Tacitus lectures and letters to Brutus," "Pericles' *Ideal State of Democracy*," Ovid's *Metamorphoses*, "the scary horror tale," "Sophocles' book on the nature and function of the gods." It is curious that three of these are non-existent books, but in subtle ways: Tacitus wrote a dialogue about orators (including the long-dead Brutus, to whom Cicero wrote actual, surviving letters); Pericles, who *was* an Athenian general, wrote nothing that survives but looms large in Thucydides, whose work includes the general's famous funeral oration, which does treat the ideal state of Athenian democracy; Sophocles only wrote tragedies, but they are often about the nature and function of the gods. Dylan's style is exquisite in these pages, and we see his typical humor, as with the comment on "Magnus," in placing the *Metamorphoses* "next to the autobiography of Davy Crockett," or with Alexander the Great's strategy of having his men marry local women: "After that he never had any trouble with the population, no uprisings or anything." Gooch's library is like a Dylan album cover, with messages and intertexts. Davy Crockett matters. Mark Twain would have been too obvious, so put in another nineteenth-century purveyor of the Americana that is so central to Dylan, namely humorist Davy Crockett. Gooch's library is also like the creative essence of Dylan's mind, unfettered by catalogs or by order. Like the characters and scenes of "Like A Rolling Stone," "Desolation Row" or "Idiot Wind," the book-titles and what they evoke come at us in a stream of consciousness manner that goes to the heart of what Dylan is, not just what he may or may not have seen in an apartment in Greenwich Village a couple of light years ago.[12]

Even the non-classical books in Ray Gooch's library have connections to Latin and other foreign languages. Finally, Dylan says he read Graves' strange book, *The White Goddess*, now mostly a textbook for wiccans and pagans, and notes "Invoking the poetic muse was something I didn't know about yet" (p. 45). Invoking the muse puts Dylan into a relation with other texts, since for Virgil and others the Muses are the connectors to other traditions, and particularly in his later work, that is what Dylan is up to. The Muses are also slippery. When initiating Hesiod at the beginning of the *Theogony* (27–8) they tell the poet: "We know how to speak many false things that seem like the truth, but we also know, when we wish, how to sing the truth." On the threshold of Ray Gooch's classical library, that is pretty much the outlook of Dylan (p. 35): " If you told the truth, that was all well and good and if you told the untruth, well, that's still well and good."

AN ITALIAN POET FROM THE THIRTEENTH CENTURY

Like Dylan, Virgil was accused of plagiarism. There is an anecdote in Suetonius' *Life of Virgil* 46 on the poet's response to the critics' charge of plagiarizing Homer: "Why don't they try the same thefts? They'll find out it's easier to snatch Hercules' club from him than a single line from Homer." Dylan successfully stole three from Virgil, so fitting T. S. Eliot's definition

---

[12] This aspect of Dylan's surreal humor, consisting of absurdist juxtaposition, has become a trademark feature of his *Theme Time Radio Hour*, for instance in Episode 1.11, "Flowers," where he gives us the following: "Tonight we're going to be talking about the most beautiful things on earth, the fine-smelling, colorful, bee-tempting world of flowers, the Bougainvillea, the Passion Flower, the Butterfly Cleradendron, the Angel's Trumpets, the Firecracker plant, we're going to be talking about *Rosa rugosa*, the Angel Face, All that Jazz, the Double Delight, the Gemini [Dylan's zodiac sign] and the Julia Child, we're going to be talking about the Knockout Shrub, the New Dawn, the Mr. Lincoln – and that's only the roses – we're also going to hit on the Silver King, the German Statis, the Globe Thistle and the Joe Pie Weed, the Violet, the Daisy, the lovely Chrysanthemum, the Arrow and the Tansy, we'll be hitting on the Bachelor's Button, the Coxcomb and the Lion's Ear, the Love in the Mist and the Victoria Sorghum [laughs], – I just made that one up – we're going to be talking about Flowers, on Theme Time Radio Hour." The list has the rhythm of a poem, and in performance comes across as a talking blues of flower names.

in our opening epigraph, "immature poets imitate; mature poets steal."
Poems/songs that are layered with intertexts reveal depths of meaning
through our recognition of those texts as we import their contexts and
receive them in their working together new images, metaphors and other
poetic or musical effects. That is true of Virgil, Dante, and Milton, and,
as we saw, it was true of Dylan's "Lonesome Day Blues" and much else
on *"Love and Theft"*. This way of writing indeed seems to be particularly
a feature of the mature Dylan, starting with *Time Out Of Mind* (1997). In
his December 5, 2004 *60 Minutes* interview he says of "It's Alright, Ma (I'm
Only Bleeding)": "I don't know how I got to write those songs." When
asked if he can still write like that he gives an interesting reply, cryptic as
usual on the subject of his art, but perhaps relevant to our theme: "I did it
once, and *I can do other things now*. But, I can't do that." [emphasis added]

Ray Gooch's library included Dante's *Inferno*, with "The cosmopolitan
man" written on the title page (*Chronicles*, p. 36). If the memory goes back
to the dramatic date of 1961, this suggests a familiarity on Dylan's part
with that Italian poet prior to the epiphany in "Tangled Up In Blue" (from
Blood On The Tracks, 1975), when later on in the evening the woman who
"was workin' in a topless place" (the singer "just kept lookin' at the side of
her face") first offers him "a pipe":

> Then she opened up a book of poems
> And handed it to me
> Written by an Italian poet
> From the thirteenth century
> And every one of them words rang true
> And glowed like burnin' coal
> Pourin' off of every page
> Like it was written in my soul from me to you,
> Tangled up in blue.

There is debate about who the Italian poet is, Dante (1265–1321) or Petrarch
(b. 1304, so not quite of the thirteenth century). Dylan himself seems
to have pointed to the latter, the author of the Laura poems.[13] Others
favor Dante, with Beatrice of the *Vita Nove* a candidate for the romantic
context. Daniel Michael, in a blog post on the topic,[14] recounts reading,
in John Ciardi's translation of *Inferno*, Canto 3.109, Dante's description
of Charon: "and the demon Charon with *eyes like burning coals*." Ciardi's

---

[13] See McGregor, "Dylan interview": "Dylan: 'I like that song. Yeah, that poet from the 13th Century.'
     McGregor: 'Who was that?' Dylan: 'Plutarch. Is that his name?' McGregor: 'Yeah'" (cited in Østrem,
     "A day above ground is a good day").
[14] http://expectingrain.com/dok/who/i/italianpoet.html.

poetic translation came out in 1954, and it is not improbable that B. J. Rolftzen, Dylan's inspirational English teacher at Hibbing High three years later, brought it to the attention of his pupil "Robert."[15] If so, that is how it may have gotten into Ray Gooch's library – where it also may have actually been.

But what is striking in Dylan's metaphor is the fact that the *words* of the Italian poet glowed like coals and poured off the page. Given our Virgilian theme, it might be worth mentioning Canto 21.94–9 of *Purgatorio*, where Dante and Virgil meet the Roman poet Statius, who is unaware he is in the presence of his own Muse, namely Virgil. For Dante's Statius (died 96 CE) the *Aeneid* of Virgil (died 19 BCE) has similar effects to those felt by Dylan's singer:

> The sparks that kindled the fire in me
> Came from the holy flame
> From which more than a thousand have been lit –
>
> I mean the *Aeneid*. When I wrote my poems
> It was my *mamma* and my nurse.
> Without it, I would not have weighed a dram.
> (John Hollander (trans.) [original emphasis])

Whatever the identity of Dylan's Italian poet from the thirteenth century, like the books in Ray Gooch's library, it is part of the general intertextuality Dylan shares with European poetry.

The texts that feed into such poetry include those of the writer himself. "Highlands" from *Time Out Of Mind* (1997) is a case in point. As many have noted, the song has an obvious debt to Robert Burns' "My Heart's in the Highlands," particularly with its chorus:

> My heart's in the Highlands, my heart is not here;
> My heart's in the Highlands a-chasing the deer;
> A-chasing the wild-deer, and following the roe,
> My heart's in the Highlands wherever I go.

Dylan alerts us in a general way ("where the Aberdeen waters flow"), and the Burns poem comes in strongly at one point in Dylan's song:

> Well my heart's in the Highlands, with the horses and hounds
> Way up in the border country, far from the towns
> With the twang of the arrow and a snap of the bow

---

[15] I met B. J. Rolftzen in Hibbing MN in March 2007, and although quite frail, and no longer physically the very cool-looking literature teacher who appears in a 1958 photo, he still had a presence. He died on July 29, 2009.

Dylan's debt is in fact fairly slight, just the five or six words with which he and Burns begin, and he has almost deliberately avoided further intertexts, replacing the objects of the hunt (deer, roe) with its agents (horse, hounds, arrows, bow), but because of those opening words, and because of the geographical specificity ("Aberdeen waters"), the presence of Burns' poem is strongly felt once noticed. Something is happening here, for Burns himself wrote of the song (as he called it) "The first half-stanza [the five words in question] of this song is old; the rest is mine."[16] These are words that Dylan could in turn say of his own "Highlands," over 200 years after Burns. Kinsley also notes that "the Air is *Failte na miosg* (*The Musket Salute*)," from Oswald's *Curious Collection of Scots Tunes* of 1740, almost twenty years before the birth of Burns.[17] Burns' song–poem is melancholic in its dwelling on absence and on a place now only existing in the memory, but it hardly rises to a level of aesthetic beauty or meaningfulness that gives its melancholy a power to affect us very much. The constant AABB rhyme, the simplicity of the repeated frames, the lack of any profound thought, these all keep it on an unsophisticated level, and it flirts with sentimentality, even achieves it perhaps, as much folk music does – which is not to detract. At the same time it is an eighteenth-century pop–folk song, and a pretty one at that. Dylan seems to have found it, and to have taken what he wanted and discarded much else, but in the process he has tied himself to the tradition in which Burns was writing – a tradition within which Dylan himself has always been working. Again, the words of Eliot with which we opened: "The good poet welds his theft into a whole of feeling which is unique, utterly different from that from which it is torn."

But the location is otherwise unspecified, and the Highlands where Dylan has already arrived in his mind at the end of the song are a refuge from a world Dylan has outgrown, though he wishes this were not so, wishes someone would "push back the clock" for him: "All the young men with their young women looking so good / Well, I'd trade places with any of them / In a minute, if I could." He's listening to Neil Young, "Thrasher" I would guess, has "to turn up the sound" which annoys those in the vicinity.

Then there is the scene in the Boston restaurant, a scene where the singer has an encounter with what looks like a second-wave feminist, a waitress who recalls in her similarity as in her difference the erotically charged and implicitly more cooperative woman who worked in the topless bar of "Tangled Up In Blue." Here Dylan seems to switch from an intertextual to

---

[16] Kinsley (ed.), *The Poems and Songs*, p. 1334, from Burns' manuscript *Notes of Scottish Song*, Dick (ed.), *The Songs of Robert Burns and Notes on Scottish Songs*, p. 48.
[17] Kinsley (ed.), *The Poems and Songs*.

an intratextual point of view. The latter exchange is a complete failure, with the two speaking at cross-purposes, and with no chance of a sharing of the pipe or reading Italian poetry. The setting initially suggests the possibility of a pick-up, but this is completely frustrated, and it is worth juxtaposing the two encounters, separated by a quarter of a century in Dylan's oeuvre, a quarter of a century in which the world had changed:

"Highlands"
I'm in Boston town, in some restaurant
I got no idea what I want
  "Tangled Up In Blue"
  She was workin' in a topless place
  And I stopped in for a beer
Well, maybe I do but I'm just really not sure
Waitress comes over
Nobody in the place but me and her
It must be a holiday, there's nobody around
  And later on as the crowd thinned out
She studies me closely as I sit down
  I muttered somethin' underneath my breath,
  She studied the lines on my face.
She got a pretty face and long white shiny legs
  I just kept lookin' at the side of her face
  In the spotlight so clear.
She says, What'll it be?
I say, I don't know, you got any soft-boiled eggs?
She looks at me, says I'd bring you some
but we're out of 'm, you picked the wrong time to come
Then she says, I know you're an artist, draw a picture of me!
  She was standing there in back of my chair
  Said to me, don't I know your name?
I say, I would if I could, but,
I don't do sketches from memory.
Well, she says, I'm right here in front of you, or haven't you looked?
I say, all right, I know, but I don't have my drawing book!
She gives me a napkin, she says, you can do it on that
I say, yes I could but,
I don't know where my pencil is at!
She pulls one out from behind her ear
She says all right now, go ahead, draw me, I'm standing right here
  She was standing there in back of my chair
I make a few lines, and I show it for her to see
Well she takes a napkin and throws it back
And says that don't look a thing like me!

I said, Oh, kind miss, it most certainly does
She says, you must be jokin'. I say, I wish I was!
Then she says, you don't read women authors, do you?
Least that's what I think I hear her say,
Well, I say, how would you know and what would it matter anyway?
Well, she says, you just don't seem like you do!
I said, you're way wrong.
She says, which ones have you read then? I say, I read Erica Jong!
    Then she opened up a book of poems
    And handed it to me
    Written by an Italian poet
    From the thirteenth century
    And every one of them words rang true
    And glowed like burnin' coal
    Pourin' off of every page
    Like it was written in my soul from me to you
She goes away for a minute and I slide up out of my chair
I step outside back to the busy street, but nobody's going anywhere
    She lit a burner on the stove and offered me a pipe

"Tangled Up In Blue" in the end also focused on the loss of relationship, though with the hope of rediscovery, but in "Highlands" things don't even get off the ground.

SMOOTH LIKE A RHAPSODY: HOMER, DYLAN, AND PERFORMANCE VARIATION

Seen from the perspective of Homeric poetics, Dylan works like a blend of rhapsode (performance artist) and a poet on the border between oral and literary cultures. To simplify, the pre-literate oral tradition becomes the *Iliad* and the *Odyssey* through the creative genius of a poet/performer, whom we can call Homer and situate in the eighth century BCE. These Homeric poems are then inscribed and are surely *read* as we read them, while they continue to be sung/performed over centuries by rhapsodes, whose performances introduce some variation and fluidity and so destabilize the fixity of the text. This variation may be detected, e.g., by observing textual variants that emerge in the third century BCE, hundreds of years after the original versions. At that period a number of scholars worked on restoring the "original" text, but in the process introduced or removed detail that changed the Homeric poems in trivial or non-trivial ways.

The inscribing of the oral poets by our Homer, roughly coincident with the invention of the Greek alphabet, may be seen as paralleled by Dylan's writing and recording of the studio version of the song. At that point, as was true with the texts of the *Iliad* and *Odyssey*, there is a canonical text. The process is somewhat like the process whereby folk song is passed on, and in both cases an authoritative text limits the scope for change. Of course, Dylan's compositions are only rooted in the prior tradition, and are not versions of it *per se*, but the relationship is clear, whether from Guthrie's version of "Who's Gonna Shoe Your Pretty Little Foot" to Dylan's "Kingsport Town" or Dylan's appropriation of Charley Patton in "High Water." Dylan's composition is, of course, transformational, and with the exception of all but two of the songs on *Bob Dylan*, and the songs on *World Gone Wrong* and *Good As I Been To You*, is inspired by his various traditions, never or rarely just giving versions of them.

Homeric performance by the rhapsodes, along with transmission of the text, over a number of centuries, introduced variation that might have been in competition with a set, written version, possibly coming together in Athens in the sixth century BCE after Pisistratus, the sixth-century BCE tyrant of Athens. In a sense Dylan is an amalgam of Homer and the rhapsode. Like Homer he is the original creator and original performer of the narratives and lyrics, whose seeds may be found in a whole range of texts from the Bible to the blues. Those versions are available to others, who in a sense also function like rhapsodes, generally departing very little from studio versions, and for the most part with a reverence for the original, reperformance of which is the aim. But Dylan himself is also rhapsode, who has performed his enormous corpus, with powers of memory that seem Homeric in scope, over the last fifty years. In a memorable three-concert stand at the Boston Orpheum on April 15–17, 2005 he sang forty different songs, repeating only one ("Highway 61 Revisited") in addition to framing his closing encores with the traditional "All Along The Watchtower," with just one middle-concert (16 July) "Like A Rolling Stone" closer, and each night throwing in untraditional lead-off encores, "Mississippi," "Blind Willie McTell," "It Takes A Lot To Laugh, It Takes A Train To Cry." It is as such a performer that he clearly defines himself. The studio version, to which he does not listen after it has been put down if we are to believe the Rome interview of 2001, does not constrain him, however, so the creative process continues from band to band and tour to tour, with endless variations of arrangement, vocal style, and, in some cases, lyrics. This is what distinguishes Dylan from singers of similar longevity, such as the Rolling Stones, or Springsteen.

The most intensive meaningful variation of lyrics is found in the songs that have seemed most autobiographical, especially the songs of *Blood On*

The Tracks, and particularly when the status of a relationship is at stake. It is as if Dylan is responding to biographical readings by essentially changing and at times radically transforming the singer's point of view. In the year he produced *Blood On The Tracks*, ten years after its original release, a live version of "It Ain't Me, Babe" makes it clear that nothing has changed, with its emphatically enunciated variations "No, no, no it *sure* ain't me, Babe" and "But it *still* ain't me, Babe." Similarly by the onset of the Christian period in 1978 "She opened up a book of poems and handed it to me" on "Tangled Up In Blue" had become "she opened up the Bible and started quotin' it to me." The *Real Live* version (1984) creates a completely different and now playful narration: "She was married when they first met to a man four times her age" (can't be Sara Lownds, right?). Or on the same version: "Then he drifted down to New Orleans where they treated him like a boy / He nearly went mad in Baton Rouge he nearly drowned in Delacroix." Gray (*Song and Dance Man* III, p. 651) has, however, noted that in recent years the lyrics have settled back to their canonical text – though the fall 2006 tour has the "She was workin' at the Tropicana [rather than 'in a topless place']" verse. The story of the variations on *Blood On The Tracks* is well known. What we officially heard from the release on January 20, 1975 differed in quite distinct ways from what appeared on 26 March 1991, when *The Bootleg Series Volume 2* presented versions of "Tangled Up In Blue," and "Idiot Wind," while *The Bootleg Series Volume 3* yielded a different version of "If You See Her, Say Hello." Bootlegs of the so-called "Acetates on the Tracks" were widely distributed. The Minneapolis sessions also produced *Blood On The Tracks* versions of "Lily, Rosemary and the Jack of Hearts." So, after more than fifteen years we were given the generally angrier or harsher New York lyrics and less upbeat arrangements that Dylan had changed when he returned to Minneapolis after recording the entire album in a few days in New York in September of 1974.

I select just two instances of performative variation, with parallels from the Homeric and the Virgilian texts. The New York "Lily, Rosemary and the Jack of Hearts" has an entire verse that would be dropped from the Minneapolis version, although it was included in *Lyrics 1962–1985*, where it stands as verse 12:

Lily's arms were locked around the man that she dearly loved to touch, / She forgot all about the man she couldn't stand who hounded her so much. / "I've missed you so," she said to him, and he felt she was sincere, / But just beyond the door he felt jealousy and fear. / Just another night in the life of the Jack of Hearts.

I myself did not hear this version until a number of years after 1975, after the narrative of the Jack of Hearts et al. had become hard-wired. What does omission or inclusion do? Essentially, the stanza slightly demystifies the Jack of Hearts, gives a glimpse through the mask, by giving us his point of view or focalization: "he felt she was sincere . . . he felt jealousy and fear." Without this stanza this is a song where mystery is much of the point, where the main actor, sometimes merging with the card itself, is generally "face down like the Jack of Hearts," where he is seen only from the outside, through the thoughts of Lily, Rosemary and Big Jim, and definitely *not* through those of the Jack of Hearts: "I know I've seen that face before," "she'd never met anyone quite like the Jack of Hearts," "she was leaning to the Jack of Hearts," "she was thinking about the Jack of Hearts." Inclusion of the verse transforms the song through the shock of telling us something about the Jack, and it is easy to see why Dylan, author of this song, of "Jokerman," of Jack Fate's benefit show (in the 2003 movie *Masked and Anonymous*), took it out, so nothing would be revealed.

Numerous passages in the *Iliad* and *Odyssey* were in the third and second centuries BCE either removed or athetized by Alexandrian scholars of that age (Zenodotus born c. 325 BCE, Aristophanes of Byzantium c. 257–180 BCE, and Aristarchus c. 216–144 BCE, the first self-ordained professors of the West), either because they had in fact been added by interpolators or because they could be argued to have been so added, and did not fit received opinions about what Homer should/could have written. The presence or absence of many of these lines has similarly radical effects on our reading of the narrative and on our involvement with that poem. Since ancient discussion of the lines is preserved (in the "Homeric scholia") we know, for instance that Zenodotus excised from his text some lines at *Iliad* 12.175–81, in which the poet sings of the difficulty of describing the clash of battle. Here is Pope's version:

> Like deeds of arms through all the forts were tried;
> And all the gates sustain'd an equal tide;
> Through the long walls the stony showers were heard,
> The blaze of flames, the flash of arms appear'd.
> The spirit of a god my breast inspire,
> To raise each act of life, and sing with fire!
> While Greece unconquer'd kept alive the war,
> Secure of death, confiding in despair;
> And all her guardian gods, in deep dismay,
> With unassisting arms deplore the day.
> Even yet the dauntless Lapithae maintain
> The dreadful pass, and round them heap the slain.

Zenodotus omitted the lines, but Aristophanes and Aristarchus put them back in, though by athetizing them recorded their view that the lines were not genuine. What they and a number of modern editors and commentators objected to was the presence of the narrating poet's voice, very unusual in this poem, particularly in such a random part of the poem rather than at the beginning, for example, where we expect to find that voice. And as with Dylan's song "Lily, Rosemary and the Jack of Hearts" the absence or presence of the lines makes a difference.

Moving from Greece to Rome, from Homer to Virgil, one of Dylan's Latin poets, we have an example of a passage present in some manuscripts, absent in others. Book 2 of the *Aeneid* tells the story of the Fall of Troy. Helen, the Greek beauty kidnapped by Paris, cousin of Aeneas, survived the fall, and Virgil's readers might have expected Trojan Aeneas, who also survived to found Rome, to have mentioned Helen in his recounting the story to Dido, Queen of Carthage – the song within the song that is *Aeneid* 2–3. Here is Dryden's translation of some of the twenty-two lines of Latin (*Aeneid* 2.567–88):

> Thus, wand'ring in my way, without a guide,
> The graceless Helen in the porch I spied
> Of Vesta's temple; there she lurk'd alone;
> Muffled she sate, and, what she could, unknown:
> But, by the flames that cast their blaze around,
> That common bane of Greece and Troy I found.

Aeneas contemplates killing her:

> Trembling with rage, the strumpet I regard,
> Resolv'd to give her guilt the due reward:

Before the narrative has to deal with the dilemma of Rome's hero and founder of the Latin race killing a woman, his divine mother appears and tells him to get on with the business of leaving Troy. Most editors now believe the lines are not genuine, or were not meant for publication, but this possibility does not detract from an essential truth: our reading of the poem and of the character of Aeneas is very much conditioned by whether or not we encounter the passage in our text.

I return now to Dylan and the end, and to his complex manipulation of how we hear and read what is the most transformed song on *Blood On The Tracks*, the song of break-up and its imagined aftermath, "If You See Her Say Hello." From the December version that ended up on the album, as everyone knows, there was an extensive change in the third verse:

If you get close to her, kiss her once for me / Always have respected her for doing what she did ["for busting out," *Lyrics 1962–1985*] and gettin' free / Oh, whatever makes her happy, I won't stand in the way / Though the bitter taste still lingers on from the night I tried to make her / stay.

In the 1992 published version of the New York outtake from 1974 we heard a more bitter and caustic song:

If you're making love to her, kiss her for the kid / who always has respected her for doin' what she did / Oh, I know it had to be that way, it was written in the cards. / But the bitter taste still lingers on, it all came down so hard.

The change from "If you're making love to her" to the less specific and less wounded "If you get close to her" delivers a more delicate touch to the song. As Les Kokay and others have noted, by the time of The Rolling Thunder Revue, at the Lakeland Florida Civic Center on April 18, 1976, the song had been completely rewritten and had become savage and unambiguous. And nine days later, at Florida State University he sang it again, with further differences:[18]*

If you see her say hello, she might be in North Saigon / *in outer space
She left here in a hurry; I don't know what she was on / I could have got her to
    her place
        [gotten over to her place?]
You might say that I'm in disarray and for me time's standing still
Oh I've never gotten over her, I don't think I ever will
A bright light from me I saw, a shattering of souls / I saw salvation in her soul
Just one of them reckless situations, which nobody controls.
Well, the menagerie of life rolls by, right before my eyes / goes by, I try not to go
We all do the best we can, which should come as no surprise / [. . . . . .] grow[?]
If you're making love to her, watch it from the rear
You'll never know when I'll be back, or liable to appear
For it's natural to dream of peace as it is for rules to break / like it is for rules to
    break
And right now I've got not much to lose, so you'd better stay awake
Sundown, silver moon, hitting on the days / shining on the haze [hate?]
My head can't toler . . . stand no more, what my heart don't tolerate / My heart
    can't
        understand no more, what my head don't tolerate
Well I know she'll be back someday, of that there is no doubt
And when that moment comes Lord, give me the strength to keep her out

---

[18] See Kokay, *Songs of the Underground.*

The fourth verse with its ending "Maybe I'm too sensitive or else I'm getting soft" was gone along with the attitude to the addressee–rival has become menacing, but the regret and the feelings are still there.

For whatever reason, Dylan did not perform the song for almost eighteen years, but on July 3, 1994 in Paris, the first concert of a European summer tour, he opened with "To Be Alone With You" (all other concerts of that year opened with "Jokerman") and followed up with "If You See Her, Say Hello." Back in the USofA, he performed it ten times between 24 August and 12 November. In the years since it has come back into his arsenal, with the fourth verse back in, while the third is gone forever from versions I have heard. As a result the addressee is no longer a rival, there is less at stake. To begin with, the versions of the lyrics were those of "Tangled Up In Blue," but over time we find a variety in the lyrics that seems to defy our reading it as a single representation of emotion, even, from the point of view of the lyrics, as a single song. The second verse gives us a whole range, from "She still lives inside of me (my mind) / I've never been alone" to "I've got to find someone to take her place, you know I don't like to be alone." As for his forgetting her we get "Don't tell her it isn't so," but also "I only wish it was so." In the fourth verse, "I've never gotten used to it, I've just learned to turn it off" is rounded out by the original lyrics but also by the hilarious "Her eyes were blue, her hair was too, her skin so sweet and soft," in New York City on August 13, 2003, protracted (I think) to "sort of, sort of... soft." This, perhaps, in case you were wondering if her hair was still red; no, it's now blue – or was that a different one? Difficulty of comprehension seems to be part of the game. We also find "I've never gotten used to it, it took me her long load[?] / Suddenly I believe you know, it's harder on the road." This same version (Augusta, Maine, August 4, 2002) also provides one of the most negative endings, even more so than in Florida in 1976. Now we have, "If she's passing back this way, and you know it could be quick, / Please don't mention her name to me, b'cause the mention of her name makes me sick." This alternates with more or less the original, more hopeful ending, and with variations such as "if she comes up with the time," to a more middle-of-the-road possibility such as (in the same New York City concert) "If she's passin' back this way, Lord and I sure hope she don't, / Tell her she can look me up, I'll either be here or I won't."

This is obviously more varied and delivers a wider range of meanings than do the classical instances we have seen. But there is a shared element in that both deal with the possibility of change and evolution through performance, a feature that is shared for instance with folk music, but not so much with poetry in recent centuries. At the end of the day, Dylan defies identification, and perhaps "singer–songwriter" works fine, just as long as we realize that works for Homer or Virgil too. Dylan has been dressing in the costume of mid-nineteenth- or early/mid-twentieth-century Americana, the world that his songs have brought back to life. But he has also been going back much further in his mind's time. I don't expect him to turn up in the toga or with any old laurel leaves on his head, but that doesn't matter since he's already back there in my mind and that's good enough for me.

PART III

Envoi

CHAPTER 10

Reception and the Classics

Christopher S. Wood

This essay was delivered as an envoi to the conference. As a talk it was meant to dispatch the audience: to liberate them from the spell cast by the conference and send them back into the world, free to assess and broadcast its achievement. In its published state the talk loses this performative quality. But even a published envoi, I hope, retains some of the privileges of paratextuality.

I will not comment on the papers systematically, but rather note some patterns. None of the classicists, it seems to me, took up Charles Martindale's challenge in its most radical form, as thrown down in *Redeeming the Text*: namely, to demonstrate the inextricability of a classical text from a present-tense reading situation. This challenge provided the original intellectual framework for this conference. Martindale wanted his colleagues to read a classical text through a modern one. Richard Thomas does this in his wonderful paper on Bob Dylan and Virgil, bringing to life "the pathos of Vergil's poetry," in the phrase of the editors of this volume, "through the dynamic recontextualization in modern song." But no one quite undertook what Martindale himself did in the paper he delivered at this conference, where he placed Ovid and Dryden in a symmetrical and mutually creative relation. A classical text, for Martindale, is never inert. Only when academic classicists acknowledge that texts are events, says Martindale, that texts move, will the field begin finally to practice a modern, paradoxical criticism willing to question the historicist dogma of the past's independence from the present.

This plea was not directed at medieval or Renaissance scholars, who habitually read the classics backwards. They know well that classical status was conferred on the ancient texts *by* the Renaissance. And in fact at the conference it was the specialists in Renaissance literature who dramatized the inseparability of the classics from their reception by forcing, as Martindale had, ancient authors and modern authors into equilibrium. Among the published papers I note Giuseppe Mazzotta's on Petrarch and Homer, and Gordon Braden's on Shakespeare and Ovid. Mazzotta, by focusing on the poet who initiated the modern project of philological recovery of the classics, actually comes close to suggesting that the ancient texts are invisible to us except through the screen of their Renaissance readings.

In *Latin Poetry and the Judgment of Taste* (2005), Martindale shifted to a more straightforward, non-ironic criticism interested basically in assigning value to literary texts. But this book targeted the same opponent that the first one had: the historicist who attempts to reconstruct the original sense of a text, in its original context. Historicism, a state of mind that emerged in the late eighteenth century in the writings of Goethe and Herder, is the belief that historical statements and acts were governed by conditions below the surface of experience, perhaps invisible to historical actors; that those conditions are permanently changing; and that historical performances cannot be assessed by timeless norms but only on their own terms. Historicism also generated a complementary insight that ended up destabilizing the project of historical reconstruction: if every historical period is guided by invisible but dynamic forces, then so too is the present. Historicism implies that our own judgments, including our assessments of the past, are not free. The past is fixed but the present is a moving platform, and so our perspective on the past, in ways that we cannot grasp from within that perspective, is always shifting. Empiricism, a set of impersonal, collectively enforced protocols for identifying and weighing historical facts, can partially correct for the shifting perspective. But literary meaning is not a quantum readily susceptible to empirical reconstruction, and so literary texts will always elude the historicist project. All Martindale is asking is that his colleagues embrace this reality. He wants them to recognize the excess of literariness that escapes empirical reconstruction, and so practice an anachronistic or Whiggish literary criticism, without apologies. As Margreta de Grazia put it in a recent essay that tracks the development of the chronological approach to the past in the writings of the philologists and historians of the Renaissance, anachronism "is the source of the critic's power."[1]

This discussion could be conducted over any corpus of texts, not only classical texts; and as a matter of fact it has been. One has the sense of having heard the whole debate already. The project of an aesthetics of reception was theorized in the 1960s and 1970s by participants in the German study group *Poetik und Hermeneutik*. American literary scholars were intensely engaged with the concept of reception in the 1980s. Since

---

[1] "Anachronism." Here de Grazia adapts a formula of Thomas M. Greene.

1990 the reception–aesthetics or hermeneuticist approach has not been conspicuous in the study of postclassical literature, not because it has been discredited but because it has been internalized. Martindale's challenge to classicists strikes an outsider as belated, though not unwelcome. It compels us to think through the problem again.

It seems clearer now that the debate is a non-debate, because each side – empiricist and hermeneuticist – creates and depends upon the other. Martindale and other hermeneuticists see empiricism as an over-rationalization of reading. Empiricism, in this view, was a well-intended corrective, inspired by the Enlightenment's critiques of religious superstition or the mystification of political authority, but misapplied to literary texts. Martindale wants to remystify reading by inviting the reader to move freely within a web of texts, a web only loosely tethered to reality outside texts. He believes that empiricism should be succeeded by an emancipated criticism. Empiricism corrected the critical abuses of medieval and Renaissance readers of the classics. But in turn it generated the appetite for a new critical freedom. Criticism, therefore, both precedes and follows empiricism. De Grazia's "story of anachronism" makes that clear. Readers were wrenching texts out of their original contexts – if it even occurred to them that texts *had* an original context – and making sense of them exactly as they pleased long before anyone suggested that the past, objectively reconstructed, ought to impose limits on present-day interpretations. The history of modern reading does not simply swing back and forth between these two modes. Rather, it is a cumulative tradition whereby each mode, critical and historicist, continually reacts and adapts to the other.

Historicism is like a mask placed over criticism, designed to block some meanings and reveal others. Moses Finley's *World of Odysseus*, for example, showed how Homer's text was structured by the sociological and economic realities of aristocracy, slavery, kinship systems, land use, and so forth. Finley himself only ever presented himself as an historian prepared to treat Homer as a reliable primary source. But his study was, of course, also an interpretation of the literary text that served as a counterweight to the neo-humanistic readings, on the ascendant after World War II, that sought universal truths in Homer. The humanistic or anachronistic approach, because it was Finley's hidden target, was therefore written into Finley's historicism. His disciplining of the critics was only a higher form of criticism. Finley's materialist reading of the *Odyssey*, meanwhile, is now affixed so firmly to the text that all future readings have to deal with it one way or another. Criticism reacts by seeking out what historicism missed, and vice versa. The two modes in the end contain one another.

That is just how a classicist, committed to the project of situating texts in time with the instruments of philology and historical imagination, might respond to Martindale: "I am already practicing criticism. Historicism entails a radical subtraction from the totality of possible readings. The idea of reading as an objective assignation of meaning guided by an empirical reconstruction of the past is in fact one of the more abstract and fanciful contrivances of modernity." Martindale would have to agree, and then concede that he is after all only asking classicists to own up to what they are doing; to concede that they have been practicing criticism all along. And at that point the debate seems to run out of steam.

I am more interested in another question. It is striking to me that a concept of the classics *per se* plays no role in the debate about reception. Both sides disavow any investment in a concept of the classics. If anything, each side accuses the other of harboring a secret allegiance to a normative canon. Martindale is basically saying that classical texts are just like any others, only older. Antiquity is just one form of alienness. All texts are "antique" in one way or another. He suggests that only pious respect for the integrity of the classic texts discourages classicists from subjecting those texts to a dynamic, anachronizing criticism. The classicists might respond that Martindale's open-ended, historically insouciant interpretations are only made possible by canonization. Here they are supported by Moshe Halbertal, who argued in *People of the Book* that canonicity liberates texts from historical context, thus making them available for free interpretation. The traditional classicist, then, is accusing Martindale not of disrespecting the canonical texts, but rather of taking advantage of their canonicity.

In this light it is easier to explain Martindale's return to basic principles of aesthetic judgment. By appealing to an ahistorical concept of judgment, he naturalizes his interpretations. In this way he responds to the classicists who suspect him of a hidden complicity with a mystified classical canon. Few will be convinced by this argument. Joseph Farrell wondered at the conference whether Martindale's critical exertions were not after all impelled by a lingering Hellenophilia, a surrender to a mere effect generated by high modernist purism.

On the basis of this volume, meanwhile, a small but significant sample, it would appear that classicists' reflexive response to Martindale's challenge is to adopt a meta-critical standpoint. Instead of re-reading the classics by way of the moderns, the classicists contributing to this volume, James Zetzel, Joseph Farrell, Robert Kaster, Richard Tarrant, Emily Wilson, and Richard Thomas, produced case studies in historical reception. These remarkable papers project a range of possible disciplinary futures for Classics:

sociologies, politics, and cultural histories of reading. Yet this is not what Martindale intended. In these papers, subtle and erudite as they are, the literariness of ancient texts is dealt with only at one degree of remove. The ones who engaged directly with Virgil and the rest are characters *inside* the scholarly narratives offered by these papers. Critical engagement with literature here is not so much the performance of historical study as its object.

No one could object if more classicists, following the lead of the authors in this volume, were to occupy themselves with histories of reading and histories of Latin and Greek pedagogy and curricula in modern societies. The project of reconstructing and purifying the ancient literary texts was central to the self-understanding of early modern European culture (Grafton and Jardine, *From Humanism to the Humanities*). Philology produced a body of works with normative authority that served as a reassuring cover for the truly dynamic aspects of European modernity, the innovations that broke with the ancient world once and for all: the printing press, the discovery of the new world, the stock market. A study of Classics as a pedagogical program would demystify the classics, revealing the canonical texts as modern contrivances, artificially isolated from a vast, lost world of spoken Latin (Françoise Waquet, *Le latin, ou l'empire d'un signe*, 1999). The survival of the classics into the twentieth century, now prepared for mass consumption not through philological castigation of the texts but through translation into modern languages, reveals the range of roles they play. The classics might be understood as a compensation for the overwhelming sense of the irrelevance of art and poetry in modern society. The classics might equally be understood as an instrument of power, functioning especially in unstable times, such as the early twentieth century, as guarantors of permanent value (Egidius Schmalzriedt, *Inhumane Klassik*). The classics always entail some *rappel à l'ordre*. Or perhaps the classics are no more than places of stillness, *loca amoena*, embedded within the chaos of modern discourse: the classics – to extend and radicalize Ernst Robert Curtius (*Europäische Literatur und lateinisches Mittelalter*) – not just as vehicles for *topoi*, but themselves *topoi*.[2] One can easily imagine the study of ancient literature taking up the questions of text-types (Franco Moretti, *Graphs, Maps, Trees*). Questions about reading habits, the materiality of the text, and the circulation of texts in antiquity have already been amply addressed by classicists.[3]

---

[2] See Hinds, *Allusion and Intertext*, pp. 5–6, here following John Hollander on allusions as echoes or "images" of text. These metaphors suggest that intertextuality involves a stilling of language.

[3] See for example Cavallo et al. (eds.), *Lo Spazio letterario di Roma antica*.

In their most radical forms these approaches fall under the rubric of "cultural studies." Cultural studies simply means a loss of confidence in the frame around the text. The literary work as the atomic unit of interpretation gives way to an unbounded textuality. Language-use is understood as a formless flow that occasionally forms eddies of literariness but quickly breaks up again. Once literariness itself is destabilized, the sheltered status of the classical canon will be threatened.

Professional academic classicists who don't finally wish to tear down the fence that protects the classics tend to lay low by bracketing the whole question of normativity. They will say, and this is a safe thing to say, that the label "Classics" is just shorthand for ancient Greek and Roman literature, which is studied in a separate academic department because the difficult languages call for special treatment. They might predict that to abandon the label and open the gates to cultural studies will encourage a slipshod approach to philology. "Classics," they are saying, is just a warning label: "Caution, don't try this at home." Whereas Martindale is saying that these texts deserve the label "classic" because they are good, or beautiful. They became classics because many readers over a long period of time found them to be good. Good modern poems, Martindale implies, will also one day be classics.

Difficulty and remoteness on the one hand, timeless literary merit on the other. Are these really robust concepts of the classics? It is remarkable that few classicists any more are prepared to defend the exceptionality of the classics not because they are remote, and not because they are good, but because they are *true*, and moreover true in a different way than modern works are true.

It is not such a strange idea. The modern work of art or literature expects it of the older work. For doesn't the modern poem almost by definition consider itself to be "true in a different way"? To be modern is not to dismiss the classics as false or overrated, but to see them as paths to truth that can no longer be retraced. To be modern is nothing other than to insist upon one's own alienation from the classics. The modern is the one who no longer possesses the classics, but only studies them. There can be no vivid sense of modernity without a correspondingly vivid sense of a lost textual home that moderns have learned to live far away from.

But the modern regrets or celebrates a lost intimacy not only with ancient texts but also with the gods that were the subject matter of the ancient texts. Virgil and Ovid were not intimate with the gods, but they were intimate with Homer, who was. At any rate Homer's text was intimate with the muffled voices, bardic, oracular, or proverbial, through which the gods spoke. The classics were closer in time to non-time. The threshold of historical memory was not so distant. The gap between the preliterate era and the classical author is measured in hundreds of years, not thousands. It is not simply a matter of the earliness of the classical text, its relative non-belatedness. To be classical really means to have written under different conditions. It means to have written before fictionality and non-referentiality became the criteria of the literary text. Ancient literary texts have non-literary or pre-literary functions inscribed inside them: they archive prayer, charm, riddle, panegyric, proclamation, treatise, catalogue, saga, and myth. The tension between the magical and the literary animates classical literary texts; it becomes the content of those texts. That is true about post-medieval texts as well, perhaps of all literature. Yet the classical literary text is different. Whereas the modern literary text defines itself as the text that declines to refer, the classical text preserves some ambiguity about its possible capacity to refer to the gods. The classical literary text is evasive about its respect for taboos. Such writing always writes over some forbidden utterance. It remembers the origins of poetry as an assertion of one view of things – for example, the immortality of the gods – over an alternative view – for example, the scandalous rumor that the gods are mortal. For Friedrich Kittler, the very thesis of the immortality of the gods was launched by writing.[4] The inscription attempted to defeat the scandalous utterance by revealing it to be mere utterance, contingent and unstable. Writing began as a prohibition against saying: it repudiated as a lie the thesis that "the gods are mortal." Kittler invokes Paul's Letter to Titus in which he asserted that Cretans are liars and thus not to be trusted when they denied the true teachings, in particular (at least in Kittler's reading) the immortality of Christ. He also invokes Ovid, who could not deny the immortality of the gods because of his imperial patrons. The classical era of literature is perhaps no more and no less than the period of the taboo on speaking the death of the gods.

The category "classics" names the idea that literature once communicated with the gods. This idea is contained within the ancient concept of hermeneutics. In his dialogue *Ion*, Plato described the poets as interpreters of the gods. Martindale, by contrast, following Hans-Georg Gadamer, takes conversation as the model of the hermeneutic engagement, a shuttling back and forth between reader and text that alters both. This is a state of civilized equipoise. But hermeneutics in the original sense is a bringing of unexpected tidings from elsewhere, from beyond the circle of

---

4 Kittler and Vissmann, *Vom Griechenland.*

interpersonal exchange. The classical texts are those that remember that the significant messages are borne in, instantaneously or even violently, though not always intelligibly. They measure the clumsy realities of human communication, time-bound and dependent on relays and inscriptions, against the angel-borne messages. The classical text, dominated by its awareness of the absence of the gods, figures the qualities of the gods as poetry: for isn't poetry itself immortal, capricious, and only dimly intelligible?

Here we begin to pry a concept of the classics apart from a repertoire of historical works. We come to understand, with Geoffrey Hartman, the almost "involuntary" fixation on the possibility of a classics on the part even of such an unclassical writer as Wordsworth:

Milton and Milton's use of the Classics recall to [Wordsworth] a more absolute beginning: a point of origin essentially unmediated, beyond the memory of experience or the certainty of temporal location. A "heavenly" origin, perhaps, in the sense of the myth . . . that the *Intimations Ode* presents and which makes a heuristic use of Plato's notion of preexistence. This recession of experience to a boundary where memory fades into myth, or touches the hypostasis of supernatural origin . . . is what preoccupies the psyche of the poet.[5]

A strong concept of the classics, then, is nothing other than a strong concept of poetry.

The classics remain a reality – more than the empty preening of an elite class of readers, more than a relic of obsolete institutional taxonomies – as long as the possibility of being classic (being intimate with the gods) remains the content of subsequent poetry. This is not the same as saying, with Thomas M. Greene and other theorists of neoclassical *imitatio*, that poetry proceeds by recombining the forms and contents of earlier poetry, and by reflecting on its own dependency. Instead, it is to point out, as Giuseppe Mazzotta does in his essay in this volume, that Petrarch learns what artists do – namely, tell lies – by attending to what the classical poets knew about the heroes and the gods, adepts of dissimulation.

The classical text is not scripture. The classical text is not the paragon that guides the ordinary, no longer classical text, but rather the prophecy of that text. Even the most scripture-like classical texts contain their own undoing – the anti-scriptural moment – inside themselves. This is illustrated by a remark of Nietzsche's: "I know of nothing that has led me more to reflect on Plato's concealment and sphinx nature than that happily preserved *petit fait* that under the pillow of his death-bed was discovered no 'Bible', nothing Egyptian, Pythagorean, Platonic – but Aristophanes. How could

---

5 Hartman, "Words, wish, worth," p. 148.

even a Plato have endured life – a Greek life which he had denied – without an Aristophanes!" (*Beyond Good and Evil*, § 28).

A robust concept of the classics will problematize both of Martindale's projects. The aestheticist approach, the application of a free Kantian judgment, is not possible because the classical text foils such a reading by setting up its own referentiality – its non-literariness – as an obstacle. The sacred text never releases the reader into freedom. And as for hermeneutics: is "reception" really the right metaphor for a confrontation with such a text, a text that does not so much emit a message as mark a "dangerous and dubious" vanishing point of meaning (Hartman on Wordsworth)? The word "reception" suggests an unenviable state of passivity.

In commenting on the debate about the reception of the classics among literary scholars, I am really only pointing to a certain lack of drama. The problem of the classics within the academic disciplines of archeology and art history, by contrast, has always been much more acute and the solutions correspondingly more drastic. The burden of art history was the dread white army of Greek and Roman statuary, risen from the ground in the sixteenth century and then endlessly cloned and imitated, infiltrating first aristocratic homes, then the public spaces of bourgeois modernity. The succession of neoclassicisms is easier to track in art than in literature because it centers on the nude and desirable body. The real erotic appeal of the sculpted body, the uncanniness of the effigy, and the ease with which a statue serves as a trophy all complicate the work of the art historian and the art critic. The European and American obsession with Greek and Roman sculpture was not finally discredited until the twentieth century when the forms were contaminated by the role they played in the Fascist cults of the body. The entanglement of art history with classical statuary was aggravated by the fact that the modern scholarly study of art was set on course in the eighteenth century by the antiquarian Johann Joachim Winckelmann, who posed the conundrum of how to explain historically the transhistorically valuable. That riddle remains programmatic for the discipline.

Today, in art history, the Greek and Roman statuary are thoroughly relativized. No scholar would assert their normativity. Art historical classicists are in fact so lacking in self-assertiveness that they have more or less retreated into a corner of their own, isolated from the rest of the discipline. No classicist proposes, in the spirit of this conference, that Greek and Roman art might profitably be read through the Renaissance and Baroque works that emulated them. But nor does any classicist dare to build a case for the unavoidability of their field, any case at all.

Greek and Roman statuary makes an immeasurably stronger claim to normativity than do the literary texts that we have been dealing with as classics. A statue is a substitute body, an effigy. A statue is a shelter for a god, an entity that otherwise escapes sensory apprehension. It occupies space just as a body does. It invites but does not satisfy a direct interpersonal engagement. Hegel saw the sculptural representation of the incarnated gods of the Greeks as the center of art because here the specific thought of art was most completely realized. The content of ancient sculpture was "the plasticity of the gods." The form of the statue perfectly realized that content. Language in attempting to redeem its materiality could only aim at, but never attain, the "absolute knowledge" of the Greek statues.[6] Art history dealt decisively with its classics by setting up the exceptionalism of the Greek and Roman statuary as its most grave taboo, and no wonder.

There is a way out of the impasse, and it might serve for literary classicists as well. The way is indicated, in gnomic fashion, in the writings on Renaissance art by the turn-of-the-century German art historian Aby Warburg. Warburg believed – really seems to have believed – that primordial experiences generated powerful pulsations of fear or ecstasy that are transmitted by pictorial formulae across time and space.[7] Warburg tracked the survival of such "pathos formulas" within networks of sculptures, paintings, emblems, diagrams, pictures of all types including modern advertisements and other images culled from the mass media. The pathos formula, for Warburg, was not a sign but a direct expression of a real force. His essential unit of study was not the work of art but the expressive formula. The formula can appear anywhere, in a museum or in the daily newspaper. From this point of view, the vertical hierarchy between the classics (high) and the rest of culture (low) breaks down. The historical or horizontal hierarchy between then and now, however, persists, because the older formula is closer to its invisible source in real experience. But if the later "pathos formula" is sufficiently replete, then the more recent image is as potent as the older image, and the linear chronology that frames all modern scholarship also breaks down.

The latecomer poet or artist who takes the ancient work of art as the key unit and "receives" it by transforming it into a new work risks missing Warburg's point entirely. For the authorial ambition of the creative imitator may interfere with the essentially expressive dynamic of the image, which punctures the frame of the work. The author is interested in protecting the

---

[6] See the remarkable analysis in Melville and Iversen, *Writing Art History*, ch. 8.

[7] Warburg, *The Renewal of Pagan Antiquity*. Among the wealth of recent commentary on Warburg, see especially Didi-Huberman, *L'image survivante*.

integrity of the work because the work serves as the material placeholder, in the world, for his or her own personhood. Perhaps only the scholar, tracing from a measured distance the paths of emotion from form to form, grasps the true shape of history. From the scholar's disinterested point of view, and this was Warburg's point of view, the poets and artists do not know what they are doing. They only transmit. The concept of the "classic" is displaced from works and re-identified as a pulsing or a flow. It is nowhere, but also anywhere.

In invoking the predicament of the art historical classicists, I really only want to take some pressure off the literary classicists. Warburg's radical disintegration of the classical work was a backlash provoked by the cult of Greco-Roman statuary, which in 1890 might have seemed as intense as ever. Literary study of the classics developed no comparably radical model, and understandably so, because their classic texts lack the iconic density of the statues. As texts the literary classics are better at dismantling themselves. Because their content is already the inaudibility of the gods, they provide the instruments of their own critique. It is understandable that literary scholars, wise in the ways of texts, react to Martindale's gauntlet with neither outrage nor breathless enthusiasm.

To be sure, some scholars would gladly undertake a relativization of the classical text far more thoroughgoing than anything proposed by Martindale or anyone else in this volume – a reduction of the text, say, to a mere effect of its embodiments in medial technologies. But in order to raise the stakes of such a demystification, one might want to begin by imagining what form a remystification of the text should take.

Bibliography

Adams, J. *Works of John Adams, Second President of the United States: With a Life of the Author by Charles Francis Adams* (Boston 1851–65).

Agrippa, H. C. *De occulta philosophia libri tres* (Cologne 1533).

Alcorn, J. and **Del Puppo, D.** "Leopardi's historical poetics in the Canzone 'Ad Angelo Mai,'" *Italica* **72** (1995): 21–39.

Anderson, C. G. (ed.) *James Joyce. A Portrait of the Artist as a Young Man: Text, Criticism, and Notes* (New York 1968).

Anonymous, "Review of John Dunlop, History of Roman Literature," *Quarterly Review* **52** (1834): 57–95. See also Everett.

Arkins, B. *Greek and Roman Themes in Joyce* (Lewiston NY 1999)

Arnold, M. *Culture and Anarchy: Essay in Political and Social Criticism* (London 1869). Reprinted in **R. H. Super** (ed.) *Complete Prose Works* (Ann Arbor 1960–77).

Attridge, D. *Joyce Effects: On Language, Theory, and History* (Cambridge 2000).

Austin, R. G. *P. Vergili Maronis Aeneidos, liber sextus* (Oxford 1977).

Baldwin, T. W. *William Shakspere's Small Latine and Lesse Greeke.* 2 vols. (Urbana IL 1944).

Baretti, J. *The Introduction to the Carmen Saeculare* (London 1779).

Barkan, L. *The Gods Made Flesh: Metamorphosis and the Pursuit of Paganism* (New Haven 1986).

Baswell, C. *Virgil in Medieval England: Figuring the Aeneid from the Twelfth Century to Chaucer* (Cambridge 1995).

Bate, J. *Shakespeare and Ovid* (Oxford 1993).

Batstone, W. W. "Provocation: The point of reception theory," in *Classics and the Uses of Reception,* **C. Martindale** and **R. F. Thomas** (eds.) (Oxford 2006) pp. 14–20.

Bawcutt, P. *Gavin Douglas: A Critical Study* (Edinburgh 1976).

Bechet, S. *Treat it Gentle* (New York 1960).

Bernard, J. D. (ed.) *Vergil at 2000: Commemorative Essays on the Poet and his Influence* (New York 1986).

Bernardi, J. E. D. *De la république ou du meilleur gouvernement, ouvrage traduit de Cicéron, et rétabli d'après les fragmens et ses autres écrits, avec des notes . . . et une dissertation sur l'origine des sciences, des arts, de la philosophie, etc., chez les Romains* (Paris 1798).

Bernardo, A. S. (trans.) *Petrarch: Letters on Familiar Matters: Rerum familiarum libri.* 2 vols. (Baltimore and London 1982 and 1985).

(trans.) *Rerum familiarum libri* i–viii. 3 vols. (Albany NY 1975).

Berry, D. H. "The criminals in Virgil's Tartarus: Contemporary allusions in Aeneid 6.621–4," *Classical Quarterly* **42** (1992): 416–20.

Blyth, C. R. *The Knychtlyke Stile: A Study of Gavin Douglas' Aeneid* (New York 1987).

Boccaccio, G. *Trattatello in laude di Dante*, **P. G. Ricci** (ed.), in *Tutte le opere di Giovanni Boccaccio*, **V. Branca** (ed.) (Milan 1974) vol. iii, pp. 455–7.

Bodin, J. *Colloquium Heptaplomeres de Rerum Sublimium Arcanis Abditis*, **L. Noack** (ed.) (Schwerin, Germany 1857).

Borges, J. L. *Labyrinths: Selected Stories and Other Writings*, **D. A. Yates** and **J. E. Irby** (eds.) (New York 1964).

Borsieri, P. *Avventure letterarie di un giorno*, **W. Spaggiari** (ed.) (Modena 1986).

Boswell, J. *The Life of Samuel Johnson.* 4 vols. (London 1799).

Bowen, Z. R. *Musical Allusions in the Works of James Joyce* (Albany NY 1974).

Braden, G. "Shakespeare's Petrarchism," in **J. Schiffer** (ed.), *Shakespeare's Sonnets: Critical Essays* (New York 1999) pp. 163–83.

Branca, V. (ed.) *Il Conciliatore: foglio scientifico-letterario* (Florence 1953).

Brinton, A. *Mapheus Vegius and his Thirteenth Book of the Aeneid* (London 1930).

Brioschi, F. and **Landi, P.** (eds.) *Leopardi. Epistolario* (Turin 1998).

Brown, S. A. *The Metamorphosis of Ovid from Chaucer to Ted Hughes* (London 1999).

Bruyas, F. *Histoire de l'opérette en France* (Lyons 1974).

Budelmann, F. and **Haubold, J.** "Reception and tradition," in *A Companion to Classical Receptions*, **L. Hardwick** and **C. Stray** (eds.) (Oxford 2008) pp. 13–25.

Budgen, F. *James Joyce and the Making of Ulysses* (New York 1934), Reprinted as *James Joyce and the Making of Ulysses, and Other Writings*, introduction by C. Hart (London 1972).

Burnett, A. (ed.) *The Letters of A. E. Housman* (Oxford 2007)

(ed.) *The Poems of A. E. Housman* (Oxford 1997).

Burrow, C. "Virgil in English translation," in **C. Martindale** (ed.), *The Cambridge Companion to Virgil* (Cambridge 1997) pp. 21–37.

Burton, R. *Classical Poets in the "Florilegium Gallicum"* (Frankfurt am Main 1983).

Calcaterra, C. *Manifesti romantici e altri scritti della polemica classico-romantica*, rev. M. Scotti, 2nd edn. (Turin 1979).

Cameron, K. *Research Keys to the American Renaissance; Scarce Indexes of The Christian Examiner, The North American Review, and the New Jerusalem Magazine for Students of American Literature, Culture, History, and New England Transcendentalism* (Hartford 1967).

Canitz, A. E. C. "'In our Awyn Langage': The nationalist agenda of Gawin Douglas's Eneados," *Vergilius* **42** (1996): 25–37.

Cappon, L. J. (ed.) *The Adams–Jefferson Letters* (Chapel Hill 1959).

Carducci, G. "Le tre canzoni patriottiche di Giacomo Leopardi," in *Edizione nazionale delle opere di Giosuè Carducci* (Bologna 1939) vol. XX, pp. 103–75.

Carne-Ross, D. S. and **Haynes, K.** (eds.) *Horace in English* (Harmondsworth 1996).

Carroll, C. M. "A classical setting for a classical poem: Philidor's Carmen Saeculare," in **R. C. Rosbottom** (ed.), *Studies in Eighteenth-Century Culture* (Madison 1977) vol. VI, pp. 97–111.

Carroll, W. *The Metamorphoses of Shakespearean Comedy* (Princeton 1985).

Caruso, C. and **Laird, A.** "The Italian classical tradition, language and literary history," in **C. Caruso** and **A. Laird** (eds.), *Italy and the Classical Tradition: Language, Thought and Poetry 1300–1600* (London 2009) pp. 1–25.

Cavallo, G., Fedeli, P. and **Giardina, A.** (eds.) *Lo Spazio letterario di Roma antica.* 5 vols. (Rome 1989–1991).

Chapman, G. *Ovid's Banquet of Sense* (London 1595).

Coldwell, D. (ed.) *Virgil's Aeneid, translated by Gavin Douglas* (Edinburgh 1964).

Commager, S. *The Odes of Horace: A Critical Study* (New Haven 1962).

Conley, C. H. *The First English Translators of the Classics* (New Haven 1927).

Connolly, J. "Review of Dugan, Making a New Man: Ciceronian Self-Fashioning in the Rhetorical Works," *Bryn Mawr Classical Review* (2006).

Cook, W. W. and **Tatum, J.** *African American Writers and Classical Tradition* (Chicago 2010).

Cortesi, L. "Epistolario di A. Mai: ripresa," in *Angelo Mai nel secondo centenario della nascita (1782–1982), Monumenta Bergomensia* (Bergamo 1983) vol. LXIV, pp. 57–303.

Cott, J. *Bob Dylan: The Essential Interviews* (New York 2006).

Curtius, E. R. *Europäische Literatur und lateinisches Mittelalter* (Bern 1948).

Davison, N. R. *James Joyce, Ulysses, and the Construction of Jewish Identity: Culture, Biography, and "the Jew" in Modernist Europe* (Cambridge 1996).

Dearing, B. "Gavin Douglas's Eneados: A reinterpretation," *Proceedings of the Modern Language Association* **67** (1952): 845–62.

de Grazia, M. "Anachronism," in **B. Cummings** and **J. Simpson** (eds.), *Cultural Reformations: From Lollardy to the English Civil War* (Oxford 2010) pp. 13–22.

DeLaura, D. J. *Hebrew and Hellene in Victorian England: Newman, Arnold, and Pater* (Austin 1969).

Desmond, M. "Bernard Silvestris and the Corpus of the Aeneid," in **A. S. Bernardo** and **S. Levin** (eds.), *Classics in the Middle Ages* (New York 1990) pp. 129–40.

Deutsch, O. E. (ed.) *Joseph Haydn: Kanons: Joseph Haydn Werke*, vol. XXXI (Munich-Duisburg 1959).

Dick, J. C. (ed.) *The Songs of Robert Burns and Notes on Scottish Songs* (London 1908).

Didi-Huberman, G. *L'image survivante: histoire de l'art et temps des fantômes selon Aby Warburg* (Paris 2002).

Dotti, U. (trans.) *Petrarca: Le Familiari* (Rome 1991).

Downing, G. M. "Joyce's use of Latin at the outset of 'Oxen'," in F. Ruggieri (ed.), *Classic Joyce* (Rome 1999) pp. 255–66.

Draheim, J. and Wille, G. (eds.) *Horaz-Vertonungen vom Mittelalter bis zum Gegenwart: Eine Anthologie.* Heuremata 7.a (Amsterdam 1985).

duBois, P. *Out of Athens: The New Ancient Greeks* (Cambridge MA 2010)

Dylan, B. *Chronicles: Volume One* (New York 2004).

Dylan, B. *Lyrics 1962–1985* (New York 1985).

Einstein, A. *The Italian Madrigal* (Princeton 1949).

Eliot, T. S. "Tradition and the individual talent," in *Selected Essays* (New York (1950) pp. 3–11.

What is a Classic? (New York 1945).

Ellman, R. (ed.) *Letters of James Joyce,* vol. III (New York 1966).

Everett, A. "Review of Mai, ed. Ciceronis de Re Publica and Villemain, La République de Cicéron," *North American Review* 8 (1823): 33–69 (anonymous in the original publication).

Farmer, R. *An Essay on the Learning of Shakespeare* (New York 1966).

Farrell, J. *Latin Language and Latin Culture from Ancient to Modern Times* (Cambridge 2001).

"Review of Martindale, Latin Poetry and the Judgement of Taste," *Translation and Literature* 15 (2006): 254–61.

Feeney, D. C. *Literature and Religion at Rome* (Cambridge 1998).

Fell, C. "Interview with Cliff Fell," *Nelson Mail,* Nelson, New Zealand, 10 October.

Finley, M. *The World of Odysseus* (New York 1945).

Fleischhauer, G. "Carl Loewes Horaz-Vertonungen op. 57," in *Bericht über die wissenschaftliche Konferenz anlässlich seines 200. Geburtstages vom 26. bis 28. September 1996 im Handel-Haus Halle* (Halle an der Saale 1997) pp. 411–25.

Fowler, A. "Gavin Douglas: Romantic humanist," in A. A. MacDonald and K. Dekker (eds.), *Rhetoric, Royalty, and Reality: Essays on the Literary Culture of Medieval and Early Modern Scotland* (Leuven 2005) pp. 83–104.

Fox, C. "Authorizing the metamorphic witch: Ovid in Reginald Scot's Discovery of Witchcraft," in A. M. Keith and S. Rupp (eds.), *Metamorphoses: The Changing Face of Ovid in Medieval and Early Modern Europe* (Toronto 2007) pp. 165–78.

Fraenkel, E. *Horace* (Oxford 1957).

Frost, W. "Translating Virgil, Douglas to Dryden," in G. de F. Lord and M. Mack (eds.), *Poetic Traditions of the English Renaissance* (New Haven 1982) pp. 271–86.

Fubini, R. "Pubblicità e controllo del libro nella cultura del Rinascimento," in P. Gilli (ed.), *Humanisme et église en Italie et en France méridionale (XVe siècle – milieu du XVIe siècle)* (Rome 2004) pp. 201–37.

Gabler, H. W. (ed.) *James Joyce. Ulysses: The Corrected Text* (New York 1986).

Gaisser, J. H. *The Fortunes of Apuleius and the Golden Ass. A Study in Transmission and Reception.* Martin Classical Lectures (Princeton 2008).

Gallo, N. *De Sanctis: Opere* (Milan 1961)

Gavazzeni, F. and Lombardi, M. (eds.) *Leopardi: Canti* (Milan 1998).

Gervasoni, G. (ed.) *Angelo Mai: Epistolario* (Florence 1954).

Gifford, D. *Joyce Annotated: Notes for Dubliners and A Portrait of the Artist as a Young Man.* 2nd edn. (Berkeley 1982).

Gifford, D. and **Seidman, R. J.** *Ulysses Annotated: Notes for James Joyce's Ulysses,* 2nd edn. (Berkeley 1989).

Gilbert, S. *James Joyce's Ulysses: A Study* (New York 1930). Reprinted (1955).
(ed.) *Letters of James Joyce,* vol. 1 (New York 1957).

Girardet, K. *Die Ordnung der Welt* (Wiesbaden 1983).

Goff, B. (ed.) *Classics and Colonialism* (London 2005).

Goldhill, S. "Cultural history and aesthetics: Why Kant is no place to start reception studies," in **E. Hall** and **S. Harrop** (eds.), *Theorising Performance: Greek Drama, Cultural History and Critical Practice* (London 2010) pp. 56–70.

Golding, A. *Shakespeare's Ovid,* **W. H. D. Rouse** (ed.) (New York 1966).

Gooch, B. N. S. and **Thatcher, D. S.** *Musical Settings of Late Victorian and Modern British Literature: A Catalogue* (New York and London 1976).

Gottfried, R. K. *Joyce's Comic Portrait* (Gainesville 2000).

Grafton, A. and **Jardine, L.** *From Humanism to the Humanities: Education and the Liberal Arts in Fifteenth- and Sixteenth-century Europe* (Cambridge MA 1986)

Gray, M. *Song and Dance Man III* (London and New York 2000).
The Bob Dylan Encyclopedia (New York and London 2006).

Graziosi, B. and **Greenwood, E.** (eds.) *Homer in the Twentieth Century: Between World Literature and the Canon* (Oxford 2007).

Green, P. (trans.) *Ovid: The Poems of Exile* (New York 1994).

Greenblatt, S. *Renaissance Self-Fashioning: From More to Shakespeare* (Chicago 1980).

Greene, E. (ed.) *Re-reading Sappho: Reception and Transmission* (Berkeley 1999).

Greene, T. M. *The Descent from Heaven: A Study in Epic Continuity* (New Haven 1963).
The Light in Troy: Imitation and Discovery in Renaissance Poetry (New Haven 1982).

Greenwood, E. *Afro-Greeks: Dialogues between Anglophone Caribbean Literature and Classics in the Twentieth Century* (Oxford 2010).

Gurd, S. *Iphigenias at Aulis: Textual Multiplicity, Radical Philology* (Ithaca 2005).
(ed.) *Philology and Its Histories* (Columbus 2010).

Gussali, A. (ed.) *Giordani. Opere* (Milan 1854–62).

Güthenke, C. *Placing Modern Greece: The Dynamics of Romantic Hellenism, 1770–1840* (Oxford 2008).
"Shop talk. Reception studies and recent work in the history of scholarship," *Classical Receptions Journal* **1** (2009): 104–15.

Habinek, T. N. *The Politics of Latin Literature: Writing, Identity, and Empire in Ancient Rome* (Princeton 1998).

Halbertal, M. *People of the Book: Canon, Meaning, Authority* (Cambridge MA 1997).

Hall, E. "Towards a theory of performance reception," in **E. Hall** and **S. Harrop** (eds.), *Theorising Performance: Greek Drama, Cultural History and Critical Practice* (London 2010) pp. 10–28.

Hammond, P. *The Strangeness of Tragedy* (Oxford 2009).

Hardie, P. R. "Contrasts," in **S. J. Heyworth**, **P. G. Fowler** and **S. J. Harrison** (eds.), *Classical Constructions: Papers in Memory of Don Fowler, Classicist and Epicurean* (Oxford 2007) pp. 141–73.

Hardwick, L. *Translating Words, Translating Cultures* (London 2000).

Hardwick, L. and **Stray, C.** "Introduction: Making connections," in **L. Hardwick** and **C. Stray** (eds.), *A Companion to Classical Receptions* (Oxford 2008) pp. 1–9.

Harnack, A. *Geschichte der königlich Preussischen Akademie der Wissenschaften zu Berlin* (Berlin 1900).

Harpham, G. "Roots, races, and the return to philology," *Representations* **106** (2009): 34–63.

Harrison, S. J. (ed.) *Text, Ideas and the Classics: Scholarship, Theory and Classical Literature* (Oxford 2001).
(ed.) *The Cambridge Companion to Horace* (Cambridge 2007).

Hartman, G. H. "Words, wish, worth: Wordsworth," in **Harold Bloom** et al. (eds.), *Deconstruction and Criticism* (London and New York 1979). Reprinted (2004) pp. 143–76.

Haynes, K. *English Literature and Ancient Languages* (Oxford 2007).
"Text, theory, and reception," in **C. Martindale** and **R. F. Thomas** (eds.), *Classics and the Uses of Reception* (Oxford 2006) pp. 44–54.

Heck, E. *Die Bezeugung von Ciceros Schrift De re publica* (Hildesheim 1966).

Hegel, G. *Introduction to the Philosophy of History*, L. Rauch (trans.) (Indianapolis 1988).

Helgerson, R. *Forms of Nationhood: The Elizabethan Writing of England* (Chicago 1992).

Hermand, J. and **Holub, R. C.** (eds.) *Heinrich Heine: The Romantic School and Other Essays* (New York 1985).

Hijmans, B. L. "*Aeneia Virtus*: Vegio's Supplementum to the *Aeneid*," *Classical Journal* **67** (1971–2): 144–55.

Hildebrand, K. "Hellas und Wilamowitz," *Die Grenzboten 69* (1910). Reprinted in *Der George-Kreis: eine Auswahl aus seinen Schriften*, **P. Landmann** (ed.) Cologne (1965) pp. 141–9.

Hildesheimer, W. *The Jewishness of Mr. Bloom = Das Jüdische an Mr. Bloom: englisch, deutsch* (Frankfurt 1984).

Hill, C. *Intellectual Origins of the English Revolution – Revisited* (Oxford 1997).

Hinds, S. *Allusion and Intertext: Dynamics of Appropriation in Roman Poetry.* (Cambridge 1998).
"Defamiliarizing Latin literature, from Petrarch to pulp fiction," *Transactions of the American Philological Association* **135.1** (2005): 49–81.

"Petrarch, Cicero, Virgil: Virtual community in Familiares 24.4," in **G. W. Most** and **S. Spence** (eds.), *Re-Presenting Virgil: Special Issue in Honor of Michael C. J. Putnam, Materiali e discussioni per l'analisi dei testi classici* **52** (2004): 157–75.

Houghton, L. B. T. and **Wyke, M.** (eds.) *Perceptions of Horace: A Roman Poet and his Readers* (Cambridge 2009).

James VI *Daemonologie* (London 1597).

Janicaud, D. *Hegel et le destin de la Grèce* (Paris 1975).

Jenkyns, R. *The Victorians and Ancient Greece* (Cambridge MA 1980).

Jonson, B. *Poetaster* (London 1601).

Kallendorf, C. W. *The Other Virgil: "Pessimistic" Readings of the Aeneid in Early Modern Culture* (Oxford 2007).

The Virgilian Tradition: Book History and the History of Reading in Early Modern Europe (Aldershot and Burlington VT 2007).

Kermode, F. (ed.) *The Classic: Literary Images of Permanence and Change* (Cambridge MA 1983).

The Tempest, The Arden Shakespeare (London 1954).

Kinsley, J. (ed.) *Robert Burns: The Poems and Songs*. 3 vols. (Oxford 1968).

Kittler, F. and **Vissmann, C.** *Vom Griechenland* (Berlin 2001).

Kokay, L. *Songs of the Underground: A Collector's Guide to the Rolling Thunder Revue 1975–6*, private publication (2000) (www.bjorner.com/RtrBook-Letter. pdf).

Kors, A. C. and **Peters, E.** *Witchcraft in Europe 400–1700: A Documentary History*, 2nd edn. (Philadelphia 2001).

Kraus, C. "Introduction: Reading commentaries/commentaries as reading," in **R. Gibson** and **C. S. Kraus** (eds.), *The Classical Commentary: History, Practices, Theory* (Leiden 2002) pp. 1–27.

Laird, A. *The Epic of America: An Introduction to Rafael Landívar and the Rusticatio Mexicana* (London 2006).

Lanman, C. R. (ed.) *Atharva-veda Saṃhitā* (Cambridge MA 1905).

de Lisle, L. (trans.) *Oeuvres de Horace : traduction nouvelle* (Paris 1873).

Leonard, M. *Athens in Paris: Ancient Greece and the Political in Post-War French Thought* (Oxford 2005).

Leonhardt, J. *Latein: Geschichte einer Weltsprache* (Munich 2009).

Lewis, C. S. *English Literature in the Sixteenth Century Excluding Drama* (Oxford 1954).

Lianeri, A. "The Homeric moment? Translation, historicity, and the meaning of the Classics," in **C. Martindale** and **R. F. Thomas** (eds.), *Classics and the Uses of Reception* (Oxford 2006) pp. 141–52.

Lombardo, S. (trans.) *Virgil: Aeneid* (Indianapolis and Cambridge 2005).

Luck, G. *Arcana Mundi: Magic and the Occult in the Greek and Roman Worlds*, 2nd edn. (Baltimore MD 2006).

Lyne, R. "Ovid, Golding, and the 'Rough Magic' of *The Tempest*," in **A. B. Taylor** (ed.), *Shakespeare's Ovid* (Cambridge 2000) pp. 150–64.

Lyons, S. *Horace's Odes and the Mystery of Do-re-mi* (Oxford 2007).

Music in the Odes of Horace (Oxford 2010).

Mai, A. (ed.) *M. Tulli Ciceronis de re publica quae supersunt* (Rome 1822).

Mandelbaum, A. (trans.) *The Aeneid of Virgil: A Verse Translation by Allen Mandelbaum* (Berkeley 1971).

Marchetti, A. "Tutta la verità sull' 'Inno a Roma' di Puccini," *Nuova Rivista Musicale Italiana* **9** (1975): 396–408.

Mariani, A. *Epistolario Luigi Mancinelli* (Lucca 2000).

Martindale, C. "Introduction: Thinking through reception," in **C. Martindale** and **R. F. Thomas** (eds.), *Classics and the Uses of Reception* (Oxford 2006) pp. 1–13.

Latin Poetry and the Judgment of Taste: An Essay in Aesthetics (Oxford 2005).

"Leaving Athens: Classics for a new century?: Review of duBois, Out of Athens: The New Ancient Greeks," *Arion* **18**.1 (2010): 135–48.

"Performance, reception, aesthetics: Or why reception studies need Kant," in **E. Hall** and **S. Harrop** (eds.), *Theorising Performance: Greek Drama, Cultural History and Critical Practice* (London 2010) pp. 71–84.

"Reception," in **C. W. Kallendorf** (ed.), *A Companion to the Classical Tradition* (Oxford 2007) pp. 297–311.

Redeeming the Text: Latin Poetry and the Hermeneutics of Reception (Cambridge 1993).

"Shakespeare's Ovid, Ovid's Shakespeare: A methodological postscript," in **A. B. Taylor** (ed.), *Shakespeare's Ovid* (Cambridge 2000) pp. 198–215.

Martindale, C. and **Martindale, M.** *Shakespeare and the Uses of Antiquity* (London 1990).

Martindale, C. and **Taylor, A. B.** (eds.) *Shakespeare and the Classics* (Cambridge 2004).

Mazzotta, G. *Dante, Poet of the Desert: History and Allegory in the Divine Comedy* (Princeton 1979).

McGregor, C. "Dylan interview," *New Musical Express* (London April 22, 1978).

McNeillie, A. (ed.) *Virginia Woolf: The Common Reader* (New York 1925). Reprinted (1984).

(ed.) *The Essays of Virgina Woolf* (New York 1986–).

Melville, S. and **Iversen, M.** *Writing Art History: Disciplinary Departures* (Chicago 2010).

Mercati, G. *M. Tulli Ciceronis de re publica libri e codice rescripto vaticano 5757 phototypice expressi*, vol. 1, *Prolegomena* (Vatican 1934).

Miller, P. A. *Postmodern Spiritual Practices: The Construction of the Subject and the Reception of Plato in Lacan, Derrida, and Foucault* (Columbus 2007).

Momigliano, A. *Secondo contributo alla storia degli studi classici* (Rome 1960).

Mommsen, T. *History of Rome*, **W. Dickson** (trans.) (New York 1911).

Moretti, F. *Graphs, Maps, Trees: Abstract Models for a Literary History* (London 2005).

Most, G. W., **Norman, L. F.** and **Rabau, S.** (eds.) *Révolutions Homériques* (Pisa 2009).

Mynors, R. A. B. (ed.) *P. Virgili Maronis Opera* (Oxford 1969).

Nadel, I. B. *Joyce and the Jews: Culture and Texts* (Basingstoke 1989).

Nagel, A. and **Wood, C. S.** *Anachronic Renaissance* (New York 2010).

Nestrovski, A. "Joyce's critique of music," in **J. Rahn** (ed.), *Perspectives on Musical Aesthetics* (New York 1994) pp. 249–90.

Nietzsche, F. W. *Beyond Good and Evil*, R. J. Hollingdale (trans.) (Harmondsworth 1990).

Nisbet, R. G. M. "Romanae Fidicen Lyrae: The Odes of Horace," in **J. P. Sullivan** (ed.), *Critical Essays on Roman Literature: Elegy and Lyric* (London 1962) pp. 181–218.

Noon, W. T. *Joyce and Aquinas, Yale Studies in English* 133 (New Haven 1957).

Norden, E. *Aeneis, Buch* VI, 3rd edn. (Leipzig and Berlin 1926).

Ó Gráda, C. *Jewish Ireland in the Age of Joyce: A Socioeconomic History* (Princeton 2006).

O Hehir, B. and **Dillon, J. M.** *A Classical Lexicon for Finnegans Wake: A Glossary of the Greek and Latin in the Major Works of Joyce, including Finnegans Wake, the Poems, Dubliners, Stephen Hero, A Portrait of the Artist as a Young Man, Exiles, and Ulysses* (Berkeley 1977).

Origo, I. *Leopardi: A Study in Solitude*, 2nd edn. (New York 1999).

Østrem, E. "A day above ground is a good day: Bob Dylan's Love and Theft" (2003) (www.dylanchords.com/professors/a_day_above_ground.htm).

Owens, J. A. "Music and meaning in Cipriano de Rore's setting of 'Donec gratus eram tibi,'" in *Studies in the History of Music 1: Music and Language* (New York 1983) pp. 95–117.

Parkinson, D. "Orpheus and the translator: Douglas' 'lusty crafty preambill'," in **A. A. MacDonald** and **K. Dekker** (eds.), *Rhetoric, Royalty, and Reality: Essays on the Literary Culture of Medieval and Early Modern Scotland* (Leuven 2005) pp. 105–20.

Patterson, L. *Negotiating the Past: The Historical Understanding of Medieval Literature* (Madison WI 1987).

Paul, J. "Working with film: Theories and methodologies," in **L. Hardwick** and **C. Stray** (eds.), *A Companion to Classical Receptions* (Oxford 2008) pp. 303–14.

Piperno, F. "Musica," in *Enciclopedia Oraziana* (Rome 1998) 3.661–77.

Pollock, S. "Future philology? The fate of a soft science in a hard world," *Critical Inquiry* **35** (2009): 931–61.

Poole, R. *The Unknown Virginia Woolf*, 4th edn. (Cambridge 1995).

Pope, A. (trans.) *The Iliad of Homer* (London 1720).

Porter, J. I. "Reception studies: Future prospects," in **L. Hardwick** and **C. Stray** (eds.), *A Companion to Classical Receptions* (Oxford 2008) pp. 469–81.

"What is 'classical' about classical antiquity?" in **J. I. Porter** (ed.), *Classical Pasts: The Classical Traditions of Greece and Rome* (Princeton 2006).

Pound, E. *Selected Prose, 1909–1965* (New York 1975).

Prins, Y. *Victorian Sappho* (Princeton 1999).

Putnam, M. C. J. *Virgil's Aeneid: Interpretation and Influence* (Chapel Hill NC 1995).
Poetic Interplay: Catullus and Horace (Princeton 2006).
Putnam, M. C. J. and **Hankins, J.** (eds.) *Maffeo Vegio: Short Epics* (Cambridge MA 2004)
Quint, D. *Epic and Empire: Politics and Generic Form from Virgil to Milton* (Princeton 1993).
"The Virgilian coordinates of Paradise Lost," in **G. W. Most** and **S. Spence** (eds.), *Re-Presenting Virgil: Special Issue in Honor of Michael C. J. Putnam, Materiali e discussioni per l'analisi dei testi classici* **52** (2004): 177–97.
Reeve, M. D. "Reception/history of scholarship: Introduction," in **S. J. Harrison** (ed.), *Text, Ideas and the Classics: Scholarship, Theory and Classical Literature* (Oxford 2001) pp. 245–51.
Reizbaum, M. *James Joyce's Judaic Other* (Stanford 1999).
Reynolds, L. D. (ed.) *Texts and Transmission* (Oxford 1983).
Ricci, P. G. (ed.) *Giovanni Boccaccio: Trattatello in Laude di Dante*, in **V. Branca** (ed.), *Tutte le Opere di Giovanni Boccaccio*, vol. III (Milan 1974).
Ricoeur, P. *Sur la traduction* (Paris 2004).
Ridley, F. "Surrey's debt to Gawin Douglas," *Proceedings of the Modern Language Association* **76** (1961): 25–33.
Root, R. K. *Classical Mythology in Shakespeare* (New York 1904).
Rossi, V. (ed.) *Petrarca. Le Familiari*, vol. I (Florence 1933).
Rudd, N. "Pyramus and Thisbe in Shakespeare and Ovid," in **A. B. Taylor** (ed.), *Shakespeare's Ovid* (Cambridge 2000) pp. 113–25.
Ruggieri, F. *Classic Joyce*, Joyce Studies in Italy 6 (Rome 1999).
Rutledge, T. "Gavin Douglas and John Bellenden," in **N. Royan** (ed.), *Langage Cleir Illumynate: Scottish Poetry from Barbour to Drummond, 1375–1630* (Amsterdam 2007) pp. 93–116.
Ruysschaert, J. "Il passaggio di Mai dalla Biblioteca Ambrosiana alla Biblioteca Vaticana," in **J. Ruysschaert** and **L. Cortesi** (eds.), *Angelo Mai nel secondo centenario della nascita (1782–1982), Monumenta Bergomensia* **64** (Bergamo 1983) pp. 11–55.
Sadie, S. (ed.) *The New Grove Dictionary of Music and Musicians*, 2nd edn. (London and New York 2001).
Saga, J. *Confessions of a Yakuza: A Life in Japan's Underworld*, J. Bester (trans.) (Tokyo 1997).
Sanadon, N. S. *Q. Horatii Flacci carmina ad suum ordinem ac nitorem revocata* (Paris 1728).
Schlossman, B. *Joyce's Catholic Comedy of Language* (Madison, WI 1985).
Schmalzriedt, E. *Inhumane Klassik: Vorlesung wider ein Bildungsklischée* (Munich 1971).
Schmid, W. "Cicerone e la filologia tedesca," *Atene e Roma* **5.5** (1960): 129–42.
Schork, R. J. *Greek and Hellenic Culture in Joyce* (Gainesville 1998).
Latin and Roman Culture in Joyce (Gainesville 1997).
Joyce and the Classical Tradition (Dublin 2002).

Scodel, R. "Review of Johnstone, Listening to the Logos: Speech and the Coming of Wisdom in Ancient Greece," *Bryn Mawr Classical Review* (2010).

Scot, R. *The Discoverie of Witchcraft* (London 1584).

Seidensticker, B. and **Vöhler, M.** (eds.) *Urgeschichten der Moderne: die Antike im 20. Jahrhundert* (Stuttgart 2001).

Senn, F. *Joyce's Dislocutions: Essays on Reading as Translation*, **J. P. Riquelme** (ed.) (Baltimore 1984).

Sheehy, E. *The Joyce We Knew*, **U. O'Connor** (ed.) (Cork 1967).

Simonetta, M. *Il Rinascimento segreto: Il mondo del segretario da Petrarca a Machiavelli* (Milan 2004).

Singerman, J. *Under Clouds of Poesy: Poetry and Truth in French and English Reworkings of the Aeneid, 1160–1513* (New York 1986).

Skretkowicz, V. and **Rennie, S.** (eds.) *Dictionary of the Scots Language* (2004) (www.dsl.ac.uk/dsl/).

Stevenson, S. "Aeneas in fourteenth-century England," in **A. S. Bernardo** and **S. Levin** (eds.), *Classics in the Middle Ages* (New York 1990) pp. 371–8.

Strier, R. "Shakespeare and the skeptics," *Religion and Literature* **32** (2000): 171–95.

Super, R. H. (ed.) *The Complete Prose Works* (Ann Arbor 1960–1977).

Tarrant, R. J. "Ancient receptions of Horace," in **S. J. Harrison** (ed.), *The Cambridge Companion to Horace* (Cambridge 2007) pp. 277–90.

  "Da capo structure in some Odes of Horace," in **S. J. Harrison** (ed.), *Homage to Horace: A Bimillenary Celebration* (Oxford 1995) pp. 32–49.

Theoharis, T. C. *Joyce's Ulysses: An Anatomy of the Soul* (Chapel Hill 1988).

Thilo, G. and **Hagen, H.** (eds.) *Servii Grammatici qui feruntur in Vergilii Carmina commentarii* (Leipzig 1881).

Thomas, H. "Musical settings of Horace's lyric poems," *Proceedings of the Musical Association* **46** (1919–1920): 73–97.

Thomas, R. F. "The streets of Rome: the classical Dylan," in *The Performance Artistry of Bob Dylan, Oral Tradition* **22**, **C. Mason** and **R. F. Thomas** (eds.) (2007): 30–56 (http://journal.oraltradition.org/files/articles/22i/Thomas.pdf).

  Virgil and the Augustan Reception (Cambridge 2001).

Thompson, R. "On choral composition: Essays and reflections," *American Choral Review* **22** (1980): 5–27.

Thornton, W. *Allusions in Ulysses: An Annotated List* (Chapel Hill 1968).

Timpanaro, S. *Aspetti e figure della cultura ottocentesca* (Pisa 1980).

  Classicismo e illuminismo nell'ottocento italiano, 2nd edn. (Pisa 1969).

  La filologia di Giacomo Leopardi, 4th edn. (Rome and Bari 2008).

Treves, P. "Ciceronianismo e anticiceronianismo nella cultura italiani del secolo XIX," *Rendiconti dell'Istituto Lombardo (Lettere)* **92** (1958): 403–64.

  Lo Studio dell'antichità classica nell'Ottocento (Milan 1962).

Tudeau-Clayton, M. "Richard Carew, William Shakespeare, and the politics of translating Virgil in early modern England and Scotland," *International Journal of the Classical Tradition* **5.4** (1999): 507–27.

"Supplementing the Aeneid in early modern England: Translation, imitation, commentary," *International Journal of the Classical Tradition* **4.4** (1998): 507–25.

Twain, M. *The Adventures of Huckleberry Finn* (New York 1981).

Vasoli, C. and **de Robertis, D.** (eds.) *Dante Alighieri. Opere minori* (Milan and Naples 1988).

Velz, J. W. "Shakespeare's Ovid in the twentieth century: A critical survey," **A. B. Taylor** (ed.), in *Shakespeare's Ovid* (Cambridge 2000) pp. 181–97.

Venables, I. "A composer's approach to setting A. E. Housman," *Housman Society Journal* **34** (2008): 71–9.

Villemain, A.-F. (trans.) *La République de Cicéron*, 2nd edn. (Paris 1858).

Vischer, E. (ed.) *Niebuhr Briefe aus Rom* (1816–1823) (Bern and Munich 1981).

Wallace, J. *Shelley and Greece: Rethinking Romantic Hellenism* (New York 1997).

Wälli, S. *Melodien aus mittelalterlichen Horaz-Handschriften. Monumenta Monodica Medii Aevi*, Subsidia 3 (Kassel 2002).

Walther, G. *Niebuhrs Forschung* (Stuttgart 1993).

Waquet, F. *Le latin, ou l'empire d'un signe: VIe–XXe siècle* (Paris 1998).

  Latin or the Empire of a Sign, J. Howe (trans.) (London and New York 2001).

Warburg, A. *The Renewal of Pagan Antiquity: Contributions to the Cultural History of the European Renaissance* (Los Angeles 1999).

Warner, R. (trans.) *Thucydides. History of the Peloponnesian War* (St. Ives 1954).

Watkins, J. *The Specter of Dido: Spenser and Virgilian Epic* (New Haven 1995).

Watt, L. M. *Douglas's Aeneid* (Cambridge 1920).

Williams, R. D. *The Aeneid of Virgil* (London 1972).

Wolfe, R. C. (trans.) *Suetonius. Life of Virgil* (London 1914).

Wood, C. S. *Forgery, Replica, Fiction: Temporalities of German Renaissance Art* (Chicago 2008).

Woolf, S. *A History of Italy 1700–1860* (London 1991).

Yeats, W. B. *Explorations*, selected by Mrs. W. B. Yeats (New York 1962).

Ziolkowski, J. M. *Nota Bene: Reading Classics and Writing Melodies in the Early Middle Ages* (Turnhout 2007).

Ziolkowski, J. M. and **Putnam, M. C. J.** (eds.) *The Virgilian Tradition: The First Fifteen Hundred Years* (New Haven 2008).

Ziolkowski, T. *Ovid and the Moderns* (Ithaca NY 2005).

  Virgil and the Moderns (Princeton 1993).

Index

Lightning Source UK Ltd.
Milton Keynes UK
UKHW02f2356020818
326704UK00007B/105/P